Remembering Angola

Portuguese Literary & Cultural Studies
15/16 Fall 2005/Spring 2006

Remembering Angola

LUSO-AMERICAN
FOUNDATION

Center for Portuguese Studies and Culture
University of Massachusetts Dartmouth

Portuguese Literary & Cultural Studies is a multilingual interdisciplinary peer-reviewed journal published semi-annually by the Center for Portuguese Studies and Culture at the University of Massachusetts Dartmouth. The journal addresses the literatures and cultures of the diverse communities of the Portuguese-speaking world in terms of critical and theoretical approaches.

Portuguese Literary & Cultural Studies (PLCS) welcomes submission of original and unpublished manuscripts in English, Portuguese, or Spanish appropriate to the goals of the journal. Manuscripts should be in accordance with the *MLA Style Manual and Guide to Scholarly Publishing* (latest version) with parenthetical documentation and a list of Works Cited. The author is responsible for the accuracy of all quotations, titles, names, and dates. Font and sizes as close as possible to the style of the previous issue of PLCS should be used throughout the text. All of the information must be in the same language (e.g., abstract, body of the article, bio-blurb). Updated specific guidelines for submission of manuscripts to PLCS (articles, short articles, review-essays, and reviews) are available at www.plcs.umassd.edu (please consult Guidelines). PLCS encourages submission of manuscripts in the form of an attached single MS Word file.

Subscription Information

The annual subscription (2 issues) for institutions is $80.00 and $40.00 for individuals. Single issues may also be purchased for $25.00. From outside the United States add $12.00 for shipping and handling.

Inquiries should be sent to *Portuguese Literary & Cultural Studies*, Center for Portuguese Studies and Culture, University of Massachusetts Dartmouth, Dartmouth, MA 02747 USA, or by email to: adamastororders@umassd.edu.

Advertising

Portuguese Literary & Cultural Studies accepts advertising that is of interest to scholars in the field of Portuguese, Brazilian, and Luso-African Studies and Critical Theory. Further information is available by contacting the Center for Portuguese Studies and Culture, University of Massachusetts Dartmouth.

Cover

Design: Spencer Ladd.

ISSN:1521-804X
ISBN: 978-1-933227-13-9

Printed by Signature Printing, East Providence, RI

This publication was made possible in part by a grant from the Luso-American Foundation.

Table of Contents

Margarida Calafate Ribeiro and Ana Paula Ferreira, eds. *Fantasmas e Fantasias Imperiais no Imaginário Português Contemporâneo*. Porto: Campo das Letras, 2003.

Claire Williams

Introduction:
"Never Again?"—Remembering Angola

Phillip Rothwell

"Nunca mais?" is the interrogative closing line of Pepetela's 2005 novel, *Predadores*. The two-word question triggers an uncomfortable chain of signification given the reflection that immediately precedes it and, more subtly, the novel it concludes. "Era noite de Natal, terceira noite de natal em paz. Não havia sons de tiros nem balas tracejantes riscando o céu, não havia conversas sobre guerra. Nunca mais?" (380). Almost three years after the assassination of Jonas Savimbi, the UNITA leader whose lust for power many blame for the prolongation of civil conflict in Angola, Pepetela's novel does not lead to an affirmation that war is finally and definitively a thing of the past in the former jewel of the Portuguese imperial crown. Rather, the novel concludes by raising doubt.

Predadores is not a narrative about the various conflicts that have raged in Angola since the 1961 uprisings against the Portuguese, although they permeate the text. It deals with what Angola has become, and the question—"never again?"—is enounced against a contemporary backdrop of predatory capitalists. The youth of these predators was spent espousing the utopian egalitarianism of the MPLA, while enforcing their very coercive and urban worldview on rural and dissenting traditions. Their middle age consisted of eliminating those who really believed in that utopia. What has become of the nation for whose birth they claimed to fight as they mature into old age?

Portuguese Literary & Cultural Studies 15/16 (2010): xiii-xxiii.

One of the most poignant lessons recent Angolan history teaches us is that structural repetition is the modus operandi of power relations. The current ruling elite is an uncanny reflection of the colonizer it overthrew. Years of conflict have made that new elite extremely wealthy. As has often been commented, the nature of Angola's resources—particularly its offshore oil reserves, first seriously exploited in the 1960s—makes it easy for multinational conglomerates to extract Angola's wealth without the consent or participation of Angolan civil society.[1] One of the ironies of postindependence Angolan history was the extent to which American oil companies effectively paid for the presence of Cuban troops on Angolan soil at the height of the Cold War. No democratic accountability has ever been exercised over Angola's immense mineral wealth and, with the connivance of the global marketplace, that wealth has been channeled into a burgeoning clientelism. Gradually, the imagination of a national project has been superseded by the predatory coarseness of Pepetela's *Predadores,* in which once-avowed ideological enemies work in tandem to profit as much as possible without being held to account.

David Birmingham offers a very damning critique of the current state of the Angolan polity as an alarmingly precise replication of the colonial era. A similarly small elite controls all the resources and resists any suggestion that they should be redistributed, shares the same Portuguese language and visceral contempt for rural Angola, has even rediscovered the same Catholic god in the post-Marxist era, and controls the mass media through fear or acquisition. Birmingham concludes, "freedom of opinion and of opportunity, which had been stifled in the days of empire, proved virtually incapable of resuscitation in the era of liberation" (Birmingham, "Angola" 184).

The 1960s' MPLA utopian vision of a new society, to be achieved through the creation of the Marxist "New Man," was flawed from its inception by its praxis. Not only did it perpetuate a tradition of gender bias, celebrating the masculine Sem Medos of Pepetela's *Mayombe,* while condemning the Ondinas, its rhetoric cloaked the transformation of the abusive power structures of the late colonial period into one of the most disheartening mimickings of social injustice in the history of postcolonial Africa. Under the catchphrases of Marxist-Leninism, rampant corruption and repression thrived. Without doubt a repeated arena for foreign intervention, the most troubling aspect of Angola's recent history is the manner in which the nation has been betrayed by those who have purported to lead it in the name of the "povo." That betrayal by those who once propounded an ideology of equality has been the negative inspiration for much of the powerful literature to emerge from the nation since independence. Writers of the stature of José Luandino Vieira, Manuel Rui, Pepetela and Ruy Duarte de Carvalho have witnessed the disavowal of the national spirit of collective liberation, not just through civil conflict, but rather with the rampant emergence of a limited, neoliberal and ultimately destructive conception of self-interest. The poverty of such a conception creates the conditions for the interrogative "nunca mais?"—the sense that peace has yet to be won for the Angolan nation.

Angola should have been a great liberation success story. To paraphrase the title of the colloquium organized by Joanna Lewis and Stephen Hart in 1994, Angola really did matter, for symbolic as well as economic reasons. In fact, Angola has a history of being somewhat overdetermined, outside its borders, at a symbolic level. Besides the Portuguese colonial imagination of an Angolan paradise, the nation attracted the imagination of the world's romantic left in the 1960s and 70s. In the early 1960s, both Che Guevara and Fidel Castro saw Angola as one of the African countries with the greatest potential for a dramatic and meaningful revolution. In 1977, the Colombian novelist and future Nobel-Prize winner, Gabriel García Márquez, published a romanticized account, distributed throughout Latin America, of Cuban involvement and revolutionary "success" in Angola, entitled *Operación Carlota.* Angola really was expected to become a revolutionary paradigm, in which unjust social structures would be replaced and opportunities extended to all its population. It was held up as such across the world in ignorance of what was actually taking place on the ground. Working against this noble imagination was a reality, also with a long history, encapsulated in a detail from a different era related by David Birmingham. The detail is that a young child could be purchased as a slave in Angola in 1906 for a "single small keg of gunpowder" (Birmingham, *Empire* 15).

This historical fact points to two repeated activities weighing down on the Angolan nation. First, it highlights the horrors of the slave trade in Angola, which continued in varied forms well after its official abolition. The demographic consequences of slavery are hard to measure. Conservative estimates claim that around a third of all the slaves who eventually reached the Americas in the modern slave trade were from Angola, and that the total number of Angolan lives lost during its practice is in excess of eight million (Tvedten 18). Second, it exemplifies an excess of armed violence that has sullied Angolan history. An unpleasant aspect of the territory's interaction with the outside world has been the repeated importation of armaments and the price paid for this importation in human and natural resources.

Yet, in the midst of injustice and oppression, Angola was, and still is, the heart of a vibrant and diverse culture. This cultural richness is central to a reimagination of a future Angola. The country's material riches are more than sufficient to raise the standard of living of every Angolan to one that would rival an average European nation. However, the legacies of both an erratic colonialism and the Cold War, mixed with the self-serving baseness of the new ruling elite, has produced a state of affairs in which Pepetela can seriously doubt the permanence of peace because the peace gained in 2002 is merely the absence of war.

Inge Tvedten points to the fundamental problem of postindependence Angolan politics: discrepancy. There has always been a discrepancy between political theory and praxis, between economic potential and actual performance, and, worst of all, between national income and indices of general human development. While the various stages of civil war can be adduced as a primary cause for these discrepancies, they have also been used too freely to overlook the general incompetence or willful corruption of elite cadres within the MPLA.

The MPLA rulers' conversion to capitalism became noticeable at its Second Congress, held in December 1985. According to Tony Hodges, it was partly inspired by "emergent class interests" (12). Hodges sees in the early praxis of the MPLA "political concepts borrowed from the USSR," which "reinforced an authoritarian, bureaucratic system of governance inherited from Portuguese colonialism" (4). This produced a prohibition on truly democratic structures. Against this backdrop of distrusting the people the rulers claim to represent, "predatory characteristics" became "highly prominent in the distorted form of capitalism that has emerged in Angola since the early 1990s" (5). If we follow Pepetela's logic, that predatory nature is now the most rigid barrier to peace in the Angolan nation.

Despite the seemingly normalized situation of social injustice characterizing Angola today, this volume aims, in part, to celebrate the nation's great cultural and historical richness—a richness that augurs well for the imagination of alternative social structures. "Remembering Angola" draws on the multiplicity of connotations associated with the verb. It is not just about reminding us of the country's troubled existence. Nor is it only about recalling its complex past, although there are articles that explicitly deal with less well studied periods from Angola's long history. This volume also takes "remembering" to mean putting pieces back together: limbs blown apart by the countless detonations of Angola's nine million landmines are a physical metonym for a national consciousness torn apart by the realization that the ideologies interfering in its sphere were nothing but vacuous cloaks for an assortment of self-interests irrationally fleecing the nation.

After so much bloodshed at the hands of totalizing epistemologies, starting with colonialism and then, in Hodges's concatenation progressing from "Afro-Stalinism to Petro-diamond capitalism," Angola needs to be rethought. The place this rethinking has already been taking place is in the field of culture. One of the most important voices in that field, a writer who, although born in Portugal, was integral to the imagination of an independent and equitable Angolan identity, is Luandino Vieira. It is now over forty years since his volume *Luuanda* so impressed the Portuguese Writers' Association that they awarded the resident of Tarrafal their literary prize, an action that led to their closure by the PIDE. This volume opens with an interview by Margarida Calafate Ribeiro of Luandino, in which he reveals the ambiguities inherent in the PIDE's prohibition of *Luuanda,* a book from which their agents simultaneously profited in a sequence of events worthy of a chapter in Pepetela's *Predadores.* Without doubt, one of the most important influences on subsequent Angolan literature, Luandino sees in the modern traits of his adopted nation, his characterizations of another era. Ana Paula Tavares's poem, "As portas de *Luuanda,"* pays homage to the cultural doors Luandino opened for those, including Tavares, who followed him. Luandino's genius was not just to give voice to those marginalized in Angolan society in the dying days of Portuguese colonialism, but through them to imagine alternate realities, in lessons as relevant today as in the dying days of Portuguese colonialism.

Another literary voice often held to be the father of the Angolan novel is Antônio de Assis Júnior. He was a member of the turn-of-the-twentieth-century Angolan cultural elite—an elite that lost its status dramatically as the century progressed and immigrants from Portugal flooded the colony. Involved in struggles for native rights, and imprisoned on several occasions, his legacy to the Angolan nation includes the novel *O Segredo da Morta* and a Kimbundu-Portuguese dictionary. Regina Claro, in her article, reads Assis Júnior as an example of burgeoning resistance to colonial practice in his social circles in the early part of the century. As a member of a group that saw its rights increasingly withdrawn by an ever-more colonially conscious Portuguese state, Assis Júnior embodies for Claro a subversive frontier, cognizant of the worlds of both the masters and the slaves. The process of "remembering" in Assis Júnior is always a strategic reorganization of a past that is long-gone in order to better understand the trauma of the present—a point as valid in today's Angola as it was at the moment the author helped to raise consciousness of Angolan identity.

The proto-nationalism of the generation prior to Assis Júnior is investigated by Jacopo Corrado. In his article, Corrado traces the development of a feisty journalistic and literary tradition among the Creole elite of the latter part of the nineteenth century. Their increasing dissatisfaction with the Portuguese state's removal of their status helps to explain their pivotal role in the raising of a specifically Angolan consciousness in the colony.

Covering a similar time period as Corrado's article, Timothy Coates investigates the peculiar penitentiary experiment undertaken by the Portuguese state when it founded the Depósito Geral de Degredados in Luanda by decree on 27 December 1881. The Portuguese state had a long tradition of deporting from the metropolis those it deemed to be undesirable. The cheap labor provided by the late-nineteenth-century deportees sent to Angola became an integral part of the policy of effective occupation of the colony at a time when the international rules of the imperial game began to prejudice Portugal's claim to an empire by historical precedence. Indeed, these "unwilling" colonizers, the *degredados*, outnumbered free immigrants to Luanda during the period of this penal experiment, which was finally deemed to be a failure and closed, in part, because of the European penal reform movement.

Angola's history is replete with examples of external factors determining the course of domestic events. Portugal's response to the changed imperial climate around the time of the 1884-5 Berlin Conference led, as Coates argues, to the establishment of the Depósito. However, another aspect of that uncomfortable colonial relationship with Portugal, particularly as it developed in the twentieth century, was the extent to which events in Angola affected and altered the consciousness of Portugal. Since the loss of Brazil, Angola had become the center of Portuguese imperial focus, at least in the abstract. When, in 1961, uprisings heralded the beginning of the wars for independence, the intransigent reaction of the Estado Novo guaranteed its eventual demise thirteen years later. By committing Portugal's youth to a series of wars across the colonies that could not be won, the Estado Novo laid the foundations for its own overthrow at the hands of its armed forces. A peculiar aspect of that war, and one investigated by Margarida Calafate Ribeiro, was the presence of Portuguese women, who accompanied their husbands on their military service. Ribeiro provides testimony from Maria Adelaide Ruano, a Portuguese woman who lived in Angola during the Colonial War. The testimony reveals the extent to which the experience of Angola raised the consciousness of "ordinary" Portuguese that something was very wrong with their own political system at home.

Isabel Moutinho's article interrogates the literary results of the Portuguese memory of that costly war in Angola. For both Ribeiro and Moutinho, the act of "remembering Angola" is intrinsic to putting the pieces of Portugal back together after an outlived colonial experiment. Moutinho points to the double role of memory in novels by Portuguese authors that recount soldiers' experiences of the colonial war. They both preserve voices as a collective memory and provide the future with a memory of events. In many ways, the texts Moutinho studies bring closure to the old narratives of the Portuguese empire in Angola with which they dialogue. They serve, for Portuguese literature, as both a postscript and simultaneously a full stop to the imperial endeavor.

Independence in Angola turned the former colony into a memory not only for those Portuguese who were sent there to fight an unjust war, but also for those born in Angola who felt forced to flee with the installation of the MPLA government and the subsequent conflicts. Indeed, exile and migration seem to have been an intrinsic aspect of the lusophone postcolonial condition, and postindependence Angola, with its wars and injustices, has produced more than its fair share of exiles over the last thirty years. One such exile is Jorge Arrimar, whose roots lie in the highlands of Huíla. As David Brookshaw discusses in his article in relation to Arrimar, the rupture with one's roots may lead to an intense urge to wander, but it also triggers the desire to return to one's origins, and is thus underpinned by the importance of memory. For Brookshaw, the exiled Arrimar's recent acceptance into the Angolan Writers' Union indicates how Angola itself is opening up culturally as armed conflict ends in the country. Arrimar's life has come full cycle, as he finally becomes a legitimized literary voice within the cultural mainstream of post-revolutionary and postwar Angola. His life has been a journey home.

The journey, as Laura Cavalcante Padilha reminds us, was intrinsic to the imagination of the process of colonization. What she goes on to demonstrate in her article is the extent to which the journey—of the subject in search of its own alterities—is part of the postcolonial trajectory of the Angolan imagination. Angolan novelists, from Assis Júnior to Ruy Duarte de Carvalho, have depicted that quest through alterity as the desire to be recognized in and as a cultural body grounded in difference. Padilha's article provides a groundbreaking theoretical basis to approach a broad range of Angolan texts that contest in innovative and affirmative, rather than simply responsive, ways the fundamental Othering question posed in Camões's *Os Lusíadas*, when the bard asks "who might these people be?" (I: 45). As Padilha shows, they are a multiplicity who confirm identity through their own Others, rather than against an Other.

Ana Maria Mão-de-Ferro Martinho continues a theoretical approach, using the gaze of Orientalism as a tool when considering that desire to be recognized in difference. In her article, she reminds us of the extent to which Angola functioned as an imperial fantasy in the Portuguese colonial imagination—a new Orient against which the colonizer sought to define himself. The elites who led the struggle for the independence of Angola idealized the nation-to-be in an equally essentialist maneuver. Martinho reads in the works of José da Silva Maia Ferreira, António Jacinto, and Ruy Duarte de Carvalho, the vagaries of what we might term the Angolan Orientalist memory.

Livia Apa reminds us, in her article, that traumatic violence knows no "after." If, as the title of Lawrence Henderson's book suggests, Angola is a history of five centuries of conflict, we can extend Apa's argument to venture that there has been an excess of the "present" in the various narrations of Angola since the first colonial moment. Apa focuses on the effects of postindependence violence in Angola on the concepts of time and space, and points out that enduring conflict has been the only shared national memory possible until very recently. During the years of civil war, the defining categories of space and time lost their ability to orientate—a side-effect of the trauma she argues surfaces in its contemporary literature.

In her article, Inocência Mata argues that the poet Adriano Botelho de Vasconcelos, imprisoned by the MPLA, challenges the totalizing discourse of the government by calling for the past to be faced. Catharsis can only come for Angola through the enunciation of dissent and the refuting of silencing homogenization. Facing the recent past does not mean, in Mata's interpretation, a nostalgic elevation of what never actually was. Rather, it allows the poet to locate a patriotic position for himself through which to rebuild, and be liberated from the power of the traumas of all-too-recent episodes of injustice in Angola.

Fernando Arenas discusses in his article the recent renaissance in Angolan cinema, providing a critical review of an innovative turn in the nation's cultural production. While the films Arenas discusses are to a great extent a coming to terms with the horror of Angola's recent past, they also bear witness, he argues, to a more universal struggle for survival in spheres of armed conflict.

One of the most profound imprints of a nation's past, and increasingly, one of its most patriotic markers is what we are led to believe is its national cuisine. More often than not, the product of cultural mixing and colonial dislocations, what one eats as the quintessence of a nation in its dish both occludes and celebrates a checkered history of prandial miscegenation. Igor Cusack, in his article, outlines how Angolan cuisine has become a tool in the armour of national ideology, celebrated in national websites, internationally marketed in cookbooks, and integral to its literature. At the same time, he demonstrates the lusotropical undercurrent of Portugal's celebration of lusophone African cuisine. Drawing on Luandino Vieira, Manuel Rui, and Pepetela, Cusack shows how perceptions of food alter in line with the conception of the national self. In Pepetela's Jaime Bunda novels, the grotesquely overweight, bumbling detective—from an era of excess among the Angolan elites—has replaced the slender body of Sem Medo—the ill-fated hero of the revolution from *Mayombe.*

Robson Dutra interrogates the evolution of Pepetela's heroes in his article. In particular, he focuses on Jaime Bunda, as an example of the inauguration of detective literature in Angola, but through pastiche and parody. As Dutra shows, the particular form of Pepetela's detective novels undermines the hegemonic discourse of the absolute—questioning the very possibility of Truth in Angola today. Bunda bears witness in his bumbling questioning to the corruption and loss of noble cause characteristic of Angolan society today. Yet, written into his characterization is always the memory of the utopian ideal that briefly appeared to be in the ascendancy as the nation was born.

Phyllis Peres continues our study of Pepetela, and concludes the studies on Angola in this volume by reminding us of a work by the author that predates the assumption of his *nom de guerre*—and subsequent *nom de plume.* Peres reads the short story, "As Cinco Vidas da Teresa," published in 1962, as a useful key to understanding Pepetela's subsequent narrative evolution. She sees the trace of Fanon in the narrative, written and set in the dying days of colonialism. Teresa's body, alongside the hidden site of the *sanzala,* becomes part of the colonial landscape, subject to violation and colonization, but also the locus of resistance. Peres's speculation of the possible reincarnation of Teresa in a sixth life, in Pepetela's subsequent fiction of critique, gives pause for thought. What would Teresa in her innocent desire to be loved think of today's Angola—the Angola of Jaime Bunda or *Predadores?* Is Pepetela's portrayal of Shirley (the black, lesbian, American FBI agent in *Jaime Bunda e a Morte do Americano*) the postcolonial version of Teresa, as she claims empathy with Africa because she bears every marker of otherness but who in reality works against difference and for the hegemony of the global market? Or might the postcolonial Teresa be Mireille—the self-serving daughter of Vladimiro Caposso in *Predadores?* The nationalities of their names point to the true nature of the revolutionary change that has hit Angola. A lusonymic Teresa—both a product and a victim of Portuguese colonialism—gives way to an anglonymic Shirley and a franconymic Mireille—markers of neocolonial American, British, and French oil company profits. At so many levels, when we remember Angola, Pepetela's question is among the most relevant: "nunca mais"?

Note

[1] Angola's first oil concession was granted in 1910. Production began in the mid-1950s in the Cuanza basin. Congo-basin exploitation began in the 1960s and the huge offshore oil reserves of Cabinda began to be exploited in 1968. See Tvedten 82.

Works Cited

Birmingham, David. "Angola." *A History of Postcolonial Lusophone Africa.* Ed. Patrick Chabal. Bloomington: Indiana UP, 2002. 137-84.

———. *Empire: Angola and Its Neighbors in Africa.* Athens: Ohio UP, 2006.

García Márquez, Gabriel. *Operación Carlota: Los Cubanos en Angola; El Che Guevara en Africa; La Batalla contra el Reich Sudafricano.* Lima: Mosca Azul y Horizonte, 1977.

Hart, Keith, and Joanna Lewis, eds. *Why Angola Matters: Report of a Conference Held at Pembroke College, Cambridge, March 21-22, 1994.* Cambridge: African Studies Centre, 1995.

Henderson, Lawrence W. *Angola: Five Centuries of Conflict.* Ithaca: Cornell UP, 1979.

Hodges, Tony. *Angola: From Afro-Stalinism to Petro-Diamond Capitalism.* Bloomington: Indiana UP, 2001.

Pepetela. *Jaime Bunda, Agente Secreto.* Lisbon: Dom Quixote, 2001.

———. *Jaime Bunda e a Morte do Americano.* Lisbon: Dom Quixote, 2003.

———. *Mayombe.* Lisbon: Edições 70, 1980.

———. *Predadores.* Lisbon: Dom Quixote, 2005.

Tvedten, Inge. *Angola: Struggle for Peace and Reconstruction.* Boulder, CO: Westview, 1997.

Phillip Rothwell is Professor of Portuguese at Rutgers University. His recent publications include *A Postmodern Nationalist: Truth, Orality and Gender in the Work of Mia Couto* (Bucknell, 2004), *A Canon of Empty Fathers: Paternity in Portuguese Narrative* (Bucknell, 2007), and *Sexual/Textual Empires: Gender and Marginality in Lusophone African Literature* (Bristol, 2004; edited with Hilary Owen). Email: philroth@rci.rutgers.edu

Articles

E Agora José, Luandino Vieira? An Interview with José Luandino Vieira*

Margarida Calafate Ribeiro
Translated by Phillip Rothwell

A Cidade e a Infância (1960) is the first book by the Angolan author José Luandino Vieira, in which various physical, social, human, and psychological geographies of the city of Luanda appear fractured by tractors and tarmac. This book began a remapping of those geographies, and was the opening salvo of a multifaceted author we came to know through successive literary developments, particularly his *Luuanda* (1965) and *Nós os de Makulusu* (1967). But before this José Luandino Vieira we grew to admire appeared, a certain José Mateus Vieira da Graça existed. He was one of the multiple faces of a man embroiled in the political project of Angolan liberation. Folded into his personality was a literary alter ego characterized by lucidity and artistic playfulness. He had several names and many written texts attached to him. His work appeared in the magazine *Sul,* in Santa Catarina, Brazil. His poems, drawings, and commentaries appeared in newspapers in Angola, or in the publications of the Casa dos Estudantes do Império. They also surfaced in the journal *Cultura.* In fact, he was just about anywhere where a group of idealistic youngsters, "unidos nas ânsias, nas aventuras, nas esperanças" launched "o grande desafio."[1]

The Portuguese Secret Police quickly imprisoned him, afraid of his unique and powerful voice. So began his multiple dislocations: from Luanda to Lisbon; from Lisbon to Luanda; from Luanda to a concentration camp in Tarrafal, Cape Verde; from Tarrafal to Lisbon—an exacting itinerary

Portuguese Literary & Cultural Studies 15/16 (2010): 27-35.

throughout the 1960s. However, his literature endured and grew more intense. It was the space he reserved for liberty. Despite being imprisoned, he circulated through the shanty towns of Luanda via his creative writing, composed in the name of the ever more inventive José Luandino Vieira.

Who was that Luanda through which José Luandino Vieira wandered? Who was that Luanda that José Luandino Vieira sought out and still craves? It was a Luanda that countermapped the colonizer's city of cement, imprinted by tractors in *A Cidade da Infância*. It was a city born through the insurmountable difference imposed by that "tarmac frontier." It was a Luanda full of all sorts, of spaces and life enacted by a *nós*, who could be Vavó Xixi and Zeca Santos, or Binda and friends, or the boys from Makulusu, or so many others who eked out a living there and aspired to be happy.

Luanda pained because of the inhumanity imposed by a colonizer. Yet, at the same time, she was beautiful in her lived humanity, captured so skilfully by Luandino in her pregnant hope of imminent change. She was embodied through Vavó Xixi shielding her grandson, Zeca Santos, who only ever wants to survive, to eat well, to wear flashy clothes, and to fall in love. She comes to life through the women of the shantytown who argue over the ownership of an egg before various levels of wisdom and power, only to agree finally to the theft of the egg *and* the chicken, at the hands of Portuguese authorities. At the end of the day, whose are the riches of that land? Whose is the land? Who(se) is Luanda? Luandino's child characters answer that question. In those spaces, in that environment, through those characters, through that language that simultaneously defines and characterizes the environment of the city, the cultural difference that demanded and justified political independence was inscribed by Luandino into the Portuguese language. Here, the incalculable force of the margin is registered, reclaiming an Other order of knowledge, an Other symbolic organization, an Other language that was never contemplated by the colonial order that imposed the wound-ridden frontier between the tarmac city and the shantytown. That Other order permeates Kianda's song, a song José Luandino Vieira attempted to reinaugurate.

Forty years ago the publication of *Luuanda* caused quite a stir. The Portuguese Writers Association awarded it the *Grande Prémio da Ficção*—a prize Luandino could not receive since he was imprisoned in Tarrafal. In fact, the prize jury would not have been able to present it to him since they were also arrested for their daring political gesture at the height of the Salazar regime. Yet, *Luuanda*'s questions remain pertinent today. Where is Luanda? Or rather, where is that Luanda declamed, lived, and offered to us by José Luandino Vieira? Who is that Luanda? Beyond the legacies of the colonial city that survive either restored or in ruins, beyond the legacies of the shantytowns, which are ever growing, beyond the smothered song of Kianda that Pepetela shows us through the anguish of the elderly of Kinaxixi, beyond the new Luanda Sul, in Luanda itself, other children exist today, whom the pained gaze of Ana Paula Tavares forces us to see:

> Olha-me p'ra estas crianças de vidro
> cheias de água até às lágrimas
> enchendo a cidade de estilhaços
> procurando a vida
> nos caixotes do lixo. ("November" 36)

New and old doors remain closed blocking entry into *Luuanda*, where some beings remain quiet and voiceless, while others devour the city, filling it with scars and wounds.

The most prestigious literary prize in the Portuguese language, the *Prémio Camões*, was awarded to José Luandino Vieira in 2006 by a jury made up of Portuguese, Brazilians, Mozambicans, and Angolans. It was in recognition of both his work and the path he has traversed. However, "intimate and personal" reasons prevented him from accepting the award. This reaction was from a man who once had only sung of hope and wanted to open doors so that the breeze and the sun might reach all the city of Luanda. What were these "intimate and personal" reasons that led him to reject such an honour? A clue may be found at the end of the interview that follows, in response to a question inspired by Laura Padilha that I put to Luandino. The answer may also be contained in Ana Paula Tavares's poem, "Luuanda," published for the first time in this volume.

"For me, reading *Luuanda* is always an exercise in pleasure and enjoyment. Every time I pick up José Luandino Vieira's work, I can scarcely contain the emotion and ecstasy I feel inside." These are the words of Laura Padilha translated from her reading of *Luuanda*.[2] When we talk about celebrating the work, Luandino Vieira reminds us what we are doing: we are celebrating something that led to the destruction and closure of the Portuguese Writers Association, in 1965.

Luuanda gained a place in both Portuguese and Angolan history as a key moment of "enfrentamento," as the poet António Jacinto put it. Its commemoration involves, for us, José Luandino Vieira sharing the history of *Luuanda*:[3]

JLV: I wrote *Luuanda* while I was in prison in 1961-62. At the time, those of us from the Baixa[4] used to hang out at three or four cultural institutions: the *Cine Clube*, the *Sociedade Cultural*, which had a journal "Cultura," part of the *Jornal de Angola*, which was the paper of the *Associação dos Naturais de Angola*. We would read loads of Portuguese and Brazilian authors, including the novelists from the Northeast of Brazil, Graciliano Ramos, Jorge Amado, and many others. I was lucky enough to get on with people who had good libraries. In the fifties, we corresponded with the magazine *Sul*, in Santa Catarina, Brazil.

Anyway, at the time, I was in prison. Writing was a good way of killing time, as well as working out the causes that had got me into that situation. Just for having claimed a national consciousness, a national identity that translated into the nationalist activities that demanded independence, there I was. It was during this time of reflection and through chats with my friends who were also in jail—some of them also writers—that I came to understand that it wasn't enough just to construct characters who had never been in our literature. I had to make them real, truer, more representative. I also came to understand that the almost involuntary impulse to alter the Portuguese language, which happened when I put words in their mouths, was the path to follow if I was to make them more believable. The language of the working-class neighborhoods where I grew up was an integral and defining part of the identities of my characters, so the path for me to follow was clearly that one. These characters were already present in Angolan literature from the end of the nineteenth century, first in novels and then in short stories. For example, Cochat Osório and António Jacinto's works already introduced other languages and "tailorings" to Portuguese. The only thing is that these characters had never been central figures in the narrative, by which I mean they were not the characters around which the plot was structured.

So I began to write Vavó Xíxi ("Vavó Xíxi e seu neto Zeca Santos"), which, starting from a relationship between a grandmother and her grandchild, tells a dramatic story about hunger. I had been going around with the story's image in my head for ages. I had known, well actually I mean, I remember a woman collecting things out of trash cans. I later discovered that she was a rich lady, from the time when the Angolan bourgeoisie got on well with the Portuguese administration, the twenties. It is the story of hunger and of a vain adolescent, of which I am very fond. It's the story I like most from *Luuanda.*

Next I remembered the huge arguments between neighbors that took place in the working-class districts, all about chicken eggs. It was all-out warfare, in which my mother took part. The backyards were right next to each other, and the chickens wandered all over them, pecking in one yard, and laying an egg in another. That's how the "Estória da Galinha e do Ovo" came into being, a tale that inevitably echoes the cliché "which came first the chicken or the egg?" Who discovered whom? To whom does an egg belong, laid by a chicken who wanders from yard to yard? To whom do the riches of Angola belong? Several traditional and institutional authorities argue and give their views, validating power relations, and the traditional authorities compare their criteria with one another in order to reach an agreement. Until the Portuguese police arrive, who no longer want just the egg, but the chicken too. In other words, they don't just want the product but the source of riches too. And when it became a case of taking away not just the riches, but also the land, everyone united against this robbery, this alienation of property. At that historical juncture, there was no alternative. The only option was war. In the short story, the future generation, the children, resolve the issue: neither the chicken, nor the egg! The moral of the story is clearly political.

The story of the boy who robs ducks ("Estória do Ladrão e do Papagaio") has to do with our life in prison. In prison in Luanda, political prisoners were mixed with common criminals. Every time someone new arrived, someone knew or else tried to find out why they were in prison. Everyone lied about just about everything, and especially about the real reasons they had been sent to prison. They always claimed they were there for "manly" deeds, such as having raped a girl, or some such thing. One day, a crippled man arrived, and I asked the guard why the poor wretch was in prison. I was told that it was because he had robbed ducks. And so I began to write the story about a duck thief, which is really a love story.

I had written these stories when a friend of mine, a lawyer, older and more cultured, came to visit and brought me work by what he termed a "great Brazilian writer." He gave me the book, *Sagarana,* by Guimarães Rosa, where I saw written the word I had chosen to call my novellas. They were not actually novellas but they were longer than a short story and they had a form totally connected to orality. The word was "estória." In the first edition, the

Kimbundu title was still in parentheses: *Musoso uá sanji ni uá diiaki*, which means a story told historically in a traditional way. A "musoso" is told and retold and, as such, it evolves as an oral narrative. I finally had a way of designating my type of narrative. According to my fellow-countryman, who knows the Kimbundu language, the anthropologist Carlos Alberto Lopes Cardoso, this is the best translation for the Kimbundu word "musoso." It means precisely this type of "estória." Also according to Lopes Cardoso, the word had already appeared in the chronicles of Fernão Lopes. And, in fact, it does. So, I was in quite good company: Fernão Lopes, Carlos Alberto Lopes Cardoso, and Guimarães Rosa. However, for me, at a quite advanced stage of writing the stories—in fact they were finished—the great lesson of Guimarães Rosa was his use of language. He confirmed my intuition. Clearly, the example of his books showed me that if the language style used was not that one then I would not be able to say what I wanted to say with those characters, nor would they be able to say what they wanted to about their relation to the world. Characters are defined with certain physical characteristics, but above all it is the language register that defines them, the way they articulate discourse or handle Portuguese. Mr. Lemos with his legal discourse, his codes, speaks a language that no one there understands. Azulhinho reads his Bible. José da Quitanda speaks Portuguese, and orders others around because he can, since he brings food and drink. Guimarães Rosa reassured me that it was legitimate, in literary terms, to construct a literary language to achieve my objective. It represented a rupture, but I think that *Luuanda* achieves a harmonious relationship between the speech of the characters and the voice of the narrator. Reading *Sagarana*, after having written my "estórias," confirmed for me that I was on the right track. I cleaned it up. I deepened it. I worked at it because "handling" the language implied having a deep knowledge of Portuguese. I quickly got the originals out of prison, in the normal way prisoners use to get stuff out. There were frequent searches of the prisoners' cells. The PIDE were always looking for evidence or ways to incriminate us. My book was dangerous material, since it had a political message written in it. The language I had used demonstrated cultural autonomy. In my characters, in my countermapping of the city of Luanda, which brought the *musseques* to the fore, cultural difference was embedded, a difference that justified claims to political independence. At the time, this made my work political. Luckily, today, all this has been overtaken by history.

My wife, Linda, to whom the book is dedicated, typed it up, and showed it to a friend who was a journalist for the *ABC*, which was the paper of the democratic liberal Portuguese. Alfredo Bobela Motta, an Angolan, a writer and one of our friends, was at the time, 1963, its editor-in-chief. He decided straight away that we should go ahead and do the book. The book was put together in the paper's printworks. The typesetter did page proofs that later did the rounds in the *musseques* of Luanda. That was the edition that reached Portugal to compete for the Portuguese Writers Association prize. I think there were some hundred copies or so, and the Casa dos Estudantes do Império distributed it. I designed the cover, a hut with dripping letters, and I sent it with the original. Later, I suggested that they could place a picture of the actual city in dim grey in the background, and in the foreground, that black hut dripping, and the title in black. My design heralded in itself a countermap of the city. In the next edition of *Luuanda*, the letters of the title became red.

Now to the so-called "Brazilian" edition. That is an incredible tale. According to the cover information, the edition was done in Belo Horizonte. In fact, this edition was done completely without my involvement by two PIDE agents, in Portugal, at a local printworks. With all the scandal, which included the destruction of the Portuguese Writers Association, the book was in great demand. These two agents made the book in Braga and distributed it, earning a packet out of it. My lawyer wanted to file a law suit straight away, and this led to another incredible episode. To cut a long story short, I lost the case, because nothing could be proved—despite the fact that everything was totally obvious. The printworks were really easy to identify by the type of paper used. Worst of all, I had to pay all the court costs. In 1972, when I republished *Luuanda*, I was living in Lisbon on parole, that is, I had to present myself to the police every time I left the city, both before going and after coming back. Marcello Caetano tried a little liberalization, and that's how the poet António Jacinto and I got out of Tarrafal and came to Lisbon on parole. I got work with Edições 70, whose editor Soares da Costa told me that I ought to do a new edition of the book. I agreed. Ten years had passed and he was convinced that everything would work out fine. A standard edition was done, and a collector's edition too, with three sketches by José Rodrigues. But three or four days after the book had been launched, the National Information Secretariat ordered its seizure. My editor appealed this decision, and the appeal was in progress when the Carnation Revolution happened. Then, all of a sudden, the book was finally free to be distributed unimpeded.

At the time of the Carnation Revolution, the original manuscripts were sold at auction to get money for I no longer know what. I only have the first set of page proofs, with the corrections of another of my friends, Manuel Teixeira Dias Carvalheiro, who had done the copyediting. About ten years ago, I went to Lisbon for a writers' roundtable, and some friends turned up with something for me. In a small black box were the page proofs of *Luuanda*, which I have to this day. The 1972 edition included some changes that were due to the fact that in the meantime I had written *Nós, os de Makulusu* and *No Antigamente na Vida*. They were ten years of learning, of living with colleagues in the concentration camp. My comrades there included the writers António Jacinto, António Cardoso, Uanhenga Xitu, and Manuel Pedro Pacavira. Uanhenga Xitu and Manuel Pedro Pacavira had never written literature before and began to write in prison, showing us their texts. Seeing how my comrades used Portuguese, and discussing this with them, helped me to mature as a writer. Also, my contact with many people who were friends in my childhood helped me a lot, as did music, the musicality of the Kimbundu language. All this helped me to clean up the text, because the 1964 edition lacked some of the markers of Angolan Portuguese. Caminho is about to republish *Luuanda*. This time, I'm not making any changes to the text. The text is finished. Also, when I read it … it was written by someone else, someone who no longer exists. So it cannot be changed. It would be an act of disloyalty to interfere with something written by someone else….

MCR: I want to end by asking, in an echo of Laura Cavalcante Padilha: "Today, almost fifty years after the text was first written, trapped in the iron fists of neoliberal globalization, we can't help but remember the famous verse of Drummond—'E agora, José?' [And now, José?]. So let us ask another José, an Angolan: Does the Cabíri continue to fly? Can Xíxi and Zeca Santos still fish today to eat tomorrow? Did Beto and Xico build the future? And what happened to Garrido, Dos Reis and Xico Futa? Where might they be? Stubbornly, only the hope hidden in the cashew nut, the *sape-sape* or the egg may, if revived, be able to provide an answer."

JLV: The Cabíris will continue to fly. It is in their nature, even if, of course, man may begin to rear them in aviaries without feathers to increase capitalist profits, given the iron fist of globalization. I see it more as a "cage," and want the best for my "little bird," which otherwise is subjected to inclemencies, dangers, rivalries and has no food or water… . Yet, it only needs to carry on whistling. Grandma and grandson, for many more centuries, will have to get their food at the margin of the banquet of Others (hidden under their tables to catch a few of the crumbs, which these Others will allow to fall in their own interests), because Beto and Xico could not build the future after all. The mistake was theirs, and it will be repeated again and again because the future cannot be built—you can only struggle in the present in order to stop our future being built by those Others. But it's good that every generation of Betos and Xicos make the same mistake, and go on struggling. Garrido, Dos Reis, and Xico Futa have grown up and multiplied. There are more and more of them. And yes, the cashew nut, *sape-sape*, and the egg continue to be the seat of hope, because, fortunately, the Others cannot defeat two things: nature and her lessons, with death as her final exam.

Notes

* I wish to express my immense gratitude both to José Luandino Vieira for granting this interview, and to Laura Cavalcante Padilha for her invaluable guidance.

1 A reference to the poem "O Grande Desafio," by António Jacinto. On the birth of modern Angolan literature, see Vieira 109. See also Tavares, "Cinquenta Anos" 128.

2 See her "Um Texto e os Máximos Sinais de Suas Palavras Mais Velhas."

3 See Orsi for an interesting exploration of "estória/história" in relation to *Luuanda.*

4 "Baixa" was the lower part of the city, inhabited almost exclusively by Europeans and their descendants. It was used in opposition to the *musseques,* which were the areas occupied almost exclusively by Africans.

Works Cited

Jacinto, António. "O Grande Desafio." *Antologias de Poesia da Casa dos Estudantes do Império, 1951-1963 Angola e S. Tomé e Príncipe.* Lisbon: Edição ACEI, 1994. 153-155.

Orsi, Maria Grazia. *Lingua, stile e società in Luuanda di José Luandino Vieira.* Diss. University of Bari, Italy, n.d.

Padilha, Laura Cavalcante. "Um Texto e os Máximos Sinais de Suas Palavras Mais Velhas." *Revista Brasileira de Literatura Comparada* 9 [Rio de Janeiro: ABRALIC] (2006). 307-22.

Tavares, Ana Paula. "Cinquenta Anos de Literatura Angolana." *Via Atlântica* 3 (Dec. 1999).

———. "November Without Water." *O Lago da Lua.* Lisbon: Caminho, 1999.

Vieira, José Luandino. "Estória de família." *Lourentinho, Dona Antónia de Sousa Neto & Eu.* Lisbon: Edições 70, 1981.

Margarida Calafate Ribeiro is author of *Uma História de Regresso: Império, Guerra Colonial e Pós-colonialismo* and co-editor of both *Fantasmas e Fantasias Imperiais no Imaginário Português Contemporâneo* and *A Primavera Toda para Ti*. Email: margaridacr@mail.telepac.pt

As portas de *Luuanda*

Ana Paula Tavares

... a porta que era preciso abrir
para chegar o ar limpo
e o sol quente outra vez...
José Luandino Vieira, *Luuanda*

Dormem os homens às portas de *Luuanda*
a mais bela
porque se fecharam as portas
e chegaram as máquinas
para desfazer a cidade.
Diante das portas de *Luuanda*
pessoas, gritos, sonhos
estão agora mudos e quietos
debaixo do calor aceso da cidade
Chegaram as máquinas
para abrir o ventre vermelho da cidade
acordar o sono dos antigos
mudar o sentido da rosa-dos-ventos.
A memória ferida de *Luuanda*
escorre um mel espesso de lembranças
como os passos dos miúdos

Portuguese Literary & Cultural Studies 15/16 (2010): 37-39.

pelas areias soltas do museke.
As máquinas entraram dentro da cidade
pela raíz
fundaram uma rede de caminhos novos
longe dos cajueiros e das árvores de protecção
Os seres da água partiram
antes das portas se fecharem
antes das vinte portas se fecharem
em cada porta um segredo
para cada porta uma palavra
O coração de *Luuanda*
já não bate virado para a baía
uma cicatriz de lama
que não cura
salpica de sangue as antigas veias
da cidade.
Os barcos do mundo fecham
a última porta
deixando um vento gelado
afastar os passos dos monas
a voz das mães
para longe de Luuanda
João–Via–Rápida está sentado
e fuma
debaixo da última mulemba
um silêncio branco
mora em cada esquina
e pesa sobre o barulho das máqinas
que devoram a cidade
as portas da fala estão agora mudas
enquanto os pássaros engordam na garganta da cidade

Uma noite inocente
deita água sobre as feridas
e leva
"à porta que é preciso abrir
para chegar ao ar limpo

e ao sol
outra vez"

Lisboa, Setembro de 2005

Letras negras em folhas brancas: A escrita da História angolana por Antônio de Assis Júnior.

Regina Claro

Resumo: O artigo analisa a resistência angolana manifesta na literatura produzida por nativos mestiços e africanos no início do século XX. O conteúdo do nacionalismo "assimilado" é examinado através de dois exemplos de Antônio de Assis Júnior: *Relato doa acontecimentos de Dala Tando e Lucala* (1917-1918) e seu romance *O Segredo da Morta: Romance de costumes angolenses* (1935).

A introdução da linguagem escrita ocidental na África foi um dos elementos mais perturbadores da dominação européia sobre diversos povos do continente. Artefato técnico de fortes conteúdos ideológicos, a escrita foi o suporte para a delimitação das fronteiras entre a civilização européia e as culturas "autóctones." Aliás, como instrumento de poder e utensílio bélico, a escrita européia reconstruiu sua África: delimitou fronteiras internas, catalogou ritos e crenças, selecionou a memória. Do mesmo modo que na América, a escrita da história foi operada por uma ação que visava silenciar as expressões dos sujeitos a quem se referia, tornava inertes os corpos sociais que examinava e pretendia inscrever seus traços culturais, tornando passivos seus dominados (De Certeau 2-27).

O processo colonial com os seus modelos "civilizadores" transformou o fio condutor da transmissão da memória, sedimentado pela tradição oral. A educação moderna, nesse sentido, principalmente nos centros urbanos, estava em consonância com o projeto de assimilação proposto pelas metrópoles e nela se sustentava a idéia de uma primazia da cultura ocidental. Mas a idéia

Portuguese Literary & Cultural Studies 15/16 (2010): 41-56.

de África apresentada, sob o filtro do Ocidente, como um todo indiferenciado, opõe-se à sua complexa realidade. Por um lado, o nacionalismo dependente de modelos sociopolíticos, desenvolvidos alhures e a utilização dos elementos do conquistador em sua cultura. Por outro, a resistência ao projeto ocidental de domínio cultural, a reavaliação do projeto colonial de assimilação e a reconstrução da identidade africana. A resistência à dominação externa opera-se, assim, no campo da ambivalência. Essa ambivalência se manifesta no dilema do próprio tempo em que a história da África deve ser inserida. A escrita da história ordena e explica os atos coletivos, conforme um conceito de tempo e duração propriamente influenciado pelas referências judaico-cristãs.

Dentro do universo da oralidade africana, as forças vitais vibram na palavra, elemento de origem sagrada, mas que se encontra intimamente relacionada com as atividades cotidianas. A palavra é, ainda, instrumento de práticas políticas, uma vez que as decisões da família e da comunidade, em muitas nações africanas, são tomadas em conjunto mediante discussão e exposição das questões. Nesse sentido, sua capacidade de comunicação possui essência diversa daquela proposta pela escrita (Leite 106).

Renovar o tempo tradicional a partir da adoção do tempo histórico, valorizar e incorporar o passado, contestar a suposição da superioridade cultural ocidental, legitimar um discurso comum e acessível que fosse produto do encontro entre passado tradicional e presente colonial e não simplesmente a continuidade de um, ou a intromissão do outro. Tal é a tarefa das elites nativas angolanas, que passaram a ocupar as redações e os círculos editoriais como trincheiras de luta emancipatória, conferindo à literatura uma responsabilidade política.

As décadas situadas em torno da transição dos séculos XIX e XX evidenciaram transformações que devassaram todos os setores da sociedade angolana. Mudanças estas, registradas pela literatura produzida pelas elites nativas, mas que também modificaram essa literatura. Tais fenômenos históricos, ao mesmo tempo em que eram registrados pela literatura, apontavam para outros modos de observar, compreender e exprimir. A percepção da experiência histórica imprimiu à produção literária uma apreensão voltada para os processos de mudança, insatisfeita quanto ao seu destino e ansiosa por assumir a sua condução. A criação literária estava colada à história e sob essa atmosfera, servir às letras também significava ser atraído para uma atuação cívica. Paralelamente a literatura passou a ser veículo de um projeto nacional. Nesse sentido, a literatura não se constituiu como ferramenta passiva somente para a instrução ou divertimento do público. Mas, se estabeleceu como um ritual complexo que, se devidamente conduzido, tinha o poder de construir e modelar simbolicamente o mundo, a nação.

A evolução histórica das elites nativas de Angola constitui um dos elementos-chave para a compreensão da história angolana nas últimas décadas. Elites que se desenvolveram durante vários séculos de interação entre europeus e africanos e que ao longo do século XIX sofreram uma deterioração geral, de estatuto e de oportunidade. Na altura, parte delas, principalmente, as elites negras e mestiças, tentou uma mobilização em defesa de seus interesses contra a progressiva marginalização econômica, social e política. O registro escrito do seu pensamento estendeu-se, aproximadamente, por duas gerações, entre as décadas de 1870 e de 1930, momento em que a censura colonial proibiu definitivamente a livre expressão.

Nossa atenção se volta justamente para o pensamento das elites nativas negras e mestiças e as formulações de um discurso unitário, num contexto adverso, ou seja, as três primeiras décadas do século XX. Nesse sentido, a obra literária do intelectual angolano, Antônio de Assis Júnior (1877-1960), se torna fundamental perante a profusão de textos com pendor propagandístico do colonialismo português, especialmente a partir do lançamento dos concursos de literatura colonial. Para além de sua obra literária, seu nome se inscreve nas lutas e reivindicações republicanas, também designadas como movimentos nativistas.

Partimos da perspectiva de que a geração de Antônio de Assis Júnior viveu e escreveu num mundo de intensas transições (geográfica, política, social, cultural, mental), onde privado e público, passado e presente, mental e social se desenvolveram numa dinâmica de fronteira. Viveu numa sociedade colonial cujo caráter mestiço estava esvaziado de legitimidade para referências de identidades afirmativas, uma vez que as referências de positividade e afirmação eram pautadas pela qualidade "superior" do branco. Nesse sentido, as sociedades constituídas no âmbito dessas relações—em condições de dominação colonial—criaram uma difícil definição de sistemas de auto-representação.

A Europa, ao mesmo tempo em que levava técnicas e invenções aos povos subjugados, os punha em contato com seu repertório conceitual, seus pré-conceitos, suas idiossincrasias, no que se referia tanto a ela própria, quanto aos povos colonizados. Esses últimos, além terem sido privados de suas riquezas, de seus territórios e do produto de seu trabalho, tiveram que assumir como sua, uma representação que era na verdade, um reflexo da cosmovisão européia que considerava racialmente inferiores os negros e os mestiços. Nem mesmo as elites nativas letradas, puderam fugir desse rolo compressor ideológico.

A construção do imaginário colonial transformava diferenças em valores, tendo como fio condutor o racismo que permeava todos os domínios desse imaginário e o "ocidentalismo," como sua metáfora de superioridade, construída e reconstruída ao longo da história.[1] A África seria o espaço colonial do silêncio (sem pensamento, sem ciência, sem filosofia) que a civilização ocidental teria que conquistar, superar, dominar, desprezando todos os conhecimentos que não se ajustassem ao modelo autodefinido, encarcerados eternamente sob a definição de tradicionais, folclóricos, exóticos, insustentáveis. Deslocando os povos africanos, com outras lógicas de conhecimento e outras histórias, para as margens da razão cristã e ocidental. Para as margens da História.

Como resultado de um processo iniciado na segunda metade do século XIX, as elites nativas negras e mestiças angolanas chegaram na década de 30 do século XX expropriadas de seu estatuto político, social, econômico, cultural. Diante da hegemonia européia, os nativos orbitando à volta das elites mais antigas, foram relegados à situação de indígenas à medida que se institucionalizava a distinção legal entre estes e os nativos assimilados, mas tendendo-se ao tratamento inferiorizante a todos os angolanos. Essas elites tentaram reagir de diferentes formas à mudança do seu estatuto. Sem possibilidades de intervenção na administração, se voltaram paras as atividades em organizações associativas.

De qualquer maneira, as elites nativas negras e mestiças dos anos de 1930 estiveram distante da imagem de passividade e silêncio que por muito tempo lhes foi atribuída. Obviamente, não houve espaço para o tom passional e direto da imprensa do século XIX. Ainda sim a despeito da censura e da violência da República e do Estado Novo, essas elites revelaram empenho em marcar posição frente aos problemas da nação, num discurso de auto-afirmação nacional possível construído nas fronteiras, por entre as tramas ideológicas coloniais. Fez parte dessa geração Antônio de Assis Júnior, escritor, intelectual, romancista, lingüista, historiador, advogado, jornalista, ativista político.

Isso nos permite questionar as divisões binárias onde as esferas da experiência social angolana foram freqüentemente colocadas. Logo, acreditamos que Assis Júnior produzia conhecimento a partir das margens, na intersecção conflituosa entre histórias e saberes. Com uma história avançando no sentido de impor seu modelo transformado em "universal" e as outras reagindo forçadas a se adaptarem a uma nova realidade. Ao mesmo tempo em que Assis Júnior construía um imaginário, descrevia o modo pelo qual percebia e concebia sua cultura e o mundo. Assim, para entendermos a produção literária e política de Assis Júnior e seu discurso de unidade, talvez seja necessário examinar os espaços intermediários, as fissuras.

As elites nativas angolanas desde a sua emergência, em princípios do século XIX, até seu declínio no século XX, construíam seu lugar cultural, social, político e econômico em espaços intersticiais que permitiam que os confrontos fossem tanto negociados, quanto conflituosos. A construção da nação se fazia em espaços de ambivalência, e de construção recíproca. O que nos permite questionar o enquadramento feito para Assis Júnior, qual seja, de uma prática política paradoxal quando criticava e denunciava os abusos da administração colonial e ao mesmo tempo reivindicava postos e funções nessa mesma administração.

Antônio de Assis Júnior firmou-se como intelectual durante a vigência da primeira República em Portugal. Seu posicionamento político e suas atividades profissionais como advogado provisionário o levaram a prisão por duas vezes, num espaço de cinco anos (1917 e 1922). No cárcere, Assis Júnior escreveu o *Relato dos Acontecimentos de Dala Tando e Lucala* onde narra sua experiência. Mais que registro do acontecimento, o autor toma a pena para defender-se das acusações que lhe foram imputadas e registrar a injustiça e abusos da administração colonial e sua profunda desilusão. [2]

Foi diretor de jornal, participou e acompanhou o florescimento dos movimentos associativos em Angola. À medida que os jornais eram fechados pela repressão colonial, o movimento intelectual foi se organizando em outras associações culturais, articulando novos códigos, adaptando-se a novas circunstâncias.[3] Em 1930, Assis Júnior elaborou os estatutos para criação de uma nova associação: a Liga Nacional Africana, sucessora da antiga Liga Angolana, e foi seu presidente em 1930, 1931, 1933 e 1935. A Liga Nacional Africana foi uma das poucas instituições organizadas pelos intelectuais nativos, nesse período, e a única com um órgão regular na imprensa angolana: a *Revista Angola*.[4]

A revista foi um espaço de debates e controvérsias sobre o que na época foi denominado de "literatura colonial," com a proliferação de obras sobre as colônias através dos concursos promovidos pela Agência Geral das Colônias, instituídos a partir de 1926. Como jornalista, colaborou ainda em diversos jornais de Luanda entre eles *A Província de Angola*, *O Angolense*, e *O Direito*. Esse último ligado à Liga Nacional Africana, onde alguns de seus membros também eram dirigentes e colaboradores do jornal. O jornal *O Direito* se posicionava como porta-voz de nativos e indígenas e, portanto, como veículo de unidade da nação.

Em meados da década de 1940, Assis Júnior colaborava com o jornal *O Farolim*, que a despeito de sua irregularidade, foi o principal veículo dos intelectuais nativos até final da década de 1940. Nesse jornal, Assis Júnior trabalhou ao lado de jovens como Agostinho Neto que, a 11 de Novembro de 1975, tomaria posse como o primeiro presidente da República Popular de Angola.

A década de 1930 foi marcada pela fase de maturidade de Assis Júnior. Não apenas a maturidade social e política, mas literária, com a publicação de sua obra mais importante, designada *O Segredo da Morta. Romance dos costumes angolenses*. Assis Júnior havia iniciado a publicação do *O Segredo da Morta* em artigos de folhetim no jornal *A Vanguarda*, em 1929, ainda no exílio, e em 1935, reuniu-os em livro que foi publicado pela Livraria Editora A Lusitana. Além das colaborações em inúmeros jornais e revistas literárias, de nos deixar um relato-testemunho, um romance e alguns pequenos contos, Antônio de Assis Júnior escreveu o *Dicionário Kimbundu-Português. Lingüístico, Botânico, Histórico e Corográfico* com edição de Argente, Santos & Cª Lda., em Luanda.[5]

Podemos considerar que Assis Júnior participou de dois momentos importantes da história angolana, talvez justamente por esse motivo, sua produção literária e atividade política estejam tão associadas à imagem de ponte, símbolo de ligação. Teve como referência, ainda muito jovem, a vitalidade da *Geração de 1880*, nas figuras de José Fontes Pereira ou Joaquim Dias Cordeiro da Matta. Como intelectual maduro, presenciou a decadência e morte dessa geração, no período de forte repressão do colonialismo português, e talvez por esse motivo seja considerado como seu último representante (Mourão 23). Assis Júnior também conviveu com os jovens "descobridores de Angola," como Agostinho Neto (1922-1979), na década de 1950.

O seu testemunho político e literário expõe não somente as diferenças, mas o abismo entre o projeto da metrópole para Angola e o projeto dos angolanos para Angola. No decorrer do *Relato dos Acontecimentos de Dala Tando e Lucala* de 1917, por exemplo, no qual o autor promete "*fazer a história com exatidão,*" estão colocadas algumas de suas posturas com relação às dúvidas acerca da metrópole como referência "civilizacional," o que imaginava para uma nação angolana e as incertezas quanto a seu papel na construção dessa nação.

O texto escrito por Assis Júnior é mais que uma reação particularista à repressão do governo colonial ou aos rumores de sua participação numa conspiração nativista. É a defesa e a declaração virulenta dos direitos e da dignidade de todos os angolanos. O impedimento ao direito à cidadania extensivo às colônias africanas, patentes na Carta Constitucional republicana, abriu espaço para a formulação do conceito de identidade coletiva.

Posto à margem, Assis Júnior se apresenta como um herói sem passado, separado das antigas tradições. Esta ruptura não acontece sem deixar um rastro de inquietação e amargura, sentimentos que o impelem a gritar seu testemunho como um apelo. Mas não é somente um discurso amargo, ele parte da amargura para construir seu discurso de auto-afirmação. À medida que vai refletindo acerca dos acontecimentos e de sua própria marginalidade, Assis Júnior dá forma a um novo grupo nacional: cidadãos que viram seus direitos lesados. Os envolvidos são tomados num plano universal, no que tange aos seus direitos, em igualdade com o universo dos colonos. Os volumes são especialmente valiosos para o historiador, por retratarem a tensão e o conflito do nativo civilizado: um homem de fronteira ou um homem "entre dois fogos," segundo o próprio Assis Júnior (*Relato* 128).

O *Relato dos Acontecimentos de Dala Tando e Lucala* se revela, portanto, como um documento em nada "silencioso" e, seu autor não se apresenta nem submisso, nem particularista, mesmo silenciado pelas autoridades coloniais. Acima de tudo, é prova de continuidade, e não de interrupção, dos protestos iniciados no século XIX e que dariam suporte aos explosivos protestos posteriores. O discurso de Assis Júnior foi construído nas fronteiras da lei que tanto defendeu; nas fronteiras da humanidade que tanto prezou. É a partir das fissuras da justiça, da humanidade e da história que se pronuncia o discurso de unidade de Assis Júnior.

A prisão é o exílio, a antítese do lugar. A partir da experiência de ser espoliado em seus direitos de cidadão, da injustiça cometida pela justiça da qual fazia sua profissão, da desumanização a que estava sendo submetido por uma política que se dizia humanitária, é que Assis Júnior abandona os antigos conceitos e historiciza sua condição. Com isso, seu universo vivido é dado como uma imagem da história. Não há distinção entre a vida privada e a vida pública. O seu próprio destino se torna uma maneira de agir na história. Seus conflitos internos se tornam dramas históricos e se ligam aos movimentos da própria nação. Em diversos momentos do texto, Assis Júnior faz explodir como um *insight*, esse sentimento de participação da história. A iminência da morte faz com que o relato de Assis Júnior se estabeleça como testemunho. Sua experiência pessoal passa a ter um poder de comunicabilidade histórica. Um momento na história apreendido em relação com uma existência particular.[6]

A despeito de sua proposta de uma narrativa exata, sem paixão e sem ornato, o que confere à obra seu tom de testemunho é justamente seu caráter parcial e lacunar. Ele não descreve os acontecimentos como simples observador que viu e ouviu. Nem simples exposição de motivos, nem simples justificação, nem simples explicação analítica de uma atividade política ou social. O que Assis Júnior nos revela nas fissuras de sua exposição é que a sua maneira de ser e viver carregava já a sua justificação: a obrigação de viver o momento revelou seu destino de homem na história.

O testemunho não é o relato indiferente de um observador ou de um cientista, mas uma comunicação, um esforço apaixonado por transmitir aos outros, que também contribuíam para a história, a sua própria emoção da história. Por isso o testemunho de Assis Júnior se torna um ato propriamente histórico, porque se desvia na verdade, da pura objetividade cientista para se situar no encontro entre uma vida particular e as pressões coletivas. Seu testemunho é o drama de uma geração, de toda uma camada sociopolítica e não testemunho de um só indivíduo.

Na feitura do texto, o processo de relembrar é de intensa descoberta e desorientação. Esse relembrar promove uma reorganização de um passado que foi dividido e separado para compreensão do trauma do presente. Dessa ambivalência, emerge uma estratégia de subversão em sua escrita. O estranhamento e o deslocamento criam espaços de reflexão antagônicos e conflituosos, que ousam extrapolar a idéia historicista de tempo como um todo progressivo e ordenado. A necessidade de "fazer a história" se fundamenta numa realidade na qual a opinião pública, seus interlocutores, destino final de sua escrita, seria incapaz de estabelecer por si só a autenticidade dos fatos: quer porque ignorasse os fatos mais essenciais; quer porque seria enganada por uma documentação manipulada ou equivocada—daí a intenção do autor de reconstituí-los.

Já no romance *O Segredo da Morta*, Assis Júnior utiliza o discurso ficcional não somente como objeto estético, como também procura transformá-lo em veículo de compreensão do homem nas relações com o mundo que produz. Parte de registros do passado da pátria para fazer uma reflexão, no presente, acerca do sentido de uma identidade nacional.

A ficção, assim como o artigo, o ensaio, o testemunho, seria o espaço privilegiado de um tenso e intenso embate. A escrita, arma obtida do colonizador, seria o antídoto fabricado do próprio veneno da conquista européia. A ficção se tornaria o campo de revelação, no seu duplo sentido de encobrir e expressar, lugar da memória e do esquecimento, da vida e da morte, do segredo e da compreensão. Meio privilegiado para a afirmação de uma identidade cultural e construção da história da nação que imaginava. Na emergência dos interstícios, provocados pela ficção, é que as experiências coletivas de nação, o interesse comunitário ou o valor cultural seriam negociados. Num processo em que o passado não seria retomado, mas refigurado.[7]

Essa mesma dinâmica de fronteira nos permite desconstruir a imagem de "ponte," para deslocá-lo do universo dos ritos de passagem ou períodos pré-estabelecidos, circunscrevê-lo dentro de um projeto intelectual específico. Ao ficcionar a história, o autor permite que sejam reconstituídos traços próprios da luta pela conquista de um espaço nacional que se apresenta no embate inevitável e violento entre colonizadores e colonizados. Um narrador onisciente organiza os fatos, relata os acontecimentos, dando voz ora a uns, ora a outros.

De um lado, colonizadores carregam seu estandarte civilizador e missionário e reivindicam para si a posse e o domínio do espaço geográfico denominado Angola. De outro, as nações e comunidades tradicionais para quem "Angola" ainda não existe enquanto um corpo territorial e cultural agregador. E entre um extremo e outro, uma nação por ele imaginada. Pois a nação de Assis Júnior, não se circunscreve à simples transposição da herança de um passado tradicional ou à mera experiência colonial. A morte e seus segredos são a expressão da experiência de confronto entre duas forças que se opõem e só é possível compreender o "segredo da morta" na sua inteireza, se o olhar puder agregar essas duas forças. No fazer a história, Assis Júnior se propõe a um trabalho de reunir e ligar partes divididas, espalhadas, ou desconhecidas.

Esses espaços intersticiais estabelecidos pela escrita de Assis Júnior, indicam o terreno para a elaboração de estratégias de subjetivação, propiciadoras de novos signos de identidade e postos inovadores de colaboração e contestação, no ato de definir a própria idéia de sociedade. A escrita reconstrói os fatos passados, mas também faz explodir, como *insights*, uma espécie de consciência, onde os lugares anteriormente definidos se deslocam para as fronteiras. À medida que elaborava e organizava suas reflexões na escrita, acerca do lugar da colônia como extensão da metrópole, deslocava e colocava em cheque esse lugar.

O "fazer história" de Assis Júnior, portanto, se constituiu como o espaço onde o autor constrói o seu lugar. Espaço marginal, movediço, intertextual, numa temporalidade descontínua, num movimento flutuante de instabilidade oculta. Esses nos parecem ser os elementos que constituem o universo no qual Assis Júnior negocia e traduz suas identidades culturais. Dessa forma, podemos apreender melhor o sentido do romance de Assis Júnior, dentro do projeto de construir a história da nação, que se manifesta também como vontade reconstitutiva. Não se busca a ressurreição de um tempo mítico. O que está em jogo é uma aposta na história. O "ser" cultural não está posto, a espera de ser resgatado, está se construindo.

De fato, a formação da nação angolana, em Assis Júnior, não caberia exatamente num único conceito definidor. Não se tratava de uma nação em que a cidadania tenha sido, mesmo enquanto idéia, uma força política capaz de forjar uma identidade. Constituía, outrossim, uma nação onde dificilmente se poderia apelar para as tradições ancestrais do "povo" ou para sua homogeneidade étnica ou lingüística. Era uma nação sem "povo," com a maior parte de seus habitantes totalmente excluídos de participação e direitos políticos, vistos com desconfiança e superioridade pelos colonos brancos. Uma nação que também não poderia apelar para a contigüidade de seu território, posto que a consciência territorial ainda se encontrava em formação.

A escrita de Assis Júnior foi se constituindo para criar a memória da nação que surgia. Assim, os heróis foram entronizados no interior de uma versão que atribuía a diferentes episódios, caráter de movimentos nacionais. Ele próprio tornado mártir, seria capaz de reconciliar passado e presente e criar uma outra imagem de nação. Diante das enormes diferenças sociais e culturais, a questão da identidade nacional permaneceu como uma questão intelectual importante. No romance, a "alma do povo angolano" foi perscrutada em várias direções, definida e redefinida na busca de uma identidade capaz de solidificar a imagem da nação. A nação de Assis Júnior não surgiria sem traumas, na medida em que comportaria dentro de si tradições em choque que deveriam ser amalgamadas, interesses de grupos que deveriam ser transpostos.

No romance, o "fazer história" e a construção de uma identidade nacional é elaborada por meio de um conjunto de artifícios, utilizados pelo autor. Ele intercala técnicas da chamada prosa erudita com elementos de elocução popular; a intervenção de uma língua africana (quimbundo) no idioma oficial (português); a oralidade, ritmos dos enigmas, provérbios e estórias, na fixidez e bidimensionalidade do papel. Que dariam uma dimensão polissêmica ao enunciado, operando assim, a instauração de todo um imaginário. Imaginário instaurado e fundamentado em formas alternativas de ruptura, de resistência e de superação.

A morte, sempre presente no imaginário e na escrita de Assis Júnior, suas representações e desdobramentos se constituiriam como importante elemento no processo de construção do discurso, pois como alegoria, possibilitava falar de uma coisa por meio de outra. No *Relato dos Acontecimentos de Dala Tando e Lucala*, seu discurso nacional emerge das fronteiras da morte, que se apresenta de diversas formas. A morte física, pois sua vida na prisão estava ameaçada e a morte política e social, pois corria o risco de ser deportado para a Guiné como indígena privado de existência civil.

No romance, a morte é entendida como fonte de poder, pois altera a ordem existente, criando as potencialidades de uma nova ordenação. É símbolo de perigo, mas também símbolo de poder. Com a desordem do espírito, dos sonhos, do delírio, aparecem comportamentos novos e forças novas. A morte se apresenta como degeneração e desequilíbrio, mas também como espaço de denúncia. Os mortos falam a verdade: advertem os vivos (**Areia 197.**). O choque das culturas desloca o discurso silenciado sobre a identidade nacional para as fronteiras, no uso da alegoria da morte. Isso porque diferentemente das sociedades africanas em que os mortos estão presentes entre os vivos, os mortos, segundo uma perspectiva européia, estão fora da ordem social estabelecida, não são mais sujeitos das relações na sociedade humana (**Oexle 29.**). É justamente nesse espaço que Assis Júnior irá atuar. Nas fronteiras do entendimento do colonizador é que ele vai dizer verdades e suas musas dar a ouvir revelações.

No espaço instaurado pela morte, Assis Júnior tenta criar um novo entendimento para a realidade do corpo social. No espaço movediço das fronteiras há a possibilidade de se pensar uma nova ordem. Num contexto de silêncio imposto, suas reflexões se encontram nos bastidores da ficção. Por meio da ficção, Assis Júnior se serve do engenho, de jogos, segredos e enigmas para a composição de uma sociedade, ao mesmo tempo em que abria alternativas para o ato de escrever a história. O autor ao historiar as estórias, compunha a história de Angola. História que pressupunha uma escrita.

A História como disciplina também trata a morte (o passado) como um objeto do saber. Mas falar dos mortos é também negar a morte, é quase desafiá-la, na medida em que a presentifica. Esse procedimento paradoxal, do trabalho da morte e contra a morte, é simbolizado pela escrita, cujo gesto tem valor de mito e de rito, posto que a escrita substitui as representações tradicionais por um trabalho de representação articulador num mesmo espaço de ausência e de presença (De Certeau 2-27).

Por outro lado o canto também nasce da memória (a Memória gerou as Musas que são as palavras cantadas). A palavra falada também é do domínio do ser, posto que presentifica. E o *aedo* (poeta) é o cultor da memória. Ao poeta-narrador é outorgado o poder de cantar o passado e o futuro. Passado e futuro que se tornam equivalentes na indiferença da exclusão, pois habitam do mesmo modo o reino noturno do esquecimento, até que a memória os recolha e faça-os presentes pelas vozes das musas. Porém, a palavra escrita com sua fixidez e precisão, aprisiona, despoja a palavra falada paulatinamente de seu poder de encantamento e a domestica no cativeiro da escritura. Mas, as fronteiras abertas por Assis Junior permitem que este sirva a dois deuses: à palavra cantada e à palavra escrita. Somente neste espaço lhe é possível fazer falar o corpo que se calou. Logo, o instrumento que cala o passado oral das estórias, no tempo da História e no espaço do papel, é o mesmo que faz falar.

A força de presentificar e descobrir pondo os seres e fatos à luz da Presença é a mesma força que oculta e encobre, subtraindo-lhes a luz e impondo-lhes a ausência. Por um lado, o esforço das Musas, filhas da Memória, está em retirar os fatos e os seres do reino da Noite, mãe do Esquecimento, e torná-los Presença. Por outro, a deusa Memória também gerou suas filhas como esquecimento "para olvídio dos males e pausa de aflições" (Hesíodo 5.55). Como força divina, manifestam os fatos como lúcida presença ou os encobrem sob o véu da similitude.

Em um contexto no qual a política colonialista portuguesa impunha a ausência, o esquecimento, e, sobretudo, o silêncio da produção literária negra e mestiça, a obra de Assis Júnior se ergue como voz. Seu projeto se transforma no fio de continuidade entre o passado e o futuro das negras letras angolanas, no caminho da escrita de sua História. A conjuntura obriga Assis Júnior a voltar-se para si e questionar seu destino presente: um passado entre fato e ficção. O romance procura novos rumos, outros destinos, em que a pátria é objeto de ficção. O universo literário assume o poder de alterar o passado para redefinir presente e futuro.

O autor conhece o poder dos vestígios. O presente não modifica os vestígios do passado. Mas o presente modifica as projeções do futuro. Ao se reportar ao passado, Assis Júnior pensa nos resultados do passado na identidade presente. E a avaliação do presente se abre para o futuro. No universo ficcional, o escritor com seu poder demiúrgico é capaz de criar, construir, reconstruir e desconstruir o mundo; e pode realizar "o que poderia ter sido." Assis Júnior parte de um corpo dilacerado que reclama união. Enfrenta mitos, reinventa-os: revisita e recria a memória numa disposição literária.

Há perguntas veladas, que perseguem a narrativa e que não se resolvem com a resolução do mistério do segredo da morta. Quando uma comunidade de indivíduos toma consciência de si própria como uma força com um destino histórico, e luta pela sua autodeterminação política? É possível pensar em unidade nacional, quando a unidade é imposta pela conquista e pela dominação? A nação nasce quando o indivíduo se sente ligado e comprometido com a terra. Ele tem que falar e pulsar por ela, crescer e multiplicar para ela, sair em defesa dela. A nação nasce de uma escolha. O romance traça essa trajetória do complexo processo de aquisição de consciência da nacionalidade através da experiência, no tempo. E de que maneira cada um estabelece seu sentimento de fazer parte de uma história nacional.

O jogo discursivo que alterna as várias vozes ficcionais, compõe um verdadeiro mosaico de propostas e sentimentos que denunciam a realidade da fragmentação do projeto colonial no passado. Ao mesmo tempo, revela as contradições do projeto nacional no presente. A organização dos acontecimentos históricos, a explicitação do tempo, demarcam a dominação e a sua negação, a exploração e a resistência.

O Segredo da Morta se apresenta como manifestação dessa dinâmica paradoxal. Nela encontramos todos os ingredientes: fascínio, dependência e rebelião. Era preciso enfrentar a tradição oral, os dialetos, as práticas cotidianas tradicionais. Enfrentar, se opor, se rebelar. Era preciso enfrentar os marcos fundadores, as guerras de ocupação, a administração colonial, a língua, a escrita e as práticas cotidianas portuguesas. O ser angolano, em Assis Júnior, seria parido a partir do enfrentamento, da oposição e da superação dessas forças ancestrais.

Os marcos de fundação, os primeiros encontros entre portugueses e africanos estão intercalados com a mitologia clássica grega e as mitologias tradicionais. Ao conjunto desses elementos se juntam um passado turvado pelo tráfico negreiro e um presente deslizante entre o auge e o declínio das elites nativas negras e mestiças. Por fim, encontramos nos bastidores da ficção, um Assis Júnior fazendo intervenções e refletindo sobre o passado, presente e futuro da sociedade angolana e da nação.

Essa diversidade é fundamental para a construção da história. Era preciso reconstruir o tempo, o espaço, as estórias. Era preciso reconstituir a trajetória portuguesa, do litoral ao interior, se apossando, delimitando, demarcando, devastando. Era preciso reconstituir a rebeldia das nações africanas e os seus obstáculos infindáveis à penetração portuguesa. Era preciso recordar a escravidão e a participação ativa de portugueses e africanos no comércio negreiro.

Assis Júnior se apresenta como um exilado de dois mundos que procura maneiras de superar os impasses de sua geração. Parece-nos marca de um pensamento que procura alternativas, coloca as verdades em suspenso e aberto aos questionamentos e reformulações na construção de uma identidade nacional. Portanto, distante da imagem de passividade que foi atribuída à sua geração. Seguramente um projeto dessa importância, no momento histórico em que viveram, não poderia deixar de se cercar de ambivalências, na medida em que o projeto pressupunha uma composição entre os diferentes grupos sociais e a afirmação de um compromisso entre passado, presente e futuro. As marcas desse empenho ficariam impressas na escrita de Assis Júnior, carregando o registro das vacilações que traduziriam as incertezas do período.

Notas

[1] Sobre o tema subalternização ocidental dos conhecimentos, veja-se: Walter Mignolo "La colonialidad a lo largo y a lo ancho: el hemisferio occidental en el horizonte colonial de la modernidad"; *Histórias locais. Projetos globais. Colonialidade, saberes subalternos e pensamento liminar*; "Os esplendores e as misérias da "ciência": colonialidade, geopolítica do conhecimento e pluri-versalidade epistémica" e John Beverly.

[2] O *Relato dos Acontecimentos de Dala Tando e Lucala* foi publicado originalmente em dois pequenos volumes pela editora Mamã Titã de propriedade da Liga Angolana. O primeiro

volume, publicado em 1917, é composto de seis capítulos em que o autor procura demonstrar de que maneira a versão das autoridades coloniais era distorcida e falsificada. A versão mascarava os conflitos de terras entre colonos e proprietários indígenas na região de Dala Tando e Lucala como revolta nativista articulada às revoltas em outras regiões, no mesmo período. A documentação forjada pelas autoridades coloniais tinha como intuito provar o envolvimento de Assis Júnior, entre outros, no movimento. O segundo volume, publicado em 1918, é composto por oito capítulos, na qual o autor se concentra em refutar ponto por ponto a versão das autoridades coloniais, a partir da recolha dos depoimentos de outros nativos acusados e igualmente encarcerados em Luanda. Além dos depoimentos, o autor se permite desenvolver suas reflexões pessoais e apaixonadas com grande veemência.

[3] As atividades das associações centravam-se na defesa dos direitos dos nativos contra as medidas discriminatórias de recorte racial, tornando-se fórum de críticas e protestos. Reivindicavam sua condição de cidadãos portugueses, reiterando as idéias pregadas pela República, queixando-se das arbitrariedades das autoridades e dos colonos. Foram fundadas dezenas de associações com fins recreativos, de instrução e de assistência, entre 1910 e 1922. No entanto, a expansão das ligas e grêmios nas colônias não foi pacífica, pois os poderes locais levantavam obstáculos à constituição das associações nativas, protelavam a aprovação dos seus estatutos e, quando lhe eram imputadas responsabilidades no levantamento das populações, puseram termo às suas atividades, cujo caso da Liga Angolana e de seu veículo de divulgação, o jornal *O Angolense*, é exemplar.

[4] A Liga Angolana foi uma das primeiras associações criadas no período republicano. Foi fundada em 1912, reconhecida e inaugurada em março de 1913, sob os auspícios do então Governador-Geral José Maria Norton de Matos. Apesar da legitimidade conferida à Liga, atestada pela presença do chefe do Governo, sua atuação foi acentuando a desconfiança das autoridades coloniais frente às elites nativas. Após diversas denúncias de participação em levantes e greves, a Liga Angolana foi dissolvida oficialmente através de decreto em 22 de fevereiro de 1922, por Norton de Matos.

[5] Esse dicionário foi escrito num total de 24 fascículos, sendo o primeiro impresso pela tipografia Mondego em dezembro de 1941, com uma tiragem de 1000 exemplares e o último impresso pela mesma tipografia em agosto de 1947, com uma tiragem de 600 exemplares. Antônio Assis Júnior. *Dicionário Kimbundu-Português. Lingüístico, Botânico, Histórico e Corográfico.* Luanda, Argente, Santos & Cª Lda, 1941: II: fevereiro/1942; III: maio/1942; IV: outubro/1942; V: dezembro/1942; VI: abril/1943; VII: outubro1943; VIII: dezembro/1943; IX: março/1944; X: setembro/1944; XI: novembro/1944; XII: março/1944; XIII: abril/1945; XIV: agosto/1945; XV: setembro/1945; XVI: dezembro/1945; XVIIfevereiro/1946; XVIII: junho/1946; XIX: novembro/1946; XX: abril/1947; XXI: maio/1947; XXII: junho/1947; XXIII: julho/1947; XXIV: agosto/1947.

[6] Naquilo que Phillipe Áries identificou como "o engajamento do homem na história." In "O engajamento do homem moderno na história" (70-88).

[7] Segundo Homi Bhabha a ambivalência inerente ao poder colonial estabelece uma situação de "entre-lugar" que é resultado do confronto de dois ou mais sistemas culturais (20).

Obras Citadas

Areia, Manuel L.R. "Antropologia da morte: uma perspectiva africana: a morte e o exercício do poder na sociedade cokwe de Angola." *Revista Internacional de Estudos Africanos* 1 (1984): 193-198.

Assis Júnior, Antônio. *Relato dos acontecimentos de Dala Tando e Lucala.* 2 vols. Luanda: Tipográfia Mamã Tita, 1917.

———. *O Segredo da Morta. Romance de costumes angolenses.* Luanda: Livraria Editora A Lusitana, 1935.

———. *O Segredo da Morta. Romance de costumes angolenses.* Lisboa: Edições 70, 1979.

———. *Relato dos acontecimentos de Dala Tando e Lucala.* Luanda: União dos Escritores Angolanos, 1985.

Bhabha, Homi. *O local da cultura.* Trad. Belo Horizonte: Editora UFMG, 1998.

Bosi, Alfredo. *Dialética da colonização.* 3ª ed. São Paulo: Cia. das Letras, 1992.

De Certeau, Michel. *A escrita da História.* Trad. Rio de Janeiro: Forense-Universitária, 1982.

Hesíodo. *Teogonia. A origem dos Deuses.* Trad. São Paulo: Roswitha Kempf, 1986.

Leite, Fábio. "Valores civilizatórios em sociedades negro-africanas." *África. Revista do Centro de Estudos africanos*18/19 (1995/1996): 102-118.

Mourão, Fernando Augusto Albuquerque. *A Sociedade Angolana através da Literatura.* São Paulo: Ática, 1978.

Oexle, Otto Gerhard. "A presença dos mortos." *A Morte na Idade Média.* Org. Braet, Herman & Werner Verbeke. Trad. São Paulo: Edusp, 1996.

Said, Edward W. *Orientalismo. O Oriente como invenção do Ocidente.* Trad. São Paulo: Cia. das Letras, 2001.

Regina Claro é mestre em História pela Universidade de São Paulo (Brasil), pesquisadora de história e literatura africana de expressão portuguesa, e autora de livros infanto-juvenis com temática africana. Desenvolve projetos de capacitação de professores da rede pública e privada na área de História da África. Email: regifla@uol.com.br

The Creole Elite and the Rise of Angolan Proto-Nationalism: 1880-1910

Jacopo Corrado

Abstract: The main purpose of this essay is to define the peculiarities of Angolan urban society and trace its evolution during the second half of the nineteenth century, a lapse of time marked by relative freedom—due to the economic crisis affecting Portugal from the definitive abolition of slavery and to the social and artistic progressive reformer impulse promoted by the Generation of 1870. This made possible the establishment in Luanda of lively journalistic activity and the production of a literary *corpus*—principally written by traders, soldiers, public officers, and landowners, born in Africa and tied both to their European and African origins, which witnessed the growth of a feeling of dissatisfaction destined to culminate in a heterogeneous set of open claims for autonomy or even independence.

This article investigates a segment of Angolan history and literature with which non-Portuguese-speaking readers are generally not familiar, for its main purpose is to define the features and the literary production of what are conventionally called Creole elites, whose contribution to the early manifestations of dissatisfaction towards colonial rule was patent between 1880 and 1910, a period of renewed Portuguese commitment to its African colonies, but also of unrealised ambitions, economic crisis and socio-political upheaval in Angola and in Portugal itself.

At that time, Angolan society was characterized by the presence of a semi-

Portuguese Literary & Cultural Studies 15/16 (2010): 57-77.

urbanized commercial and administrative elite of Portuguese-speaking Creole families—white, black, some of mixed race, some Catholic and others Protestant, some old-established and others cosmopolitan—who were based in the main coastal towns. As well as their wealth, derived from the functions performed in the colonial administrative, commercial, and custom apparatus, their European-influenced culture and habits clearly distinguished them from the broad population of black African peasants and farm workers. In order to expand its control over the region, Portugal desperately needed the support of this kind of non-colonizer urban elite, which was also used as an assimilating force, or better as a source of dissemination of a relevant model of social behaviour. Until the nineteenth century, great Creole merchants and inland chiefs dealt in captive slaves, bound for export to Brazil via São Tomé e Príncipe and the Cape Verde islands. The tribal aristocracy and the Creole bourgeoisie thrived on the profits of overseas trade and used to live in style, consuming large quantities of imported alcoholic beverages and wearing fashionable European clothes.

In the early twentieth century, however, their social and economic position was eroded by an influx of petty merchants and bureaucrats from Portugal who wished to grasp the commercial and employment opportunities created by a new and modern colonial order, anxious to keep up with other European colonial powers engaged in the partition of the African continent. This study considers the "first intellectuals," the early printed publications in the country and the "precursor Africans" who, feeling the need to raise their roots to higher dignity, wrote grammars and dictionaries but also poetry, fiction and, of course, incendiary articles denouncing exploitation, racism, and the different treatment afforded by the colonial authorities to Portuguese expatriates and natives. They were fully aware of the fact that their past function as a link between the few rulers sent from the metropolis and the African inland tribes was indispensable to the perpetration of the colonial system, and that the system guaranteed them a privileged condition as well as exposure to European culture. On the other hand, they were thwarted by the impossibility of achieving the highest social standing in their own homeland. Their first reaction was the invention of a new identity, introducing the term "children of the country," or "sons of the country," and the adjective "*Angolense*" in order to define themselves in clear opposition to both the Portuguese and the "uncivilized" black natives.

With the rise of both black nationalism and armed struggle still in the future—as well as the international recognition attributed to acclaimed contemporary writers such as Pepetela and Luandino Vieira and, in general, to the Angolan militant literature of the second part of the twentieth century—the period of Angolan history that is at the centre of this investigation still presents wide open spaces. Moreover, the literary production that flourished during those years is generally dismissed as minor colonial literature or, at best, celebrated by the apologists of the colonial empire as the outcome and evidence attesting to the existence of a multicultural, intellectual, Creole elite, originating in proverbial and overrated Portuguese plasticity. According to this reasoning, the idealized pervasive practice of interracial marriage was irrefutable proof indicating a total absence of racism among the Portuguese.

It is no surprise that the end of the colonial period coincided with a call to reafricanize the new political elites governing Angola and with the banishment of any kind of syndrome evoking Lusitanity, let alone the recognition of the intellectual vibrancy and legitimacy of a distinct Creole perspective.

When speaking about contemporary literature, for instance, Angolan book reviewer Luís Kandjimbo does not consider as authentically "Angolan" the well-known novel by Pepetela, *Yaka*, wondering if it can indeed be defined as a colonial novel, since it emphasizes "a kind of alterity built upon a fictional discourse in which, as absolute protagonist, the [Creole] Semedo family symbolizes the *other* in a society where black characters are reduced to mere walk-on figures or objects of observation [...]. The preponderance of a vision subduing history and its real actors deprives the novel of any worthiness, bringing into question whether it could belong to the genre classified as historical novel" (61-62).

Pepetela was born and raised in the colonial society as a white Angolan, but this did not prevent him from joining the national struggle for freedom against the Portuguese (1961-74). *Yaka* is his novel portraying the Benguela Creole society from the end of the nineteenth century to the eve of independence. An exacerbated defence of Africanness would equally exclude from Angolan literature the commitment of some contemporary writers aiming to piece together this important but neglected phase of Angolan history, such as José Eduardo Agualusa and Arnaldo Santos. In any case, as noticed by Cosme in his 2001 essay *Crioulos e Brasileiros de Angola*, at the present time any memory other than the genuinely black African one can hardly be appreciated in Angola. These days, the concept of Creoleness, as a sort of caution or royalty granted by Portuguese colonization, is no more than a rhetorical figure destined to fade away with those who still aspire to any historical right of compensation for the biological discrimination and cultural interdiction suffered in the past or for the political prescriptions that turned them into "Portuguese-others" (Cosme 57).

This attitude seems to be confirmed by the demolition in 1999 of the primary emblem of the Creole past dating back to the nineteenth century: the mansion that once belonged to the powerful mulatto mistress of Luanda Dona Ana Joaquina dos Santos Silva, *Ná Andêmbo.* She was a slave trader, rich from the fortunes of ships, *fazendas*, and buildings owned both in Brazil and Angola, and an authentic patroness of Creole society until her death in 1859.

The claims of autonomy and independence expressed at a time of profound changes affecting Portuguese society and colonial policies during the period examined were the expression of just a tiny fragment of Angolan urban society. They were involved in the slave trade and deeply integrated into the colonial system, to which they supplied the subordinate administrative body of the province and the middle and low ranks of the armies sent to fight in the countless *Guerras Pretas* [Black Wars] waged by Portugal to subdue unruly and rebellious tribes. Moreover, their demands were not direct evidence of an original sprouting of national consciousness as much as they were inspired by the echoes of the liberal ideals that could reach, covertly packed below deck, the harbours of Luanda and Benguela through the merchant ships proceeding from Brazil or Europe, ideals that were often assimilated in a quite disorderly and confused way.

It is also evident that the overwhelming majority of the inhabitants of the country were completely excluded from the formulation of these claims, and that the same happened for the concept of the country itself. At that time, the notion of Angola was grounded on the limited—if compared with the actual size of the country, that is, the territory claimed by the Portuguese at the end of the nineteenth century—surface of the land effectively occupied and "civilized" by the colonial rulers: the towns of Luanda, Benguela, Moçâmedes and related districts, the river Kwanza region and a few more garrison houses, trading posts, fazendas and frontier-like small inland settlements.

This first wave of dissidence was most assuredly born and raised inside the colonial milieu itself and was promoted by a local and heterogeneous urban social stratum that embraced and opposed at the same time both their European and African background. Consequently, it seems that the fate of the so-called "civilized" Africans was to be eternally confined in a sort of limbo that precluded any possible access to either the metropolitan or the African world.

Nonetheless, we are facing the first sign of "modern" resistance to colonial rule in Angola and that cannot be ignored, neither for the historical and cultural worthiness of the texts produced, nor for the development of a cognitive inquiry into the discourse of nativism, proto-nationalism, and nationalism, without neglecting the influence wielded by these forerunners over the following generations. Already in 1891, for instance, the only and anonymous issue of the satirical journal *O Tomate* featured an article entitled "*Independence of Angola.*" Its main purpose was to capture the family connections and interrelationships that took place during the whole colonial period between the "sons of the country" of the coast and the rebel African chiefs based in the hinterland.

For the first time, the protagonists of the resistance against Portuguese penetration were cheered as heroes (Cruz e Silva 11-12). Almost one century later, MPLA founder Mário de Andrade, interviewed in 1982 by the French sociologist Christine Messiant on the birth of Angolan nationalism, said: "Those who later followed the path of nationalism—and I am talking about the first small group, the core—shared, generally speaking, an important source, that is the familial source. I mean that all of us were aware of the generation belonging to the final part of the last century and its cultural expression, be it political or simply literary. My father, for example, owned all the books, *Voz de Angola clamando no deserto* among them and all the old articles published in the *Luso-Brazilian Almanac.* We can say that we were nourished by the ideas of that generation" (Andrade 189).

These ideas are also a starting point for a more extensive reflection about the effective meaning, at least as far as Portuguese colonial and postcolonial studies are concerned, of paradigmatic categories such as cultural, linguistic, and racial hybridism or of the concept of Creoleness, for they are the expression of a transcultural, autochthonous society emerging in urban or semi-urban spaces and characterized by the fusion of distinct migratory streams.

These are spaces where Portuguese, Brazilians, other Europeans, Bantus, traders, missionaries, and slaves shared a common condition of eradication from the homeland, and lived in a "double trance made of disadaptation and readaptation, deculturation or exculturation, acculturation or enculturation: the synthesis of all has to be found in the field of transculturation, where human beings, economies, cultures and aspirations felt themselves estranged, provisional and changed, as migrant birds over the country" (Pacheco 203).

Furthermore, the relevance of the role played by a literature sprouting in such a milieu is evident today. In addition to its contribution to the enrichment of the discourse about the formulation of issues related to cultural and postcolonial studies, and to the deepening and understanding of basic concepts such as "nationalism" and "Creole," the importance of its seminal function relative to the birth of Angolan literature and to the settlement of the dichotomy existing between colonial and national literature is beyond doubt. An abrupt definition of all poetry and fiction written in Angola before 1948 as simply colonialist, exotic and assimilationist overseas literature, retaining only aspects such as alienation, descriptiveness, or the Portuguese colonial point of view, seems to be a gross historical and cultural deformation since, even as far as Angola is concerned, the rise of national consciousness is a slow and deep maturation process.[1] Generally, this rise of consciousness contributes to a series of ethnic, social, religious, political, and ideological factors and is unlikely to start suddenly on the eve of independence. It starts through the observation of the differences existing between the land, the people, and the colonizer country. It goes on through the acquisition of awareness in respect to problems related to the colour of skin, through the rejection of injustice. It creates its own traditions and historical events and, from then on, it claims independence and state organization.

In contrast, since the present study aims to make its way through a cultural, ethnic, and social border zone, we run the risk of underrating a huge barrier in relation to issues regarding a lusophone context. Beyond the difficulties of finding sources and information retrieval, due to the thirty-year-long civil war following the declaration of independence of Angola in 1975, the way leading to a well-grounded interpretation is full of obstacles caused by the exposure to exploited and abused interpretative patterns concealed behind myths, traditions, and rhetoric smothering Portuguese overseas expansion. The unavoidable clash with powerful myths fuelled by Lusotropicalism or by a well-established, centuries-old colonial rhetorical tradition, for instance, have characterized and affected the Portuguese vision of its own overseas empire, rendering the celebration of a presumed widespread Creoleness according to propagandist demands.

The most pernicious tendency affecting Lusotropicalism—a special affinity for the tropics that the Portuguese, according to the Brazilian sociologist Gilberto Freyre, entertained to a greater extent than other Europeans—is probably the association of all the former Portuguese dominions under a common idea of joyful miscegenation. That would be the effect made possible by the innate capacity of adaptation peculiar to the Portuguese abroad and by the expansion of their faith and values by means of a cultural dialogue that, rude and all-loving at the same time, ensured a space of interaction between Europeans and natives. It is a tempting and easily exploitable theorization that does not bear up to more exhaustive examination. Comparing realities such as the Brazilian and the Angolan seems a quite daring operation, even if solely under a sociological point of view, as Gilberto Freyre did. The original colonization of Brazil, for instance, was executed through the establishment of a feudal system based on donations. The *capitães*, who were both landlords and managers of property, could dispose of resources allowing them to buy or hunt for slaves and feed them, build quarters and plantations, equip private armies, raise forts and hire garrisons.

Quite different was the fate of the poor settler coming—and often forced to come—from Minho or the Azores Islands, who disembarked alone and semi-naked on the African coast with no protection or resources to help him face the unkind climatic conditions and find his way through the wilderness.

The first encounter and a disruptive colonization

The starting point of the troubled colonization of Angola coincided with the first encounter between Europeans and subjects of the so-called Kingdom of Congo. It occurred in 1482 when King D. João II sent a young commoner named Diogo Cão with an assortment of stone pillars surmounted by the cross of the Order of Christ and carved with the royal arms to mark the capes he should discover. When Diogo Cão stumbled on the Congo River, he was actually looking for something else: a passage around Africa into the Indian Ocean. He travelled to the mouth of the river, where he set up a pillar, left four messengers to search for a great king about whom he had heard and took four natives back to Portugal. Back in Lisbon, King D. João knighted Diogo Cão and appointed him to be the commander of a second expedition, sent out to recover the messengers, whose foremost assignment was to establish amicable relations with the Congolese.

Those friendly relations facilitated the settlement of missionaries, traders and soldiers, but the attempt to christianise the Kingdom of Congo through the conversion of subaltern chiefs proved ephemeral. In addition to that, the slave extraction and export, which subsequently developed, soared to 60,000 in the first two decades and to 345,000 from 1506-1575. Portuguese intentions to maintain good relations with the Congo people were rapidly sacrificed to profit (VV. AA. 50).

In 1575, carrying credentials from King D. Sebastião, Paulo Dias de Novais landed on the Ilha de Luanda in command of a fleet of seven ships carrying a hundred families of colonists and 400 soldiers. The following year, de Novais moved to the mainland opposite the island and established the settlement that was to become São Paulo de Assunção de Luanda. What attracted de Novais to the area was the prospect of controlling the legendary silver mines of Cambambe, a utopia that fuelled Portuguese dreams and desires for a long time. Luanda and the São Paulo settlement offered a sheltered port in an excellent spot very close to the river Kwanza, the supposed route to the mines (VV. AA. 75).

Over time, this area became the departure point of the *Kwata Kwata* wars to capture slaves—*Kwata* actually means "to catch" in the Kimbundu language—and the assembly and loading point for slave ships bound for Brazil. Basically, the development of Brazilian sugar plantations and the exploitation of Brazilian gold mines towards the end of the seventeenth century utterly depended on slave labour provided by Angola. The brisk trade in slaves brought more colonists and the settlement grew. There followed a long period in which Brazil and Angola were intimately connected under the aegis of the Portuguese crown, whose African policies were dictated by the economic interests of its South American dominion. Portuguese colonial policies had to take into account the fact that the administration of such a vast portion of land with so little available Portuguese manpower could not do without the use of local collaborators.

Angola understandably attracted few permanent settlers. The territory was portrayed as savage and forbidding and Europeans generally regarded the climatic and sanitary conditions as prohibitive. Malaria was rampant throughout the land and the colony well deserved its reputation as a "white man's grave." The practice of miscegenation and cultural assimilation was the only means by which the Portuguese could respond to the pressure exerted by rival colonial powers but, more than that, it ostensibly provided the only chance of survival for the small number of colonizer agents, overwhelmingly male, sent to make their way in such an adverse environment.[2] Portuguese men absorbed African legacies through intermarriage, giving birth to a society—unique in the African context—in which mulattos enjoyed some kind of status.

Here lies the stepping-stone towards the formation of the so-called urban Creole elites and the first important clarification to underscore. Even if we are going to deal predominantly with the cultural aspects involved in this kind of society, it has to be recalled that the life of the colony was completely focused on trade and colonial administration, and that the concept of "cultural elite" has always to be subordinated to the concept of "economic elite."

According to Ana Mafalda Leite, Portugal had no other option but to reach working compromises with the Afro-Portuguese local "oligarchies," for they had already travelled inland and so had a better knowledge of the land's physical and social geography, adapted as they were to the local populations, with whom they used to trade (Leite 105). By the middle of the eighteenth century, a significant proportion of "sons of the country" and mulattos were already occupying positions within the middle cadres of administration and armed forces, operating as a buffer between emissaries of the metropolis and the native population, who were divided into nine major ethno-linguistic groups: Kikongo (or Bakongo), Kimbundu, Lunda-Quioco (or Tchokwe), Mbundo (or Ovimbundu), Ganguela, Nhaneca-Humbe, Ambo, Herero, and Xindonga. All were more or less hostile to external penetration and periodically embroiled the Portuguese in insidious small-scale conflicts, preventing them from reaching an effective detribalisation of the hinterland and discouraging the creation of more extended settlements or the implementation of *fazendas*. Until the end of the nineteenth century the overwhelming majority of whites were confined to Luanda and a handful of coastal towns, such as Benguela—founded in 1617—and later Moçâmedes—founded in 1840.

The abolition process

The progressive loss of the network of trading posts along the Asian shores,[3] followed in 1821 by the more traumatic loss of Brazil, forced Portugal to make the most out of the remnants of its empire. However, it was by now plain that the traditional purely mercantilist approach to the exploitation of the African territories was no longer an alternative to the model set up by rival colonial powers, nor did it have a chance to survive the advent and implementation of capitalism.

The analysis by René Pélissier confirms that Portugal, at that time, completely lacked human, financial, and technical resources, coherence, and stability in the colonial administration. In Angola, the majority of whites and mulattos—without disregarding the active role played by the so-called "civilized" blacks during the following Portuguese colonial expansion as the backbone of colonial militias—often felt abandoned to themselves by a busted, impotent, or indifferent metropolis.

The persistence of the plundering mentality among them was a frequent cause of conflict (Pélissier 107). The troubled steps leading to the abolition of slavery heightened social tensions and worsened the economic crisis affecting the agonizing Portuguese empire. In the 1830s, the Portuguese government appointed a progressive prime minister, the former minister of the navy, Marquis Sá da Bandeira, whose most important reform was the abolition of the slave trade in 1836. The decree could not be enforced adequately—it took Britain's naval intervention to put an end to the activity in the middle of the nineteenth century—and, above all, it did not include any kind of provision against slavery within Angola.

Between 1854 and 1858 Portugal passed a series of cautious decrees aimed at reducing slavery in Angola. Government slaves were freed and the 1858 proclamation declared that all forms of slavery should be abolished by 1878. Legislation was passed to compensate owners and to care for the freed people, but many of the colonists found ways to circumvent the decree, so that the actual conditions of labour did not change significantly (Colecção 151-52; qtd. in Brásio, *Vol. 2* 44-47). The de facto servitude of Africans in Angola continued until the end of the colonial period and later was one of the leading reasons for a sharp rise in nationalist feeling during the prolonged colonial war.

Urban society

At the top of the mid-nineteenth-century Angolan socio-economic pyramid were the traders who enriched themselves thanks to the slave traffic and barter with the interior. They were established in Luanda's mansions, dominated the import-export trade and were associated with—and played havoc with—political power (Torres 60).[4]

The properly defined white population was far from numerous—only 1830 people estimated in 1846—and this probably affected its impact in terms of influence and extension of power. In contrast, the mulatto population—about 5,770 people at the time[5]—*grosso modo* identified itself ideologically, politically, and economically with the whites, together forming the preponderant element in urban Angolan society. White traders owned the land and managed the capitalization of their activities connected to the Atlantic trade with Brazil, Europe, and the United States. Since the Portuguese occupation, trade had always been instrumental to the existence of the colony. It is not surprising then if more than one governmental resolution strongly jeopardizing local capital—the abolition of the traffic—or openly advantaging the metropolitan bourgeoisie—protectionist customs policies—encountered resistance, which was able to put back the enactment in the colony of decrees considered as a nuisance to the interests of local businesses.

It is important to underline that a remarkably high proportion of the white population was composed of convicts or enriched ex-convicts. Most of those who survived their sentence returned to Portugal but those who enjoyed some measure of commercial success running small businesses or trading with the natives remained, creating roots—that is, mixed race families—and consolidated specific interests that diverged more and more from metropolitan policies such as, for instance, demonstrating strong opposition to the laws enacted by Sá da Bandeira that were leading to the progressive abolition of the slave trade (Torres 61).[6]

From a sociological and psycho-sociological point of view, we can observe how a wide segment of the economically preponderant population was formed by individuals who can be divided into convicts, poor settlers, and *mestiços*, all rejected by the metropolitan society. From that rejection derived, if not a fracture, certainly a series of deep tensions. It cannot be forgotten that the local colonial society was also layered between "civilized" and "non-civilized" people. The first definition grouped the whites, regardless of their social, economic, and academic standing, and the acculturated mulattos and blacks who had adopted European habits and customs. Black people who kept on living according to the native way of life, that is to say "those who, born overseas from native mother and father, could not differentiate themselves through their own education and customs from the common representative of their race," were judicially considered as "non-civilized."[7] This division obviously caused various frictions because of the social and racial discriminations implied, and the resulting concerns rapidly found vent in the local press, and were backed on one side by the settlers aiming to safeguard the *status quo*, criticising the authorities if they allowed mulattos and blacks to intervene in the colony's public life and, on the other side, by the Africans, protesting against social injustice and claiming social emancipation.

In 1890, the journalist José da Fontes Pereira suggested, in an article published in the *Arauto Africano*, that if the British wanted to trade with the "masters of the country" they had better address themselves directly to Africans, and not to the Portuguese. But who were these "Africans"? Retailers and civil servants; provincial senate and provincial government officers, magistrates, clerks, copyists, and subordinate staff; customs treasurers, agents, collectors, and scribes; lawyers and court-room employees; garrison, recruiting-centre, and fortress commanders, warrant officers and privates; chaplains, minor, and regular canons, deacons and parish priests; land or estate owners: here is an outline of the range of positions and, consequently, of the scale of power reached by this Euro-African elite during the cycle of slavery and its slow decadence over the course of the nineteenth century. The conjunction of these sectors enables us to understand how this kind of colonial bourgeoisie was deeply rooted in Angola and disconnected from the metropolis, and how its economic links were far stronger with Brazil—or better with the Brazilian colonial bourgeoisie involved with the traffic—than with Portugal.

In conclusion, on one side, the colonial bourgeoisie and the metropolitan bourgeoisie were complementary but, on the other, far from sharing a constant and absolute reciprocal identification, they were divided by deep divergences and opposing economic interests. From the mid-nineteenth century, a constantly increasing number of Portuguese settlers started to disembark, but on land they found this already well-established and—if not cultivated—at least literate local bourgeoisie, Portuguese-speaking, mixed race, Catholic, cosmopolitan, and composed also of mulatto and black people. Adelino Torres refers to the existence of an authentic *colonial bourgeoisie* mainly based in Luanda and Benguela which embraced a class of proprietors employing servile or indentured manpower and possessing assets, material values, capital, prestige, and influence in the colony, regardless of any possible interest or possession held in Portugal or Brazil, and of the ethnic group to which they belonged.

Other than the coffee plantation owners, clearly an elite among the colonists, the Portuguese settlers were poor, unskilled, and uneducated, and, on the whole, they failed to succeed as agriculturists. Unable to compete with Africans and without resources, they moved to the cities and survived as best they could by doing menial jobs. Their presence invariably led to an atmosphere of racism and petty discrimination that affected both black African people and the Creoles of the cities, who of course did not remain silent.

The "free press" period

The tumultuous period of the Portuguese civil wars (1828-1834) led the metropolis to bankruptcy. At the end of the conflict, the economy was sluggish, unemployment was high, but the formation of a new cabinet coincided with the spread of a sort of liberal spirit. In 1836, a law passed by Prime Minister Sá da Bandeira extended to the Portuguese overseas possessions the right to print publications that could diffuse essential legal, commercial, and general information to the residents of the colony.

The first rudimentary newspapers turned out to be the main vehicle for local literary proclivities. Luanda and Benguela rapidly became centres of intense cultural activity and of social and political agitation, hosting debates in which French revolutionary ideals were openly supported and developing an advancing will to achieve political autonomy. *O Boletim Oficial*, an official journal founded in 1845 by Governor General Pedro Alexandrino da Cunha, was the starting point of the development of journalism that, supported in the beginning by the small local European elite, was destined to take root in the capital and to rapidly increase during the following decades. By the end of the century, a total of 46 periodicals had been printed, as recorded by Carlos Ervedosa (Ervedosa 28). A decree enacted in 1856 legalized the "free press" in the overseas dominions and, in 1866, the first issue of *A Civilização Africana* was published, a small self-funded weekly publication dedicated to administrative, economic, industrial, and commercial concerns, which inaugurated the second phase of the history of Angolan journalism.

The definition of "free press" is, of course, quite rough if applied to Angola, and it is more correct to say that "settlers and locals tended to define as 'free press' the publications issued by private printers, in order to distinguish them from the official governmental gazette" (Ervedosa 25). If it is true that a certain number of publications saw the light during the second half of the nineteenth century, it is also true that their life was never easy, colonial censorship being constantly on the watch.

Just to mention a few episodes that had a strong impact on the local public opinion of the time, in 1842 a printing press had been loaded in Lisbon and bound for Luanda, where it was supposed to be installed. The Portuguese authorities, fearing such a powerful asset in the hands of the natives, decided to turn aside the ship and let it sink off the Moçâmedes coast with its precious cargo. The owner of the printing press was a Joaquim António de Carvalho e Meneses, a mulatto, coming back to his native land to assume the post of secretary-treasurer in the capital of the colony. Journalist José da Fontes Pereira's comment shows how the presence of the Portuguese was substantially felt as a burden, hindering every kind of enhancement in the country: "aware of the power that such a skilled politician could deploy using a weapon [the printing press] that is so dangerous to the interests of the metropolis, in Portugal they preferred to lose a State ship rather than allow this engine of civilization to disembark in Luanda!"[8]

In 1867, António Urbano Monteiro de Castro, Alfredo Mântua, and Francisco Pereira Dutra, popular journalists and editors, were condemned for the crime of abuse of the free press; the latter did not survive his imprisonment. In 1873, the governor general of Angola approved a warrant released by the Luanda council administrator. The premises of the newspaper *O Mercantil* were shut down and any valuable materials confiscated. In 1881, republican journalist José da Ressurreição Arantes Braga was condemned to 40 days imprisonment for sedition. In the same year, issue number 1 of *O Echo de Angola* was the first periodical entirely edited and funded by Africans (Coelho 107-08).

With the launch of the "free press period" the colony of Angola enjoyed a sort of intellectual euphoria. Both "sons of the country" and creolized Portuguese found in this kind of journalism, devoted to the taste for controversy and to the defence of local values and interests, the way to express their heterogeneous positions about politics, trade, but also art, culture, and social criticism, and to uphold their economic and administrative interests against the arrogance shown by some governors, at variance with the most reductive metropolitan policies.

Periodical publications such as *O Arauto Africano*, *A Província de Angola*, and *O Echo de Angola* were the expression of a generation whose primary distinction was a fierce autodidactism, since higher education was beyond reach for most of its writers and because, generally speaking, it was impossible to pursue further education after completing the first two years of secondary school without leaving Angola.

To this end, the presence of Protestant missionaries was crucial, since they made a reality out of the ideology of "self-sufficiency" by opening school rooms where they would valorise local knowledge and oral literature, which they even tried to fix into written languages, drawing up grammars and dictionaries. Most of the missions were established in the northern part of the country, where Portuguese penetration was superficial and the colonial authorities had no choice but to tolerate the thriving of foreign commercial enterprises and missions, which helped the locals involved to develop a critical sense and to take into consideration their African roots, serving as a testing ground for the creation of a national literature.[9]

The Berlin Conference and the times of the 1890 Ultimatum

The abolition of the slave trade coincided with increased Portuguese expansion in Angola. Expansion began in 1838 with the conquest and establishment of a fort at Duque de Bragança (present-day Calandula), east of Luanda. By the mid-century, the Portuguese had extended their formal control still farther east to the Kassanje market near the Cuango River. In 1840 the Portuguese founded the town of Moçâmedes (present-day Namibe) on the coast south of Benguela. The Portuguese also attempted to gain control of the coast from Luanda north to Cabinda through military occupation of the major ports. Because of British opposition, however, they were unable to complete this attempt and never gained control of the mouth of the Congo River.

The cost of military operations to secure economically strategic points led in 1856 to the imposition on Africans of a substantially increased hut tax, which for the first time had to be paid with currency or trade goods rather than with slaves. As a result, many Africans either refused to pay or fled from Portuguese-controlled areas. By 1861, in any case, the Portuguese lacked the resources for continued military expansion or economic development, and most of the interior remained in the control of African traders and warriors.

From the late 1870s through to the early 1890s, Portugal promoted a renewed program of expansion in the interior. Part of the impetus came from the Lisbon Geographical Society, founded in 1875 by a group of industrialists, scholars, and colonial and military officials. In reaction to the activities of the society, to the subsequent wave of popular concern for the colonies diffused through the country, and to the growing interest among Europeans in colonial adventures, the Portuguese government allotted large sums for public works in Africa and encouraged a minor revival of missionary work (Papagno 100-01).

During the 1870s, an advisory commission to Portugal's Ministry of the Navy and Colonies conceived the project to link Angola on the Atlantic coast with Mozambique on the Indian Ocean coast, counting on the support provided by the Portuguese government, which aspired to control a solid strip of territory across the central part of the continent.[10] Portugal was, in fact, unable to gain effective control of the hinterland. Aware of French and Belgian activities on the lower Congo River, in 1883 the Portuguese occupied Cabinda and Massabi north of the Congo River, towns that Portugal had long claimed. In the same year, Portugal annexed the region of the old Congo Kingdom. Seeking to uphold these claims against French and Belgian advances in the Congo River Basin, Portugal negotiated a treaty with Britain in 1884. The other European powers, however, rejected it.

At the Berlin Conference of 1884, the participants established in principle the limits of Portugal's claims to Angola, and, in later years, a series of treaties with the colonial powers in control of the neighbouring territories delineated Angola's boundaries. The west coast territory acquired by Portugal included the left bank of the Congo River and the Cabinda enclave. In 1890, however, Britain delivered an ultimatum to force Portugal's withdrawal from Nyasaland (present-day Malawi) and Rhodesia (present-day Zimbabwe and Zambia).

The nominal occupation of large areas of the ocean coast by the Portuguese was a clear obstacle to the claims of rival colonial powers, while the inner parts of the continent remained unseen and still uncharted. The political and financial problems affecting the Portuguese crown made easier a shift in the balance of power in Africa. In addition, the Berlin Conference internationally established a variation of the overpowering policy from the traditional right conferred by original discovery to the right granted by effective occupation.

The Berlin Conference, whose four main issues were the commercial opening of the Congo region, the suppression of slavery in that area, the freedom of navigation on every African river, and the procedures to follow for the future occupations on the continent, imposed the right of effective occupation. In this way, the recognition, on the part of aboriginal chieftains and natives, of the sovereignty exercised by a European power over the territories traditionally belonging to one or more ethnic groups prevailed over any validity of the historical rights claimed by Portugal (Allain 23).

By the end of the conference, it was universally clear that untenable Portuguese dreams of glory had to be abandoned and that the presence of ruined outposts would no longer guarantee full—nominal—dominion of a territory. The approach to the overseas resources had to be rapidly overturned in order to avoid the otherwise inevitable perspective of losing also the remnants of the empire.

During the last twenty-five years of the nineteenth century the course of events seemed to quicken. The British ultimatum, the subsequent formalisation of the Portuguese empire and the entrenchment of Lusitanian patriotism led, in a desperate attempt to scoop foreign competition, to the implementation of some meaningful changes in the administration of the colonies. The pressure of the "scramble for Africa" and the British threat, together with the European demand for raw materials and tropical products, were powerful stimuli for investment in Angola's vast potential wealth.

In 1892, a protective tariff was introduced, which led to a significant increase in trade between Portugal and Africa. That increase was particularly marked for Portugal's exports to Africa and for African exports to third countries, shipped through Portugal as re-exports (Lains 10). After the abolition of slavery, the production of export goods such as coffee or cotton required measures to tie the population to the land. A successful and effective colonization could not proceed without strict control of the African populations, not only because it was necessary to provide a labour force for the plantations, but also because it granted a huge tax revenue. In 1899 a new labour code was imposed on all African natives in the form of a "moral and legal" obligation to work (Lains 15-16).

The 1892 tariffs and the 1899 labour code were the landmarks of the new colonial regime imposed by Portugal on its African colonies. Perhaps the adoption of these measures, which brought important benefits for Portuguese colonization, was delayed simply to strengthen the bargaining position of the country during the scramble for territory and the diplomatic negotiations concerning African borders in the 1880s. It was evident by now that the government's interest in Africa had sharply increased, as is shown by the fact that the position of governor general of Angola, for instance, obtained a new status that attracted men who managed to impose a tighter administrative control over the territories.

In this way, a penal colony such as Angola was gradually transformed into a colony of occupation, to the detriment of the thousands of *contratados*, contract workers employed in the plantations in a semi-slave regime, but also of the Creole elites, progressively forced to cede rights, privileges, and positions to the new administrative, military, and commercial staff who arrived from the metropolis.

The fall of the Creole elites

At the turn of the century, a series of decrees gradually established that the issue of any kind of publication, periodical or not, had to be considered as a crime of "free press abuse." As the repressive measures adopted by the metropolis and the subsequent worsening of the basic rights situation in the colony roused the reaction of *Angolense* intellectuals, Portuguese colonial policy was consolidated by new internal wars and occupations, by the countrywide installment of administrative units and by the enhancement of economic development. Although there were fewer than 10,000 whites in Angola in 1900, there had been a substantial increase in white female immigration. The male-to-female ratio that year was slightly more than two-to-one.[11] Concomitantly, there was a drop in the ratio of *mestiços*-to-whites. Whereas *mestiços* had outnumbered whites in 1845 by more than three-to-one, in 1900 this ratio was reversed. Of course, black Africans still constituted more than 99 percent of the population, even if their number reportedly declined from an estimated 5.4 million in 1845 to about 4.8 million in 1900, although scholars dispute these figures. Even today, Angola's census problems are far from being solved.

In the late nineteenth century, Africans still controlled trade in the plateaus of the interior, despite Portuguese expansion. The Ovimbundu proved highly successful intermediaries on the southern trade route that ran from the Bié Plateau to Benguela. The Ovimbundu were more competitive than the *sertanejos* (people of the frontier, as Europeans and their usually mulatto representatives in the rural areas were called), who often had to pay tribute and fines to African chiefs if they wanted to cross their territories. By the mid 1880s, the Ovimbundu by and large had replaced the *sertanejos*. The Tchokwe and Imbangala[12] also took advantage of their positions in the interior to extend their control over the region's trade. Nonetheless, by the late 1800s, Portuguese encroachments and the imposition of European rule limited the political freedom of these Africans and diminished their prosperity.

Immigration changes came into full effect and competition for places that were traditionally the prerogative of Luso-Africans became ruthless, upsetting the previous politico-economical and socio-cultural schemes. The recently arrived settlers forced both old towns and small demographic nuclei to undertake new economic and cultural activities and, crushed by the colonial wave, black and mulatto natives tended to quit the towns and recede to the *musseques* (shantytowns). Consequently, the role model provided by the journalistic activity that previously invigorated the social life of the colony and by the, even if troubled, diffusion of local and small periodical publications gradually lost its fundamental role. Once it had become clear that the local political debate that had stimulated so many young *Angolenses* was outmoded, and that internal and export trade, demographic development, and the new pace assumed by society gave life to concerns that could have been hardly satisfied by a periodical press, the local colonial bourgeoisie had to let go of the control of its environment. It was no longer possible to liven up the political life of towns like Luanda and Benguela with such small resources.

In 1909, the journal *O Angolense* was suppressed, due to a misunderstanding between its founding members, Francisco das Necessidades

Castelbranco—director—Augusto Silvério Ferreira and Pedro da Paixão Franco—editors—and Eusébio Velasco Galiano—publisher—and by a legal process to which the journal was subjected. In 1913, Governor General Norton de Matos ordered the suspension of the *Independente* and *A Verdade*, deeming that they posed a profound material danger to the colony's stability. The suspension endured several months and the Cortes of Portugal were summoned to discuss the matter.

Finally, a decree issued on 31 July 1916 established the application of precautionary censorship to periodicals and other publications, to be exerted by districts and council commissions (Lourenço 7). The gilded age of the Creole communities was definitely over.

Notes

1 1948 is a year marked by the foundation of the cultural movement known as *Movement of the New Intellectuals of Angola*, or "*Vamos descobrir Angola*" [Let's discover Angola], whose purpose was to give expression to popular concerns and to promote the emergence of black African consciousness.

2 The male-female ratio among whites in Angola was around 2:1 in 1900 (Bender 52). However, in 1869, the Spiritan missionary Hippolyte Carrie was firmly convinced that the recently founded town of Moçâmedes would be the only salubrious spot on the coast and therefore the best place to start a new mission. Aiming to persuade his superiors about the harsh conditions affecting other Angolan towns, he supported his views by quoting the following extract: "White women, there are none. Nor could there be, for they'd die for sure, especially if they were still of age to give birth. Until now, there is not a single case in which a white woman or child has survived after delivery" (qtd. in Brásio).

3 By 1640 the Portuguese pepper empire in Asia had entered its twilight years. Despite this economic decline, India featured as a romantic colossus in the Portuguese popular imagination. The empire of the east still contained fifty-odd beachheads, fortresses, trading factories and islands stretching from the Zambesi to the Pacific, including Ormuz, Diu, Damão, Goa, Cochim, Malaca, East Timor, and Macau (Birmingham 43).

4 According to the data collected by the Portuguese economist the following activities were exercised in Luanda in 1845:

Wholesale houses … 33

General stores … 35

Wine, oil, and retail sellers … 107

Informal retailers selling on the streets … 113

Water-selling houses … 16

Bakers ... 7

Apothecary's shops … 5

Butchers … 5

Cigar factories … 1

[5] Data confirmed in Lipski and in Bender.

[6] It is interesting to note that, from 1859-60, the emancipation of the "Angolan homeland" becomes a concern for the restless sons of the country, labelled by Torres as "non-white civilized people," even if they did not know exactly whether to give life to a Republic of Angola or join the Brazilian Republic—or the United States of America. The latter hypothesis suggests the need to maintain a strict contact with slave-buying countries.

[7] As established through decree in 1894 by the General Government of the Province of Angola, according to Lourenço (2).

[8] See Pereira, qtd. in Pacheco (141-42).

[9] The speech given by the Minister of Foreign Affairs, Count de Castro, during the Chamber of Deputies session on 14 March 1866, shows the effects of the lack of Portuguese military forces on the northern coast of Angola: "American, British, French and Hamburger trading posts deal with the natives to our detriment, for they don't pay a penny for embarked and disembarked goods. That produces a considerable loss, since our traders, having to pay heavy customs duties, cannot compete in any way with foreign traders. It must be said that the importance of Angola resides entirely in its trade: if we cannot make the most of it, there's no reason for us to go on" (qtd. in Brásio, *Vol. 1* 295-96).

[10] Between 1877 and 1879, Serpa Pinto made the first expedition from coast to coast led by a Portuguese from Benguela to Durban. This expedition, however, did not have official support from Lisbon and, more importantly, it crossed areas not claimed by Portugal.

Between 1884 and 1885, Capelo and Ivens, this time with official support, crossed the continent, along a strip between parallels 15º and 18º (south), from Moçâmedes, in southern Angola, to Quelimane, in northern Mozambique. Two years later, with the apparent agreement of the German government, the Foreign Office in Lisbon produced the famous rose-coloured map, claiming that portion of territory that would unite Portugal's two colonies in southern Africa.

[11] The statistics for 1900 are found in Bender (20).

[12] The Imbangala were not a distinct ethnic group, but a sort of cult that held together bands of mercenary soldiers who lived both by general rapine and by hiring themselves out to the highest bidder. They operated in the Kimbundu-speaking world and were also consciously and openly cannibals.

Works Cited

Allain, Jean-Claude. *La Conférence de Berlin sur l'Afrique 1884-1885.* Paris: Centre des hautes études sur l'Afrique et l'Asie modernes, 1985.

Andrade, Mário de. *Sur la première génération du MPLA: 1948-1960. Mário de Andrade, entretiens avec Christine Messiant, 1982. Lusotopie.* Bordeaux: Institut d'Etudes Politiques de Bordeaux, 1999.

Bender, Gerald J. *Angola under the Portuguese, the Myth and the Reality.* London: Heineman, 1978.

Birmingham, David. *A Concise History of Portugal.* Cambridge: Cambridge UP, 1993.

Brásio, António. *Spiritana Monumenta Historica Series Africana/Angola (1596-1867).* Vol. 1 Pittsburgh, PA: Duquesne UP, 1966.

———. *Spiritana Monumenta Historica Series Africana/Angola (1868-1881).* Vol. 2. Pittsburgh, PA: Duquesne UP, 1968.

Coelho, Sebastião. *Angola, história e estórias da informação.* Luanda: Executive Centre, 1999.

Colecção da Legislação Novíssima do Ultramar. *Rapport sur l'abolition de l'esclavage dans l'outremer Portugais.* Lisbon: n.p., 1876. Brásio, António. *Spiritana Monumenta Historica Series Africana/Angola (1596-1867).* Vol. 1 Pittsburgh, PA: Duquesne UP, 1966.

Cosme, Leonel. *Crioulos e Brasileiros de Angola.* Coimbra: Novo Imbondeiro, 2001.

Cruz e Silva, Rosa. *O nacionalismo angolano, um projecto em construção no século XIX?* Moscow: Institute for African Studies (IAS), 2000.

Ervedosa, Carlos. *Roteiro da literatura angolana.* Luanda/Havana: União dos Escritores Angolanos, 1985.

História de Angola. Porto: Afrontamento, 1965.

Kandjimbo, Luís. *Apologia de Kalitanji.* Luanda: INALD, 1997.

Lains, Pedro. *An Account of the Portuguese African Empire 1822-1975.* Lisbon: O'Brien and Prados, 1998.

Leite, Ana Mafalda. "Angola." *The Postcolonial Literature of Lusophone Africa.* Ed. Patrick Chabal. London: Hurst & Company, 1996. 103-164.

Lima. *Ensaios sobre a Estatística das Possessões Portuguesas.* Lisbon: n.p., 1846.

Lipski, John M. "Portuguese Language in Angola: Luso-creoles' Missing Link?" Presentation at the annual meeting of the AATSP. San Diego. 9 Aug. 1995.

Lopo. *Para a história do jornalismo em Angola.* Luanda: n.p., 1952.

Lourenço, João Pedro da Cunha. *A dinâmica e o estatuto dos jornalistas em Angola no período da "Imprensa Livre" 1866-1923.* Luanda: União dos Escritores Angolanos, 2002.

Pacheco, Carlos. *José Da Silva Maia Ferreira: o homem e a sua época.* Luanda: União dos Escritores Angolanos, 1990.

Papagno, Giuseppe. *Colonialismo e Feudalesimo, La questione dei Prazos da Coroa nel Mozambico alla fine del XIX secolo.* Torino: Piccola Biblioteca Einaudi, 1972.

Pélissier, René. *De la colonisation Portugaise moderne en Afrique.* Paris: Centre des hautes études sur l'Afrique et l'Asie modernes, 1985.

Pereira, José da Fontes. "*A independência de Angola, VI.*" *O Futuro de Angola* year 3 no. 56 [Luanda] (1886).

Torres, Adelino. *O Império Português entre o real e o imaginário.* Lisbon: Escher, 1991.

Jacopo Corrado holds a PhD from the University of Essex. He is the author of *The Creole Elite and the Rise of Angolan Protonationalism 1870-1910* (Amherst, NY: Cambria Press, 2008). He is currently working on a post-doc at the Universidade Federal do Rio de Janeiro, researching the connection between abolitionism and republicanism in Brazil, Angola and Portugal. E-mail: jacopo_corrado@yahoo.it

Preliminary Considerations on European Forced Labor in Angola, 1880-1930: Individual Redemption and the "Effective Occupation" of the Colony[1]

Timothy J. Coates

Abstract: Forced colonization of Angola using European convicts from 1880 to 1930 was a bold experiment by the Lisbon authorities, motivated by an increasing population of criminals and the international scramble for colonies in Africa. It held the promise of solving both these dilemmas while providing the labor needed for development.

"If we hope to develop a colony, it is a fact that this is not achieved with forced penal colonization… " (Junior 16).

Introduction

This article stands at the crossroads of two large avenues of historical writing on the nineteenth century: penal reform and New Imperialism. To date, this has been a lonely and rather obscure corner in the literature, especially on the Portuguese in Africa. This article will outline how (largely) white European forced labor provided by convicts became commonplace in the Angolan colony by the end of the nineteenth and first thirty years of the twentieth centuries. The process of exiling convict labor to Angola sheds light on several aspects of Portuguese society, penal reform in Portugal, and the overall colonization efforts of the Portuguese in Africa, especially Angola. Penal exiles (*degredados*) sent by the Portuguese judicial system to the African colonies during the nineteenth and twentieth centuries are yet another link

Portuguese Literary & Cultural Studies 15/16 (2010): 79-105.

that connected Portugal to its African holdings. *Degredados* also formed links between and among colonies. Aspects of crime, criminals, and criminality in Portugal are really only now being explored by social scientists. The very important connections they formed have not yet received the attention they merit. This is equally true for both the early modern and modern periods.[2]

This project developed from my previous work on early modern crime, convicts, and forced and state-sponsored colonization. After concluding at 1755, I began to question what happened to the use of *degredo* (penal exile) after that date. Part of that answer was the use of internal exile within Portugal to the little town of Castro Marim (see below). However, internal exile and what I call "The Castro Marim story" then led me to penal reform in nineteenth century Portugal and the creation of the *Depósito Geral de Degredados* in Luanda (see below). This imperial prison housed convicts (mostly) from Portugal, from all the other colonies (except Mozambique, which had its own prison), as well as foreign criminals sentenced by Portuguese courts. The creation of the *Depósito* was the last and one of the most creative phases of the Portuguese use of exile as punishment.[3]

The research for this work has been planned in three stages. This article appears at the end of the intermediate stage, after my research in Lisbon was completed. Many of the more interesting questions, and certainly much more about the individual convicts and the day-to-day running of the *Depósito*, will only be possible to investigate after consulting archival material in Luanda: the final phase of this study. Hence, the use of *preliminary* in the title. This article will not be able to answer all the questions it raises. It will, however, describe the overall situation, take a first look at some numbers, and speculate about their meaning and impact in the colony of Angola.

A problem of sources

One of the major frustrations, as well as rewards, of this study is that it covers a new area of research on Lusophone Africa. There are very few pertinent secondary sources. I have already mentioned above the lack of works on crime and criminality. Studies done on Angola during this period (1880-1930) have little or nothing to say about the *Depósito*. In spite of their relatively large numbers, *degredados* are sometimes mentioned but only in passing. There have been no studies done on either the *Depósito* as an institution or the impact of its inmates and their labor in Angola. Understandably, historians of Angola have focused on much broader issues affecting greater numbers of the African population, such as the forced labor of Angolans, resistance to colonial rule, and the struggles for independence. Nevertheless, there are two welcome exceptions to this overall pattern. Gerald Bender's seminal study of the failure of Portuguese colonization in Angola, *Angola Under the Portuguese*, includes a discussion about *degredados* and the *Depósito*. One of the requirements of the commander of the *Depósito* was to submit an annual report to the military High Command in Luanda. One such report, Junior's *O Depósito de Degredados*, was published in 1916 and contains a great deal of information about the institution. However, his report ended in 1915 and is not an institutional study, nor was it intended as such. The availability of primary sources is not as clear. The *Depósito* and the Angolan military that administered it produced massive amounts of documentation. Some of this material (a very small percentage I suspect) made its way to Lisbon and is scattered among the holdings of the *Arquivo Nacional da Torre do Tombo* (ANTT), the *Arquivo Histórico Ultramarino* (AHU, where at least in theory all the material should be held), and the *Arquivo Histórico Militar*. Criminal records, as well as several batches of appeals from *Depósito* inmates, are held as well in the ANTT. The military sections of the *caixas* (boxes of loose documents) of Angolan materials in the AHU for this period are notable for containing virtually nothing from the *Depósito*.

As a result, this study has had to start at square one, determining answers to the most fundamental questions: how many *degredados* were sent to Portuguese Africa from 1822-1932? How many of these were sent to Angola? How many were registered in the *Depósito*? What crimes did these convicts commit and what sentences did they receive? What was their overall presence in the colony? What did they do while there? How were they supervised and what was their daily reality in Luanda? Did they become the colonizers envisioned by Lisbon? Why or why not? These are the questions that go to heart of this study. Before turning to those, a few words about the historical background of exile and its importance and longevity in the Portuguese world can lead us to Angola and the *Depósito* in the 1880s.

The punishment of exile in Portuguese society

Forced exile (*degredo*) was a constant feature of Portuguese society from the creation of the nation state in the High Middle Ages. Prior to 1415 and the beginnings of Portuguese expansion overseas, *degredo* was instituted in the legal codes as internal exile to one of several towns or villages along the border with the other Iberian kingdoms (i.e., Galicia, León, Estremadura/Castilla, and Andalucia). Typically, each town had a cap placed by the crown as to how many *degredados* could reside there. Frequently, those *degredados* convicted of more serious crimes (e.g., heresy, treason) might be excluded from some towns and specifically directed to others. With the conquest of Ceuta in 1415 and the Portuguese push into the south Atlantic, the judicial system incorporated some of these new holdings as sites to receive convicts. After the Inquisition was established in Portugal, its tribunals coordinated their sentences of exile for sinners with the manpower requirements of the state. Convicts and sinners manned the navy's galleys, while others staffed many of the forts and other outposts in the Portuguese Atlantic, such as Cacheu (Guiné), Luanda, and forts in the interior of Angola along the Cuanza River. No site could rival São Tomé Island. Its economic importance in both the developing Atlantic slave trade and sugar production made it an important outpost of the Portuguese Atlantic. Because of the tropical diseases faced by Europeans who attempted to reside there, São Tomé quickly became a quasi-penal colony during early modern times. Convicts and sinners from mainland Portugal were exiled there in (relatively) large numbers. They, in turn, supervised slaves laboring to produce sugar.

By the 1650s, *degredados* were omnipresent throughout the global Portuguese Empire, and the sentence of *degredo* was handed down with great frequency by the High Courts in Porto, Lisbon, Salvador, and Goa. Later these would be joined by a fifth court established in Rio de Janeiro. Criminals from Portugal were sent where their presence could achieve the maximum for the crown and where free immigration could not attract sufficient colonizers. This meant the few remaining presidios in North and West Africa, Cape Verde, São Tomé, Luanda, and the fringes of the Brazilian colony (Maranhão, Nova Colônia do Sacramento) all received European and Brazilian convicts up to the time of Brazilian independence in 1822-24. In Asia, the High Court in Goa sent its criminals to remote locations along the Indian Ocean littoral. In keeping with the overall patterns established by the European courts, the more serious the crime, the more distant (from the court) the site of exile. In Asia, this meant Mozambique Island or perhaps Timor. Minor infractions were punished with internal exile. In Asia, this might mean a sentence to Diu. In Brazil, it might mean being forced to live in Rio Grande do Norte. In Portugal itself, internal exile came to mean obligatory residence in the little town of Castro Marim, in the extreme SE corner of the Algarve.

Notably, exile to Angola during early modern times was reserved for serious criminals. A sentence of five to eight years in São Tomé or Angola, or ten years in the galleys was, in reality, a life sentence.[4]

This loosely structured system worked remarkably well throughout the early modern period. Judicial costs were part of the sentence whenever the convict could afford to pay them. The system cost the state very little, other than transportation. Oversight was minimal. Convicts had the opportunity to rehabilitate themselves by providing labor (normally as soldiers) until they completed their sentences. Once that had occurred, convicts could obtain certificates of completion from local judges and return home or reside wherever they chose. The system also provided a powerful and effective method of social control. Those who transgressed society's norms would be sent far away, exiled from family, friends, hometown, and all the networks that supported him or her. Most convicts (then as now) were male but *degredadas* (female convicts) do appear here and there in the records. *Degredo* was a powerful double-edged sword: merciful but cruel. The punishment of *degredo* cast a long shadow over Portuguese society. Approximately 50,000 Portuguese convicts and sinners received this sentence by one of the courts during the 200 years from 1550 to 1755. Considering the small size of the Portuguese population (even including Brazil and the other colonies), *degredo* was a punishment with a powerful impact on the individual and an equally useful tool for maintaining the Empire (Coates, *Convicts* 183).

In the period from 1755 to Brazilian independence, Portuguese courts produced an additional 200 to 250 *degredados* annually. This would mean an additional 14,000 to 17,000 convicts were on the move in the Empire. Throughout the nineteenth century up to the 1880s, *degredados* were sent in fits and starts to any of the five remaining colonies in Africa. Internal exile continued to Castro Marim, at least until the 1850s.

Totals for this period (1824-80) are difficult to estimate because of the incomplete and piecemeal nature of the records. The early nineteenth century was not a fortuitous time in Portugal. The French invasions and civil war did nothing to aid in detailed record keeping. In 1823, there were 288 prisoners in Limoeiro (Lisbon's main jail) and Belém awaiting transport to Cape Verde (106), Angola (82), India (59), Benguela (22), Mozambique (13), Angoche (2), Príncipe (2), São Tomé (1), and Pará (1) (ANTT, MAEJ, maço 403, doc. 11). In the documentation that I have been able to find (summarized here as Table 1), Portuguese courts were sentencing approximately 285 convicts each year, to all the former colonies, including the Atlantic Islands and India. Another 20 to 25 convicts sentenced to internal exile in Castro Marim would have to be added to these figures, at least until the 1850s. This unplanned scattering of convict labor would come to a rather abrupt halt in the 1880s. By that point, the Portuguese State and Inquisition had sentenced approximately 115,000 people to some form of *degredo* in the Portuguese World from 1200 to 1880.[5]

Table 1: Exile Locations and Numbers of Portuguese Convicts Sentenced to Degredo from 1837 to 1872

Location	Men	Women	Total
Terceira	1	0	1
Santa Maria	1	0	1
São Tiago	842	42	884
São Vicente	10	1	11
Guiné	18	0	18
São Tomé	627	13	640
Luanda	5,809	200	6,009
Ambriz	79	2	81
Moçâmedes	36	0	36
Benguela	0	160	160
Lourenço Marques	2	1	3
Moçambique	1,350	69	1,419
India	907	2	909
Total (%)	9,682 (95%)	489 (5%)	10,171

Source: ANTT, Ministério de Negócios Eclesiásticos e Justiça (hereafter MNEJ), folio 448, part 5

Penal reform in Portugal

Until the middle of the nineteenth century, the Portuguese legal code remained the *Ordenações Filipinas*, originally published in 1602. The course of the second half of the century saw the legal code reformed and modified. Each time, the code defined *degredo* overseas in more narrow and in more restricted terms until the logical outcome was the creation of overseas prisons designed to supervise *degredados* and their labor. The first major revision was in 1852 and the only distinction in overseas locale was to either "western" or "eastern" (Portuguese) Africa. These distinctions signified the western (Atlantic) colonies of Cape Verde, Guiné, São Tomé, and Angola (called "first degree" *degredo*) versus the eastern or Indian Ocean colony of Mozambique (second degree). It was only when they were specifically sentenced to Portuguese Asia (i.e., India, Timor, and Macau) that European *degredados* would not be sent to Africa. The major problem with this legal code was that it lacked any sort of direction, supervision, or intended purpose for the convict once he or she arrived in the colony. Additional legal reforms of 1864, 1867, 1884, and 1886 corrected this oversight and created the first real prisons in Portugal. New sentences linked prison time in Portugal to be followed by *degredo* to one of the African colonies. The death penalty was abolished in 1867 along with the punishment of public works. *Degredo* was seen as "a complimentary or auxiliary punishment, always temporary" (Moreira 152). By 1867, the various African *degredo* locales were further refined legally by the difficulty faced by Europeans to adapt to their climates. Cape Verde, São Tomé and Princípe, Luanda, and Moçâmedes were the easier, first degree sites. Bissau, Cacheu, Benguela and Mozambique (Island) were the more difficult, second degree locations.

Included in the 1869 reforms was the overseas penal colony, "instituted especially for the moral expiation of the delinquent" (Moreira 157).[6] The solution was to create an overseas prison designed to achieve this lofty goal. This was the legal background that led to the creation of the *Depósito* in Luanda and eventually a second similar (but more modest) *depósito* on Mozambique Island.

The mission of penal reform and the redemption of the "corrupted" individual (i.e., the convict) through lengthy reflection over time (i.e., penitence) in a penitentiary followed by supervised work overseas was then augmented and became the solution to several practical problems:

> Europe finds itself with an enormous number of criminals, not knowing what to do with them after abolishing the death penalty [...] the current political environment among nations, which translates into struggles for colonies [...] the labor crises caused by the lack of indigenous labor [...] and finally the Latin fantasy [...] of colonial assimilation are the main causes that allow convict labor, something that is both useful to the colony and which regenerates the delinquent. (Telles 8)

Therefore, many aspects of penal reform in nineteenth century Portugal supported the continuation of a centuries-long practice now linked with penal transportation to the colonies. In 1883, *degredados* were prohibited from being sent to Lourenço Marques, since they "escaped to the Transvaal and prejudiced the development of the city and the good name of the province [of Mozambique]" (Moreira 165). In 1862, convicts from Cape Verde were no longer sent to São Tomé, and, in 1872, they were banned from the island of São Vicente (Cape Verde). By the 1880s, Angola became the colony of choice and the former military presidio of São Miguel was transformed into the overseas penitentiary envisioned by lawmakers. However, not just lawmakers had turned their attention to the colonies in Africa. "From the 1870s to 1910, a more complex and diversified urban bourgeoisie moved to the center of the political stage in Portugal, with a much more direct interest in the colonies" (Clarence-Smith, "Myth" 172). Legal scholars, lawmakers, those interested in penal reform, politicians, businessmen, and others began to focus on penal reform and the emerging Portuguese solution of forced colonization of Portuguese Africa, especially Angola. Clarence-Smith has very clearly and succinctly outlined this combination of Portuguese interests, which formed before the Treaty of Berlin, leading to what he calls, "aggressive Portuguese Expansionism" (Clarence-Smith, "Portuguese" 172).

One of the more articulate positions on this subject was adopted by Francisco Xavier da Silva Telles, the Secretary-General of the *Sociedade de Geografia de Lisboa* (not surprisingly one of the principal organizations encouraging Portuguese colonial development). Silva Telles had some first-hand experience in Angola with *degredados*, working there as a medical doctor. In 1901, as the head of the Lisbon Geographical Society, he organized a conference on Penal Transportation and Colonization. Two years later, he published a long article with the same title in which he developed the pros and cons of penal transportation as then currently practiced by the Portuguese in their African colonies. Silva Telles made a number of fine distinctions among the various types of convicts sent to Africa. Vagrants and others called '*addidos* were not part of the official statistics he used to compile his overall totals (see Table 3). Also excluded were *deportados*, or deportees (most guilty of political crimes, especially anarchism). In addition, his figures (the official government statistics) ignore *degredados* already in the Angolan colony before 1883 as well as military *degredados* (Telles 36-37).

The realities of the Angolan colony

The second half of the nineteenth century in Angola was a time of economic transition. The end of the slave trade (by 1850) had temporarily stunted the local economy and agricultural production for export from the colony was slow to develop. In 1844, exports were at a low of 201 *contos* (201,000$00). "Coffee, palm oil, palm kernels, and groundnuts in northern Angola, and cotton in southern Angola, were the main staples which replaced slaves during these years, together with ivory, wax, and rubber from the far interior. In 1874, Angola's exports reached a peak of 2,671 *contos*, compared to 830 *contos* in 1825 at the height of the Atlantic slave trade" (Clarence-Smith, "Myth" 169).[7]

A more effective administration of the colony was needed, combined with an improved infrastructure for Luanda (port, roads, waterworks, etc.) as well as for the colony as a whole (e.g., railroads, copper mines). Additional troops were need for the colonial army. Convicts would provide part of the labor needed to achieve these overall goals, to provide "the obligation to ensure the establishment of authority" required in the Treaty of Berlin.

The European/Portuguese segment of the population of Luanda during this period was modest. As can be noted in Table 2, in the period from 1880 to 1930, the percentage of the European population reached its peak of 32% in 1898. Far more typical were the figures for the other years, which are all below 15% of the total. While the total numbers of *degredados* were modest when compared with these figures, they formed a significant element of the European population, especially in Luanda. Orlando Ribeiro has estimated that "At the end of the nineteenth century, *degredados* represented 12% of the white population, living in Luanda with a startling liberty. Many were owners of restaurants" (Ribeiro 132). As we shall see, their percentage of the European population of Luanda may have been higher than this. Silva Telles estimated that two-thirds of the European population lived in Angola as a result of a judicial sentence (Telles 82).

Table 2: The Population of Luanda, 1850-1930

Year	Europeans	Africans	Total
1850	830	11,885	12,715
1887	2,000	12,500	14,500
1898	4,898	10,350	15,248
1923	3,709	19,010	22,719

1930	6,008	39,001	50,588 (5,557 mestiços)

Sources: For 1850, 1887, and 1889, *Anuario Estatístico (*qtd. in Martins, *Vol. 1* 95.) For 1923 and 1930, see Amaral pp. 2, 5.

In 1893, the governor of Angola advised Lisbon on the pressing need to construct more houses for *degredados* and their families arriving from Portugal. Luanda, he said, had around 900 *degredados.* Around 304 men and women were already housed in the Fortress of São Miguel (divided into 5 companies), while he lacked room for an additional 257 people, including 114 dependents.[8] Presumably, the governor was well informed as to the total number of *degredados.* If his figure of 900 is correct, they represented 6% of the total population and 18% of the Europeans in Luanda. Only a couple of years later, in 1904 and 1905, there were slightly over 900 new *degredados* arriving annually. Their percentage of the European population could only have been rising (Martins 125).

Convict or *colono* (free state-sponsored immigrant), the life for Europeans in Angola during this period was demanding. The most common diseases in the colony were malaria, smallpox, dysentery, and a long list various fevers (Governo Geral de Angola 19-99). "After illness caused by malaria, without a doubt, alcohol poisoning is the enemy that produces the greatest number of victims, indigenous as well as European, in all of Africa" (Joaquim Vieira 18-19). Alcohol, its production, sale, and consumption were an important aspect for the Portuguese. "Europeans consider alcohol indispensable for living in Africa. Many mix their water with *aguardente* [firewater] or other spirits" (Joaquim Vieira 19).

Both the *Sociedade de Geografia* as well as other smaller societies had quite specific plans as to what types of colonists and how many were needed in the Angolan colony. In the various congresses (1924, 1934) and meetings that took place both at the turn of the century as well as into the 1920s and 1930s, it was clear that *colonos* should be people with farming backgrounds who would emigrate with their families. Sites should be well chosen and all the necessary preparations completed for their arrival.

Actually, the Portuguese crown had followed a long series of experiments in state-sponsored colonization in Angola during the nineteenth century. Colonists from Pernambuco in 1849, Germans in 1857, military colonies in 1859, Boers from South Africa in 1880-1926, and colonists from Madeira in 1884 all made attempts to form colonies in the Angolan interior. With the exception of the Chibia colony of 1885, they all failed for the same reasons that later colonies would perish: the lack of planning, arable farmland, experienced farmers, demand, and transportation for any crops produced.[9] The Chibia colony was the exception and, interestingly, its success was due to the high demand of its chief product: *aguardente* made from sugar cane. As soon as they were prohibited from making distilled spirits, the colony's fortunes also declined.

Suitable housing was another issue as well:

> Houses for *colonos,* places where they will certainly spend more than half their time, should be planned with great care. They should be well situated to take advantage of sunlight and wind. They should be kept clean and should be large enough to be healthy. They should be designed with the needs of tropical hygiene in mind. Unfortunately, the vast majority of the houses in Angola, even those in the capital, are very far from meeting these conditions. (Governo Geral de Angola 9)

The *Depósito Geral de Degredados*[10]

The *Depósito* was created by decree on 27 December 1881, which amended the legal code of 1869. One of the ideas behind its creation was to imitate the (then recent) success of the British in providing cheap manpower for its Australian colony. The Portuguese were also students of the French experiments in Guiana and New Caledonia. The *Depósito* would be the central hub of *degredo* and cheap labor, labor that would facilitate the "effective occupation" demanded by the terms of the Treaty of Berlin. The piecemeal and unfocused use of convicts that had been occurring since 1824 would now come to an end; the *Depósito* and its military administration would provide the control and direction (so completely absent) over this rabble. These were some of the basic objectives the state had in mind when it created the *Depósito* and placed it specifically under military command. Unfortunately, neither control nor direction would be forthcoming.

Both the opening and the eventual closing of the *Depósito* can be directly tied to larger events taking place outside the colony, namely the Treaty of Berlin and penal reform movements in Europe. The demise of the *Depósito* resulted not from the failure of the system or because of its cost but from the global depression beginning in 1929-30.

By the end of the nineteenth century, ships making the 24-day voyage from Lisbon to Luanda arrived twice a month. From time to time throughout the year, the government would send *degredados* from Lisbon in batches (Castel-Branco 116). Once on land, they would be turned over to the guards at the *Depósito* to be registered into the *livro da matrícula* (registration book) maintained by the commander. This was the theory of how the system was supposed to work. Silva Telles states that the majority of convicts were totally unsupervised and unregistered (Telles 81). Faria Blanc Junior (the prison commander in 1915) suggests the same in his recommendations.

The internal organization of the *Depósito* was along military lines, with convicts assigned to one of five squadrons according to ethnicity, gender, and crime. The First and Second Companies were composed of male European convicts, the Third Company of male convicts from the colonies, the Fourth was made up of all female convicts, and the Fifth was for male vagrants from Portugal (*vadios*). Vagrants were the most problematic of all those sent to Angola. Not surprisingly, the state vacillated between sending them to Luanda or saving the expense and keeping them in Portugal. In the period prior to 1915, between one and two hundred were sent each year, but when the 1915 report was published, the commander noted that "vagrants are not sent here anymore" (Junior 24).[11] *Vadios* are also not included in any of the official totals for *degredados*. Legally they were guilty of being idle, not working, rather than of having done something more criminal. Their absence from the figures further compounds any understanding of how many Europeans were sent to labor in Angola. Whatever totals are reflected here then must be viewed as preliminary since the number of *vadios* was significant.

The main *Depósito* was housed in the Fortress of São Miguel in Luanda. The decree that created the *Depósito* called for dependent institutions to be established under the direction of the Luanda *Depósito Geral.* The first such sub-*Depósito* was established in Benguela, which functioned in this capacity until it was closed in 1907. In 1882, 43 people "sent from Portugal" founded the colony of Júlio de Vilhena in the town of Pungo Andongo. In 1883, the Angolan government created the Cacolo-Calondo (Malange) penal colony and a second colony, Esperança, the next year. In 1885, an agricultural penal colony named for Rebelo da Silva was opened in the interior. The last effort to establish these colonies was in 1894 when the military created the penal colony of Mochico to lessen the demand placed on the *depósitos* in Luanda and Benguela. All these colonies ended quickly and in failure for the same reasons as attempts earlier in the century (see above) (Magalhães 36-38). Perhaps the most significant of these was the general dearth of planning and the complete lack of agricultural knowledge on the parts of the prospective convict colonizer.

The short life of the sub-depository in Benguela aside, it is really Luanda and the Fortress of São Miguel that are at the center of forced colonization in Angola. The regulations for the *Depósito* were periodically updated: 1881, 1883, 1886, and 1907. The *Depósito* was a military base with the intention of providing labor. All convicts, in fact, had to perform some sort of work and all had to wear uniforms, including straw hats with ribbons showing their matriculation numbers (see Photo 3).

How many *degredados*?

This is the most basic and most problematic question to answer. As mentioned above, the official statistics did not include two critical elements: (1) the number of convicts already present in the colony, and (2) vagrants, political deportees, and those sentenced by military courts.

Table 3: Total Number of Convicts Entering/Leaving the Depósito Geral

Year	Male	Female	Total	Already Present	Left	Total
1883	245		245			
1884	320	35	355			
1885	74	13	91			
1886	69	20	89			
1887	48	17	65			
1888	41	9	50			
1889	89	11	100			
1890	100	10	110			
1891	110	40	150			
1892	165	25	190			
1893	250	40	290			
1894	140	30	170			
1895	149	20	169			
1896	140	12	152			
1897	148	20	168			
1898	128	17	145			
1899	134	17	151	979	83	938
1900	No data	No data	No data	938	37	975

Year	Male	Female	Total	Already Present	Left	Total
1901	979	161	1140	975	95	880
1902	113	15	128	880	188	820
1903	275	17	292	820	152	960
1904	167	20	187	960	384	763
1905	144	19	163	763	183	743
1906	116	10	126	743	197	672
1907	195	18	213	672	186	699
1908	133	9	142	699	286	555
1909	212	21	233	555	122	666
1910	231	19	250	666	137	779
1911	304	19	323	779	298	804
1912	141	12	153	804	215	742
1913	283	20	303	742	190	855
1914	113	12	125	855	143	837

These figures only include registered *degredados*. They do not include *vadios*.
Sources: 1883-1889: Graph 1 in Telles.
Governo Geral da Província de Angola, *Annuario Estatistico. 1899.*
1901: Governo Geral da Província de Angola, *Annuario Estatistico. 1901*
1902-1914: Junior 64.

In Photo 4, it is possible to appreciate the internal organization of the *Depósito*. At the entrance, after passing though the guard house (noted as number 5 on the original) and past the commander's residence (2), the areas at the front of the prison were reserved for female convicts (3, 4) and dependent children (11). At the opposite end of the prison were the barracks for the four male companies (21, 22, 23, and 24) near the kitchen (20) and garden (*horta*). In between we find the parade grounds (*parada*), barracks for the guards (12, 13), and the various convict workshops (26, 28). Those *degredados* assigned to work in the *Depósito* made a surprising variety of goods. Their sale of these items turned a tidy profit for the *Depósito*. Inmates made shoes, clothing, furniture, locks and keys, tin articles, brooms, washed clothing, and bound books. In the six-year period from 1909 to 1915, these goods and services gave the *Depósito* a net profit of over ninety *contos*.

We also know a bit about the meals served to those working in the *Depósito*. Faria Blanc Junior tells us that he made every effort to serve healthy balanced meals, which (in 1915) daily cost the *Depósito* twenty-six *centavos* for European convicts, twenty for Africans, and twelve for dependents.

One of the more interesting documents uncovered in Lisbon shows us exactly what these *degredados* were eating in 1931, at the time the *Depósito* was on the verge of closing.

Table 4: Total Expenses for Foods for the Depósito Geral de Degredados for August 1931.

Provider	Foods	Price (Escudos?)	Consumed Units (kilos?)	Total Price
State Bakery	Bread	2.10	10,331	21,695$10
State Butcher	Beef			
	First quality	5.8	3,330.35	19,316$03
	Second quality	3.8	273	1,037$40
José Nascimento Ribeiro	Sugar	1.96	615.06	1,205$51
	Yellow beans	1	671	671$00
	Butter beans	.89	1,218	1,084$02
J. J. Melo	Garlic	3.49	11.4	39$786
	Paprika	16.85	18.5	311$725
Manuel do Nascimento	Rice	2	1,907	3,814$00
	Sausage	13	583	7,579$00
	Firewood	.09	4116.8	3,705$12
Beltrão Pena	Salt	0.19	792	150$48
	Vinegar	1.68	734	1,233$12
Setas & Irmão	Onions	1.84	719	1,322$96
	White beans	1.08	607	655$56
	Tomato paste	3.2	591	1,891$20
	Pepper (powder)	22	156	343$20
Céu Rodrigues	Lard	6.5	777	5,050$5
	Potatoes	1.13	12,232	13,822.16
	Yellow beans	.85	687	583$95
J. F. Rita	Coffee	2.49	30699	764$405
	Pasta	4.7	1,683	7,910$1
Gomes & Irmão	Fresh pork	6.09	598	3,641$82
	Salted pork	5.92	200	1,184$00

S. Leal	Salted pork	5.25	594	3,118$50
Conc. Setas	Chick peas	3.49	721	2,516$29
	Beans	2.95	207	610$65
José F. Ribeiro	Olive oil	9.96	856	8,525$76
	Codfish	8.55	657	5,617$35

PROVIDER	FOODS	PRICE (Escudos?)	CONSUMED Units (kilos?)	TOTAL PRICE
Various	Fresh greens	.8	15,284	12,227$20
	Green beans	.8	1,166	932$80
	Game	2.5	1,395	3,488$87
	Fresh Greens	.6	220	132$00
	Fresh fish	2	209	418$00
	Fresh fish	2.25	206	463$50
	Fresh fish	2.2	239	525$80
	Fresh tomato	.5	77	46$20
	Wine	3.5	131.4	459$90
	Olives	4.5	14.6	65$70
	Tips paid to suppliers			480$00
Total				138,640$67

Of this total, the Ministry of Justice owes 83,968$60, the Ministry of the Interior owes 45,711$20: 8,918$22 for vagrants, 36,792$98 for civil cases; the Colony of Mozambique owes 2,059$73; the Colony of Cape Verde owes 6,580$03; the Colony of Guinea owes 207$85; and the Colony of São Tomé owes 93$87.
Expenses for September 1931 were for the same foods from the same suppliers but the overall total was slightly less: 120,013$86.

Source: Arquivo Histórico Militar, second division, second section, box 161, document 22.

Table 4 provides a general impression of the foodstuffs being consumed by inmates. However, due to the current lack of information, it raises a number of unanswerable questions as well. For example, without knowing the daily expense per inmate in 1931, it is not possible to know how many *degredados* were present in the *Depósito* at the time of these expenses. Without a great deal more financial information regarding the *Depósito*'s overall expenses and income, it is hard to appreciate the cost of a month's meals. For example, Faria

Blanc Junior does not include overall income and expenses in his published report. We can see that the *degredados* did appear to have a balanced diet, high in protein (note the amounts of beef and fish). Assuming this list was augmented with fresh fruit and vegetables from the *Depósito*'s garden (see Photo 4), it would appear to be a healthy diet. Supplying the *Depósito* with these goods must have been a lucrative series of contracts for the Luanda businesses listed.

What do they do in the colony?

All convicts were in one of three situations regarding work: licensed (to private parties), working directly for the state or towns, or working in the *Depósito.* In the first two cases, the convict was not fed or paid by the *Depósito.* Those working for the *Depósito* received daily rations and bread as well as two *centavos* daily for their expenses, such as to purchase soap or to pay the barber. All convicts had to pay a percentage of their income into several obligatory funds, including one for repatriation.

The numerous comments made by travelers, government officials, and military commanders suggest that *degredados* were everywhere in the colony and in large numbers in the cities, especially Luanda. After looking at how they were assigned for work in the colony, perhaps it would be more to the point to ask, "What did they not do?" A detailed listing in 1901 shows that the *Depósito* and the colony had 993 *degredados.* They were working in a variety of governmental and civic positions throughout the entire colony. Just to mention a few of the larger examples, fifty-seven were assigned to the troops in Benguela, twenty-four were in the Fortress of São Pedro da Barra (a place of secondary punishment), thirty-three were working for the Luanda telegraph company, thirty-four were employed by the Luanda town council, eleven were working for the police (!), seventeen in the Governor's Palace, twenty-seven were in the armory, and thirty-nine were employed in houses of the military. Of the 993, 127 (almost 13%) were "absent" (Governo Geral da Provincia de Angola, *Annuario 1901* Table 66).

Few had kind statements to make about the *degredados* sent to Angola. "Almost all are individuals with evil instincts; their habit is to practice crime. For them, *degredo,* far from being a punishment, is a benefit or the realization of a dream. It is not difficult for them to run off into the interior and live with the natives or to find a bit of coastline to make an escape" (Matos 141).

Not all were as unkind in their judgements about *degredados* sent to Angola. One former military commander who had *degredados* working for him had high praise for them. He stated, "Many times I had *degredados* under my command and, to do them justice, I never had better or more humble workers. The only incorrigible ones were the vagrants" (Magalhães 38).

Exiting the *Depósito*

Other than completing their sentences or by an untimely death, the only legal method of exiting the *Depósito* and the clutches of the state was by receiving a pardon. Awarding pardons or commuting the time remaining of sentence was a long-established practice of the old regime. Royal weddings and births of children in the royal family were frequently associated with blanket pardons for prisoners awaiting their sentences. This practice was continued after the installation of the Portuguese Republic (1910). Each year on the anniversary of the Republic (October 5), the President would announce the list of those who had been pardoned for their crimes. Inmates in the *Depósito* were well aware of this practice and attempted to bring their plights to the attention of the highest officials in the land. After 1910, annual batches of their petitions for pardon made their way up the chain of command from the director of the prison, to the Governor of Angola, and then to the Ministers of Overseas and of Justice (and presumably to the President) for consideration. Letters requesting pardons were frequent enough that the *Depósito* developed a printed form for the commander's use.

The letter from Francisca Rosa, inmate number 6126 of the Fourth Squadron is typical. Rosa was eighteen when she sent her petition in 1915, having been in the *Depósito* since 1911. She was guilty of the crime of infanticide, having been sentenced (27 August 1910) in her native district of Bragança to six years of prison to be followed by 10 years of *degredo* or to 20 years of *degredo* (only, with no jail time). Later that same year (1910), on 4 November, she received a partial pardon, reducing her twenty-year sentence by one-third. She arrived in Luanda in 1911 and now petitioned the President for a pardon in honor of the fifth anniversary of the Republic. In his accompanying report, the *Depósito*'s Commander noted that, other than a minor infraction committed when she first arrived, her behavior had been good and that she "appears to want to reform herself." Her behavior was in sharp contrast to that of another member of the Fourth Company, the twenty-two-year-old Mathilde de Jesus from Castelo Branco. Mathilde had been in the *Depósito* since 1907, having received a similar sentence (and reduction) for the same crime of infanticide. Mathilde, however, had been punished on three separate occasions in the *Depósito* for insulting guards and for her insolent attitude. The commander noted that "she is not well behaved and shows no signs of repentance." Petitions such as these from 1915 are both fascinating as well as ultimately disturbing. Young women such as these, uneducated, unmarried, were without the necessary economic and social resources to deal with the birth of an unwanted child. Their lives were, at best, severely marred (if not altogether ruined) as a result.

The sixty-eight letters, which form this batch from 1915, are a particularly rich source (ANTT, MAEJ, folio 729/5). Of these, sixteen are from female convicts and fifty-two are from men. The relatively high percentage of female petitioners (23.5%) is significant. Did they believe the state would be more likely to pardon a female? Was the nature of their crimes (mostly infanticide or murder) somehow more understandable, somehow more pardonable? These sixteen women were guilty of first degree murder (*homicídio voluntário,* six cases), infanticide (five), poisoning (three), theft with murder (one), and simple theft (one). Their ages range from the eighteen-year-old Francisca Rosa (mentioned above) to Antonia Valente, aged 50. On the low end, their sentences were three and a half years for one case of infanticide to twenty-eight years for the same crime or for murder.

The youngest of the male petitioners was Anselmo Pinto da Silva from Chouca, aged seventeen, convicted of theft and sentenced to six years of *degredo* in Africa. The oldest was the sixty-three-year-old Manuel Antonio Estebuinha from Odemira. He was also guilty of theft and had received a sentence of five years and three months of *degredo* to Africa and a fine for three months at ten *centavos* daily. Sentences of years of *degredo* plus a fine were common for the others convicted of theft or murder, presumably to repay the victim or family. Theft and murder are the most typical offences of this lot, with a couple of unintentional homicides (second or third degree murder), assaults, and arsons. The normal sentence for first degree murder was eight years in prison in Portugal, followed by ten to twenty years of *degredo* in Angola. The least severe sentence handed down to a man in this group was four and a half years of *degredo* for theft. Many others combined prison time in Portugal (the time of penitence and reflection), additional years of prison overseas, to be followed by years of labor in Angola (reform and redemption through work).

In many ways these letters are from typical inmates. The average male convict was in his late twenties and was guilty of murder. Women were in relatively small numbers and were normally convicted of murder or infanticide.

Similar (although smaller) lists of petitioners exist for scattered years in the nineteenth century and then seem to pick up during the first years of the Republic (i.e., 1910-1918). It is impossible to know the outcomes of these petitions without seeing the files held by the *Depósito*. Judging from the lists of those granted pardons by the President each October 5, it would appear that those from the *Depósito* in Angola had little luck. Pardons for them were rarely if ever awarded. In spite of this reality, petitions continued to arrive each year.

What did the *degredados* do when they left the *Depósito*? Did they remain in the colony and become the European colonizers envisioned at the beginning of this process? Chapter 6 (articles 52-60) of the Mozambique *Depósito*'s 1905 Regulations is worth quoting at some length here, since it responds directly to the issue of European colonization and state-awarded land:

> Those convicts familiar with agriculture who prove to be rehabilitated will be allotted a free plot of land owned by the state. The state will determine which land will be allotted to the convict. Each of these plots of land will be a dependency of the prison.
>
> The plot of land will be cultivated to the best of the ability by the convict or by workers that he will hire.
>
> This concession of land will be done by the governor-general after he has received all the necessary information from the commander of the prison and the local authorities regarding the convict's ability to work and his general behavior. The land awarded under this concession will only be leased to the convict during the period of his sentence. It will only become his after his sentence is completed.
>
> This concession of land will be voided and the land will return to the property of the state in the event that:
>
> 1. The *colono* does not begin to cultivate the land within one year of the date of concession,
> 2. The *colono* begins cultivation but abandons the land,
> 3. The *colono* leaves the land before ten years have passed.
>
> In the event that the *colono* dies, the land will become the property of his wife and children. If the *colono* does not have a wife or children, it will return to the state.
>
> Those *colonos* who do not have the financial means to begin cultivation of the land will be given farming implements, seed and other necessities by the prison, which will also continue to feed and clothe them for the first year.

> 1. The items furnished by the prison will be repaid by one third of the harvest. Those convicts who complete their sentences can obtain equal concessions if they prefer to remain in the province [of Mozambique].
>
> During the first five years of the concession, the *colono* will not have to pay any sort of tribute [i.e., taxes] for the land. After that time, they will have to pay the same as all other property owners.

On the other hand, did they return to Portugal? In either case, did they return to their criminal ways, or did they follow the straight and narrow path leading away from the judicial system? Did the presence (or absence) of their families influence this decision? Faria Blanc Junior in his report suggests that many *degredados* did remain in the colony. One of his main suggestions to his superiors was to "make it more difficult for prejudicial individuals to remain in the colony." He also suggested tightening the supervision of the *degredados* and not allowing them the current one-year grace period to request return passage to Portugal, paid for by the *Depósito*'s repatriation fund (Junior 15-17). The 1915 Commander had few kind words to say about *degredados* and marriage. His view was that nothing good would result from those who brought their wives and children with them from Portugal. The vast majority of these wives, he claimed, were women of dubious moral character who may seek a new life of disgrace. Marriage between convicts was no better; European ex-convicts marrying Angolans "did not result in anything worth mentioning" (Junior 12-14). Better and more complete answers to these questions await further investigation.

Was the *Depósito* a success or a failure?

Júlio Ferreira Pinto, himself a *colono*, had a couple of comments about the effectiveness of the *Depósito* in general and *degredado* labor in Angola. Writing in 1926, he stated that the *Depósito* was created in Luanda because of egotism and lack of reflection. He suggested sending *degredados* instead to Cape Verde, since this would lower the transportation costs from Lisbon. Keeping them in the *Depósito* or allowing them to roam the streets of Luanda as vagrants did not have the desired regenerative effects. If the Republic wanted to continue sending them to Angola, he suggested agrarian or industrial colonies in the interior (Pinto 155-158). As we have seen above, the state did attempt a variety of planned colonies in the interior, but due to a lack of planning or foresight, none were successful. In fact, they were quickly abandoned after only a year or two.

In terms of the *Depósito* as an institution of penal reform, it is clear even from this distance that it failed miserably. It never had sufficient personnel, funding, or the physical space required to achieve its basic duty of housing and administering the pool of *degredados* sent to Luanda. Because of this, *degredados* wandered freely in Luanda with little or no supervision. Some became merchants while others returned to their criminal ways and caused no end of havoc in the capital city. Many others simply disappeared into the interior.

The *Depósito* had a triple mission of removing the offenders from Portuguese society, keeping their corrupting influences far away from Europe, reforming the convicts into honest citizens, and making them useful to the Angolan colony through their labor. Given their relatively large numbers within the European population and the multitude of tasks in which they were engaged in the colony, their labor was significant; the *Depósito* was a success when judged on that aspect alone. However, the *Depósito* created another problem for the colony, as a number of administrators and others at the time mentioned; the presence of convicts and of the *Depósito* itself cast a dark shadow over Angola. Thus, it made *Luanda* and *Angola* synonymous with *penal colony*, retarding large-scale free immigration.

In the decree ending *degredo* to Africa for European convicts, the government concluded that the experiment had been a failure. "The old system [...] failed completely. The shipment of criminals to the overseas provinces [...] was transformed into a dead weight" (Qtd. in Bender 92). Salazar based his decision on cost (Bender 92). For sure, transporting the convicts and providing the expenses required to administer the *Depósito* were expensive. Cost, however, was not a factor when the *Depósito* was first planned. It seems unfair to dismiss it as a failure based on cost alone. In addition, the inmates provided labor and made a variety of goods sold on the market in Luanda. Further study will be needed to determine if the institution actually spent more than it received for its numerous goods and services.

Degredados formed upwards of 60% of all white immigrants to Luanda during this period and outnumbered free immigrants until after 1930 (Bender 87n86). There is no question that they had a large impact in Luanda and by extension in the Angolan colony until the closure of the *Depósito*. However, it is also clear that they did not provide the stimulus to free immigration that had been so carefully planned in Lisbon nor did they provide the social impact envisioned in the 1880s.

What happened to *degredo* as a punishment?

Degredo continued in one form or another in the Portuguese legal code until 1954. The end of the *Depósito* came in 1932. European convicts would remain in Portugal in domestic prisons and agricultural colonies, such as the *Colónia Penitenciária* in Alcoentre (near Santarém) and the *Colónia Penal Agrícola António Macieira* in Sintra. By 1933, each of the colonies was slated to have its own prison, where it would house convicts sentenced by its courts. The two smallest colonies of São Tomé and Macau would send their convicts to Angola and Timor, respectively. Angolan convicts (joined by those from São Tomé) would be sent to a smaller facility in Roçadas in southern Angola. Mozambique had its own penal institution: the *Depósito Geral dos Sentenciados* opened in 1894 and housed in the Fortress of São Sebastião on Mozambique Island. Its regulations and objectives mirrored those of its sister prison in Luanda, although it would appear that the numbers of *degredados* sent there never approached the Angolan totals. By 1951, the prison on Mozambique Island was removed from military control and transferred to Lourenço Marques under the judicial system. Eventually, each colony would construct a prison for its own convicts and *degredo* between colonies would end.

The punishment of exile to Africa was replaced by the *Estado Novo* with a prison sentence, which, in the case of political crimes, was still often to be served in Africa. This would lead to the creation of Tarrafal, the infamous prison in Cape Verde, where Salazar's regime would send some of its most vocal and famous critics.[12] The *Depósito Geral de Degredados* and Portugal's experiment with European forced labor in its largest and most promising African colony quickly became historical oddities, curious footnotes in Angolan history. After 1938, the Fortress of São Miguel, where the *Depósito* had functioned, was transformed into a museum, a picture post card site promoted by the Angolan Information and Tourism Board (see Photo 2). Later during the struggle for independence, it would revert to use by the military. Forced colonization using convicts was forgotten after Angola attracted free immigration from Portugal later in the century.

Conclusion

The forced colonization of Angola in the period from 1880 to 1930 was a bold experiment by the Lisbon authorities, motivated by an increasing population of criminals at home and an international scramble for colonies in Africa. Convict labor held the promise of solving both these dilemmas while providing some of the cheap labor needed to develop the economic potential of Angola and stimulate free European immigration from the homeland. The large numbers of convicts and the state's inability to effectively control them or direct their labor meant that this fifty-year experiment was doomed from its very beginnings.

In many ways, the *Depósito* was a failure. However, if its goal was to set the stage for the future economic development of the colony, looking at the course of Angolan history from 1930-1960, the sacrifices made by inmates of the *Depósito* have yet to be fully understood or appreciated.

Notes

[1] The research that made this article possible was conducted in 2002 with a grant awarded by the Arquivo Nacional da Torre do Tombo (ANTT) and the Luso-American Development Foundation. At that time, I was honored to be invited by the Universidade de Lisboa, Centro de Estudos Africanos, to offer a graduate seminar on "Degredo para Africa Portuguesa no Século XIX." In that seminar, my students and I explored much of the secondary literature and began the archival work that led to this article. Special thanks are due to Professors Isabel de Castro Henriques and João Medina. A second research trip to Lisbon in 2005 was funded by a College of Charleston Faculty Research grant.

[2] For very solid examples of this small but growing literature for the modern period, see Vaz, Relvas, and Pinheiro; Relvas; Vaz; and Bastos.

[3] On Mozambique, see the *Regulamento do Depósito Geral dos Sentenciados da Provincia de Mozambique*; for *degredo* in early modern times, see Coates, *Convicts*, and Pieroni and Coates.

[4] See the unique work of Maria Eugénia Martins Vieira for examples of *degredados* sent to Angola from 1714-1757. Her work is an examination of one register of *degredados* sent to Luanda during that period. However, it is important to remember that Angola was only one of many such sites in the Empire.

[5] This figure assumes 80 convicted annually from 1200 to 1400 (16,000), 100 annually from 1400-1550 (15,000), 50,000 exiled from 1550-1755, 250 annually from 1755 to 1824 (17,000), 285 annually from 1824-1880 (16,000), plus internal exile to Castro Marim from 1755-1850 (2,400). This very brief summary of *degredo* in Portuguese society cannot do justice to the many facets of the system. I have developed these at some length in *Convicts and Orphans*, and with Geraldo Pieroni on internal exile in *Castro Marim*. For the transition to the use of the first Atlantic colonies as exile sites, see Coates, "Crime and Punishment" 119-140.

[6] The 1869 legal reforms were largely the work of Luís Augusto Rebelo da Silva, the noted nineteenth-century author, historian, philosopher, and legal scholar. Moreira, *O Problema*, 157.

[7] Clarence-Smith is citing J. Monteiro, *Angola and the River Congo* (London, 1968); G. Pery, *Geografia e estatistica geral de Portugal e colónias* (Lisbon, 1875) 358; and Hammond,

Portugal and Africa, 1815-1910, A Study in Uneconomic Imperialism (Stanford, 1966) 51.

[8] See volume 2 of Martins (appendice documental [unnumbered pages], from *Arquivo Histórico Ultramarino*, Angola, box 871, dated 13 Oct. 1893).

[9] On the earlier congresses, see Barcelar; Ferreira; Giraúl; and Sasportes. For an in-depth discussion of these and more recent attempts by the Portuguese state at colonization (into the 1960s), see Feio (15-21).

[10] Note the rather odd use of the word *depósito* [depot or armory] for the two prisons in Africa. Prisons in Portugal were *penitenciárias* [penitentiaries], not *depósitos*.

[11] See also Relvas 102-03.

[12] On Tarrafal prison, see both Aquino and *Tarrafal: Trabalho colectivo*.

Works Cited

Amaral, Ilídio de. "Subsídios para o estudo da evolução da população de Luanda." Separata da revista *Garcia de Orta* 7.2 [Lisbon] (1959).

Aquino, Acácio Tomaz de. *O segredo das prisões atlânticas*. Lisbon: Regra do Jogo, 1978.

Barcelar, João. "O problema do transporte penal." *Segundo Congresso Colonial Nacional*. Lisbon, n.p., 1924.

Bastos, Susana Pereira. *O Estado Novo e Seus Vadios*. Lisbon: Don Quixote, 1997.

Bender, Gerald J. *Angola under the Portuguese: The Myth and the Reality*. Berkeley: U of California P, 1978.

Cardoso, Manuel de Costa Lobo. *Subsídios para a história de Luanda*. Luanda: Museu de Angola, 1954.

Castel-Branco, João Bentes. *Guia do colono para a Africa Portugueza*. Porto: Typografia da Empresa Literária e Typografica, 1891.

Clarence-Smith, W. G. "The Myth of Uneconomic Imperialism: The Portuguese in Angola, 1836-1926." *Journal of Southern African Studies* 5.2 (April 1979): 165-80.

———. "The Portuguese and Spanish Roles in the Scramble for Africa: An Economic Interpretation." *Bismarck, Europe and Africa. The Berlin Conference 1884-1885 and the Onset of Partition*. Ed. Stig Förster *et al.* London: Oxford UP, 1988. 215-27.

Coates, Timothy J. *Convicts and Orphans. Forced and State-Sponsored Colonization in the Portuguese Empire, 1550-1755*. Stanford: Stanford UP, 2001.

———. "Crime and Punishment in the Fifteenth-Century Portuguese World: The Transition from Internal to Imperial Exile." *The Final Argument: The Imprint of Violence on Society in Medieval and Early Modern Europe*. Ed. Donald J. Kagay and L. J. Andrew Villalon. Woodridge [UK]: Boydell & Brewer, 1998. 119-40.

Feio, Mariano. *As causas do fracasso da colonização agrícola de Angola. Comunicações*, série de *Ciências da Terra* 7. Lisbon: Instituto de Investigação Cientifica Tropical, 1998.

Ferreira, Dinis. *A colonização europeia em Angola*. Lisbon: Tipografico Colonial, 1922.

Giraúl, Visconde de. *Ideas geraes sobre colonização europea na Provincia de Angola*. Congresso Colonial Nacional. Lisbon, n.p., 1901.

Governo Geral da Provincia de Angola. *Annuario Estatistico da Provincia de Angola. 1899*. Loanda: Imprensa Nacional, 1901.

———. *Annuario Estatistico da Provincia de Angola. 1901.* Loanda: Imprensa Nacional, 1905.

Governo Geral de Angola. *Guia Médico para o Colono de Angola.* Loanda: Imprensa Nacional, 1908.

Junior, Hermenegildo Augusto de Faria Blanc. *O Depósito de Degredados.* Loanda: Imprensa Nacional, 1916.

Magalhães, A. Leite de. *A colonização e desenvolvimento de Angola.* Lisbon: Journal da Europa, 1925.

Martins, Maria João Rodrigues. "São Paulo de Luanda, 1870-1910: Alguns tópicos sobre saúde, urbanismo, e quotidiano." MA thesis. U of Lisbon, 1994. 2 vols.

Matos, João da Silva. *Reforma penitenciária.* Lisbon: Sousa Neves, 1885.

Moreira, Adriano. *O Problema Prisional do Ultramar.* Coimbra: Coimbra Editora, 1954.

Pieroni, Geraldo, and Timothy J. Coates. *Castro Marim: da vila do couto à vila do sal.* Lisbon: Sá da Costa, 2002.

Pinto, Júlio Ferreira. *Notas e commentários dum colono.* Lisbon: J. Rodrigues & Companhia, 1926.

Regulamento do Depósito Geral de Sentenciados da Provincia de Moçambique. Lourenço Marques: Imprensa Nacional, 1905.

Relvas, Eunice. *Esmola e Degredo. Mendigos e Vadios em Lisboa (1835-1910).* Lisbon: Horizonte, 2002.

Ribeiro, Orlando. *A colonização de Angola e seu fracasso.* Lisbon: Imprensa Nacional, 1981.

Santos, Nuno Beja Valdez Thomaz dos. *A Fortaleza de S. Miguel.* Luanda: Instituto de Investigação Cientifica de Angola, 1967.

Sasportes, Simão. *A colonização branca.* Tese presentada ao primeiro Congresso da Colonização. Lisbon, 1934.

Tarrafal: Trabalho colectivo de sobreviventes do Tarrafal. Lisbon: Caminho, 1978.

Telles, Francisco Xavier Silva. *A Transportação Penal e a Colonização.* Lisbon: Sociedade de Geografia de Lisboa, 1903.

Vaz, Maria João. *Crime e Sociedade. Portugal na Segunda Metade do século XIX.* Oeiras: Celta, 1998.

Vaz, Maria João, Eunice Relvas, and Nuno Pinheiro, eds. *Exclusão na História. Actas do Colóquio Internacional sobre Exclusão Social.* Oeiras: Celta, 2000.

Vieira, Joaquim Francisco. *Os três maiores inimigos do colono português em Africa.* Lisbon: Imprensa Nacional, 1902.

Vieira, Maria Eugénia Martins. "Registro de cartas de guia de *degredados* para Angola (1714-1757). Análise de um códice do Arquivo da Câmara Municipal de Luanda." BA thesis. U of Lisbon, 1966.

Timothy J. Coates is author of *Convicts and Orphans: Forced and State Sponsored Colonization in the Portuguese Empire, 1550-1755* (Stanford, 2001) and *Castro Marim, da vila do couto à vila do sal* (Sá da Costa, 2002). An associate editor of *Portuguese Studies Review,* he has been awarded the Order of *São Tiago da Espada.* He is a Professor in the history department at The College of Charleston (South Carolina). Email: CoatesT@cofc.edu

Photo 1.
"São Paulo da Assumpção de Luanda."
Engraving by Caetano Alberto. In *O Occidente* Vol. 6 (1883) 76.

Photo 2.

"The Fortress of São Miguel." Original photo from the Angolan Information and Tourism Board. Published in Nuno Beja Valdez Thomaz dos Santos, *A Fortaleza de S. Miguel* (Luanda: Instituto de Investigação Cientifica de Angola) 63.

Photo 3.

"Men of the Second Company," in Junior (28).

Photo 4.
"O Depósito de Degredados," in Junior (endpapers).

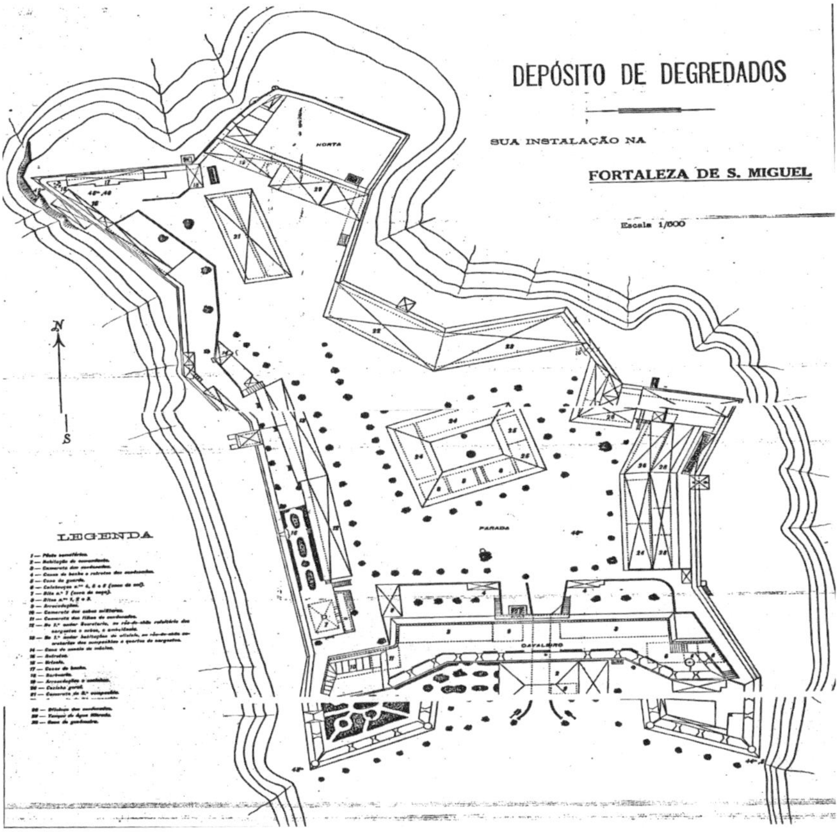
DEPÓSITO DE DEGREDADOS
SUA INSTALAÇÃO NA
FORTALEZA DE S. MIGUEL
Escala 1/500
HORTA
PARADA
CAVALEIRO
N
S
LEGENDA

Testimony to the Presence of a Woman in the Colonial Wars in Africa (1961-1974)

Margarida Calafate Ribeiro

Below is the testimony of Maria Adelaide Ruano, a Portuguese woman who lived in Angola during the colonial war there. Like many other women, she accompanied her husband to the continent on his military service.

Margarida Calafate Ribeiro took her testimony as part of a research project underway at the Centro de Estudos Sociais (University of Coimbra), which centers on the role of Portuguese women during the colonial war. She is grateful to Maria Adelaide Ruano, for both her willingness and her generosity. Margarida Ribeiro and Phillip Rothwell are responsible for translating the testimony into English.

I am the second daughter of a happy marriage. I was born in July, 1947, in Nelas, but when I was just three months old we moved to Figueira da Foz, where my parents, who were originally from Beira, made a living in business. Figueira was the city of my infancy and youth. I lived there until I went to university. It was a very pleasant city. You could go for walks a lot; you could play in the streets; I was very happy there. Even today, Figueira is a very special city for me. I would spend winter at school, at the cinema, going to small parties at friends' homes, typical activities for Portuguese cities in the provinces. And in the summer, the town became totally cosmopolitan. Waves of Spaniards and French would appear—there were a lot of foreigners, and the casino. In the summer, at least twice a week, I would go to the casino,

Portuguese Literary & Cultural Studies 15/16 (2010): 115-25.

you know, there was so much glamour about it: the dresses, the jackets, the shows, the summer nights.

I had a very traditional education, strict in terms of permissible behaviour, ethics and morals, and also politically, even if it was characterized by a certain degree of open-mindedness, it was an "open-mindedness" in quotation marks. At home, we discussed politics openly, and on the whole, we were not happy with things as they were. My father was very liberal, even when it came to religion. I would go to mass, but if I didn't, it was no big deal. However, we were absolutely forbidden to discuss politics outside our home, because there was a kind of consciousness of the fact it was a no-go area, a kind of fear and knowledge of the consequences that could be unleashed as a result of a less than prudent public expression of what we were actually thinking.

I came to Lisbon to take the university entrance exam when I was just sixteen, and I stayed in residence halls run by nuns. My movements were more or less controlled, even if discretely, but they were controlled. Later, when I came to Lisbon permanently to study, it was the same story. I could only go out at night with the expressed permission of my parents. Every time I wanted to go to the cinema, I had to ring up and ask them. When I say it like that, it sounds like we were completely conventional and that my education was conventional, but, in actual fact, my parents never said no, I couldn't go out. However, these control measures existed, as was to be expected given the era in which we lived, and it was part of the way we were.

The course I had chosen, Economics and Business, was not offered at Coimbra, which would have been the natural choice for someone who lived in Figueira da Foz. My departure for Lisbon was initially a big shock for my father. It was also for my mother, but especially for my father. At the time, in 1965, the idea that students were all in revolt was common currency, the idea that they were against everything and everyone. And because of this, right from the beginning, my parents made it perfectly clear that I was there to study and that I should not get involved in politics. This was one of the greatest fears of most of the parents of my generation.

I usually rang home every day, and, at least once a week, my father would warn me: "You know that whatever happens, we will be there for you, now don't get involved in any politics." At the time, it was more normal to hear fathers say: "If I find out that you are there"—referring to Caxias—"I will leave you there to rot."[1] After having warned me off politics, he would paint the darkest picture possible of what the PIDE prisons were like. I think any youth would have been terrified by his account. I was certainly afraid. But, despite these warnings, my relationship with my parents was very good. We have to see things in the context of the 1960s. There was nothing more natural than children asking for permission from their parents. In fact, I had no sensation of being tightly supervised. My requests were always granted, I don't think my parents ever said no to me. There was a natural and healthy hierarchical logic underpinning relationships. Of course, despite my father's entreaties, there was a palpable atmosphere of tension that engulfed the university and this tension was very important to me. He was, in fact, right, there were fireworks in the air and I had just arrived in a glass bubble. Today, it all seems like a caricature, but just to let you know what it was really like, I'm going to tell you about a small incident that happened. When I came to Lisbon to do the university entrance exam, I sat at my desk, and the attendants brought us ashtrays so that we could smoke during the exam. I was shocked. At school in Figueira da Foz it was absolutely forbidden to smoke. Our smocks had to cover up our knees, and although the classes were mixed, during the breaks, we were separated from the boys. Then suddenly, they come and place an ashtray on my desk so that I can smoke during the exam. This was my first shock, something as simple as that. But it was through that that I realized I was in another world, a world that intimidated me at first, but that also excited me.

As far as politics were concerned, I was pretty naïve. For instance, I used to believe, in fact I really believed, that what appeared in the newspapers was the truth. What total naivety! I could not imagine that a journalist would write a news article, and put his byline on it, and, in fact, be writing an utter lie, or a partial lie or a misleading truth by omission. Sometimes, we would argue over politics, and I, quite innocently, would say, "But I read this in the paper," to which the reply would come that it was an out-and-out lie. While at university, I became aware of my own naivety. I became conscious that things were not as I had assumed or as they seemed to be, and that there were certain things about which one did not speak, but that still existed. I did not like Salazar, but neither was I particularly critical of him, probably because I had nothing with which to compare him. My relationship to him was rather dubious, or ambiguous: I thought things were in a poor state, I was aware of this, but I had no clue of exactly where or how, even if I identified our lack of freedom and development as a pretty fundamental problem. I was conscious of the fact that we were stuck. When Salazar died and Marcello Caetano was named prime minister, I was really happy. There were great expectations around him, he was a younger man, perhaps more in tune with the era. This was our hope.

All this acquisition of a more politicised perspective on the way we lived had a lot to do with the degree course I had chosen. The School of Economics [*Instituto de Ciências Económicas e Financeiras*], in Lisbon, was one of the most open-minded. First of all, because we studied aspects of development, and then, because we had professors who opened up our minds, not in an in-your-face way, but with the subtlety with which they positioned themselves in relation to the material studied and in regard to anything to do with economic development. We would talk about agriculture, trade, industry, and in so doing, Portugal's own backwardness became blatant. It was through our studies that we felt and thought that we ought to be in a better socio-economic position and the reason we had not attained it was due to political factors. The faculty at the school was one of the most irreverent, in fact, perhaps because the very material we studied showed us clearly our undeniable backwardness in all its glory. However much you did not want to notice it, it was impossible not to see it.

The majority of my colleagues were men. It was around the time that I went to university that there began to be more women, something that was a determining factor for the era. As well as politics, the discussion of which still terrified my father, we would go to parties, to the cinema, we would listen to music, and read a lot. At the time, French culture was dominant. We would listen to John Holiday, Greco, Aznavour, we would read French authors religiously. But I also remember reading Manuel Alegre, his *A Praça da Canção*, which was banned. I happened to buy a copy of *A Praça da Canção* here in the center of Lisbon, I can't remember the name of the bookshop any more, I remember the place, maybe it was Bertrand's. Anyway, it was one of those books that one did not ask for at the front of the store. We would have to go to the back, where we would ask for it, they would wrap it up, and then we would pay. I also read *O Canto e as Armas*. That was a book that was widely read at the time, although not by the general public, in fact I would say not even by most of those at university. Not every student read *A Praça da Canção*. The School of Economics was very politicised, as was the Technical College [*Instituto Superior Técnico*] and the Faculty of Medicine. I'm not really sure about other disciplines and faculties. I think there were small numbers of politicised scattered across the student population.

I think I first heard of the colonial war while I was at school. But the first memory I have is of the problem in India. When the Indians took control of Portuguese India, in 1961, it terrified me, since, a little before, soldiers had gone to India, and there were already rumours circulating. My fear was because my father was still very young and people began to speak of the possibility of mobilizing conscripts for India. I was still young, and the idea of my father going to India was horrific. As far as Africa is concerned, what I first heard were stories of terrorists. Then, of course, from the moment that I met my husband, the war was ever present, it was something between us.

I met my husband while I was still at university. I met him through some colleagues, at some parties that we used to go to. He was a soldier, a pilot, in fact. Our affair was initially very short. We fell out after hardly any time, three or four months. Then he went to Guinea, and I more or less kept up with him while he was there. In the middle of his stationing in Guinea, he came back to Portugal, and he began to follow me around again. We got back together, and a short affair followed, a year or so.

At that time, our prospects for the future were not as clearly laid out as they are these days. My aim was to finish my degree and get a job, preferably a good job. Travel was out of the question, unlike nowadays. We may have thought of travelling but working and being married were what was expected, and what was more or less on every woman's mind. Everything was so different from today, when everything is planned out. People marry with fully furnished houses, in move-in condition. We used to marry and then go and live in rented houses, we would buy a little furniture, and then gradually things would be organized, we would bumble along. No one would dream of waiting until you had everything prior to getting married. Marriage was the aim, a liberation and an emancipation. It was the beginning of a new life, a life run by us, in accordance with our tastes, our actions and our wills. And that was really important.

The story of my marriage is interesting and obviously has a lot to do with the colonial war. In guerrilla warfare, helicopter pilots are invaluable. There were very few of them, and during the war, in Guinea, in some areas of Mozambique and in certain areas of Angola they were essential. So obviously, they were mobilized very quickly. After a few months in Guinea, my husband was transferred to Angola. It was then that he declared that he wanted to marry me. He did not want to go overseas again on his own. So he went to speak to my father. My father was utterly opposed, as was my mother.

Actually, my mother's reaction was really negative. My father was upset, he could not see how I would finish my degree, and he argued that the majority of people who interrupt their studies never finish. I think he imagined me married in Angola, having children, and he could not see how I would be able to finish my degree. For my mother, the issue was a lot simpler: she simply did not want me to go to Angola, because she was afraid. However, I thought that if I loved him, and I did love him, it was both my desire and my obligation to go with him. In fact, I thought it was terrible that he should go alone. We neither wanted, nor, if the truth be told, would we have accepted that possibility. And so I went. I packed my bags, interrupted my degree, and went.

We were married in October 1969 and went on our honeymoon with my husband constantly phoning his base to find out when he would have to go to Angola. So, I married knowing that very soon we would be leaving for Africa. My mother, once she had come to terms with the fact that my decision to marry was not negotiable, and having accepted that I would leave for Africa, made me a special trousseau to take with me. I already had a good trousseau, full of the nice things that girls have, but my mother thought it was not suitable for Africa. So, she bought me a suitcase with a red bottom (I can still see it today) and filled it with embroidered towels, kitchen utensils, all that kind of stuff. Everything was really pretty, all matching, but it was not as good as my original trousseau. When I married, I did not even set up a home here, because we were supposed to be going to leave immediately. However, we kept on having to wait. We eventually rented a house here, and since my godfather was an officer in the army, he arranged some furniture for us. We bought what was essential, and my parents lent us the rest, and we remained living in Portugal until July. I left for Luanda on 19 July 1970. My husband had left in June.

As far as I was concerned, in the beginning, the war was perfectly justified, but, actually, while I was still at university, falling in love with my husband, who was a soldier by profession, and even more so when I went to Angola, I began to be wrought by the complexity of the situation: it was so ambiguous, it really made me feel uncomfortable and worried me a lot. When I arrived in Angola, and saw what its reality was and heard that slogan "Angola é Nossa" [Angola is Ours], I remember saying: "Well the bit that is mine, I'm more than happy to give up completely, and get out of here straight away." Perhaps it was childish, now that I think about it, but there was in my innocent phrase a large dose of realism. So, my position, confronted with what I was forced to live and faced with that land that they said was ours, became extremely ambivalent.

In my family, there was no tradition of being in the military, unlike in many Portuguese families. As far as my family was concerned, my husband was the first soldier we had had, unlike his side of the family, which boasted a military tradition. Both his uncle and his older brother served in the armed forces. Actually, both he and his brother were pilots. His brother passed away when he was twenty-two years old in an accident in Portugal that, as it happens, didn't even involve a plane. At the time, in order to be a pilot, the dream he had always had, meant being in the military.

I have to confess that I really didn't like the time I spent in Luanda. I spent much of the time at home, and, if I could, I would erase that time from my life. I didn't like it because my husband was always flying dangerous missions, and so it was a high-risk lifestyle. For instance, in every month, he would be at home maybe ten days, and those ten days would be scattered over the month, he would go away, then be back for three days, then go away again. And as well as the missions he had, there were the emergencies, the urgent evacuation of the wounded. There was no such thing as Saturday or Sunday. Twice during his posting, so that I could spend Christmas with him, I had to fly four thousand kilometres by plane to the ends of the earth, to Cuito Cadaval. It was a tiny village of three houses made from limestone and rock.

I ended up feeling really isolated, so I decided to matriculate in the university, because I wanted to finish my degree. I had promised myself this, and also my father. So, I matriculated, over there, in the university. I started attending the classes, but, in the meantime, became pregnant, and had a really difficult pregnancy. I would vomit every day several times, without fail. In the fourth month of the pregnancy, the doctor suggested the possibility of an abortion, because I was even thinner than I had been at the beginning of the pregnancy. I couldn't go anywhere, because I spent all my time vomiting. At the time, I was twenty-two. Then, there was a cholera outbreak in Luanda. Up until then, my mother had been taking all the vaccines to come and help me in Angola but, faced with the outbreak of an epidemic, it was more sensible for me to go to Portugal, to the metropolis as we used to say then. My daughter was born in 1971, in Coimbra. I vomited immediately after she was born, and thus I brought a close to the whole process—of my pregnancy and of my vomiting. Then I went to my parents' home, and after a month, I returned to Angola. Today, I would never go to Angola with a month-old baby.

My mother wisely advised me to stay in Portugal for a few months, but I could only think of my husband, and the work he was doing all alone. I neither wanted, nor was able, to leave him over there all alone. And despite the fact that he was away a lot, as I said earlier, it was so great when he arrived home, and we were there waiting for him. So I went back. I always, or nearly always, flew with TAP. The Air Force had houses over there, but there were not enough for the number of people stationed in Luanda. We had to rent a house, and the Air Force gave us a fridge, a stove, and a few other things that I can't remember any more what they were. I never liked the atmosphere in the mess. Only when I first arrived did I go there, but I stopped going almost straight away. There was a lot of gossip and a type of social life that really didn't interest me.

I centered my life on my home: I had a black maid with whom I got on well and who was indispensable for me with the baby. Now that you ask me, I never had the sensation that she could be the enemy. We had a normal relationship, and in spite of that dreadfully tense situation in which I lived, I never looked at her with distrust. Actually, in regard to all this stuff about relations between blacks and whites, it's really interesting because they were always saying that racism does not exist, and this was a blatant lie. I remember an incident, which really impacted me and showed me the true nature of interpersonal relations in Angola. I went to the pharmacy, and there was a black girl there. The pharmacist, as soon as he had seen me, asked me what I needed, completely ignoring her. I pointed out to him that that lady was there first. He said to me without thinking that that was irrelevant, she could wait regardless. I was shocked, and thought that his attitude might explain a certain animosity among the settlers against the military. The arrival of the military in great numbers, and often with their families, profoundly altered the pattern of social relations that had been followed by the settler community. The way they thought that one being was inferior to another, in other words, the way they based their social structures on inequality. The main argument that the settlers used against the military was that the soldiers were there to make money and nothing else. This judgment of theirs right from the start did nothing to foster good relations with the soldiers, especially since it was not true in most cases. I never saw blacks mistreated, but racism definitely existed, you just had to open your eyes to see it. Only once did I see a black driving a good car, apparently as its owner. Blacks drove the taxis or buses, and went by bus. There were no blacks in the cinema, for example.

In Luanda, my circle of friends was greatly reduced. I would hang out with some of my husband's colleagues, and their families when they were there. But no one mentioned the war. The war was a topic of concern, of anguish, of fear, and of silence, however paradoxical that may seem. There was an enormous amount of worry about it. To quote the mantra of the era, the more involved in operations our husbands were, the more discrete we should be. Sometimes, my husband and I would talk about it, but that was extremely rare, mainly because I was not in favor, as I said earlier, I always thought that land simply wasn't mine. But my position was ambiguous. Obviously, what I wanted when there was an offensive was that our side would win. My husband was on our side. But to me it was very obvious that that land had to be independent, and in my opinion, as it was causing me a great deal of pain, the sooner the better. As far as I was concerned, the end of the war meant independence. That the Africans should get their land was absolutely legitimate. When I saw the settlers arguing against us—I knew two or three couples—I would say to them: "So why don't you arrange your own army to defend what you think is yours?" Let them take the fate of that land into their own hands. Of course, that would not have been a good idea either. It would have been like the Rhodesian solution, a solution that did not work. But it was really easy to criticize when others had gone over there, and were the ones who suffered the ambushes, the ones who lost their friends, the ones who saw the mutilated corpses. I rarely spoke of politics, but I did blurt that out, so that things became a little tense. But even among my natural peers, that is, among the colleagues of my husband, mine was a lone voice; my views were not shared and I was well aware of this. At a certain point, given everything that was going on, I really wanted to go home.

My husband held a more ambiguous position: he heard what I had to say, but defended the view that that land was ours. I never told him that he should not go out on a mission, but I did not like it when he did. Everything was so riddled with contradictions, not just at the personal level, but also in public too. For example, with the outbreak of war, previously inconceivable rights were granted to blacks, in terms of educational possibilities, employment and health benefits. My husband would talk all about this, about the great work being done, showing me that without our presence, these were populations that would be more vulnerable, more unprotected, less developed in medical and educational terms. I recognize that this is true, but to use this as an argument to justify that war, and therefore, all those sacrifices on both sides… I simply was not convinced.

My husband's job was really hard work; it was physically and emotionally exhausting, since it was so closely linked to the worst consequences of war. He was in high-risk situations, but also rescue missions. Maybe because of this, I don't know, despite the way the war developed, he never became discouraged in his dedication to his work. His actions were crucial, and meant a great deal to the lives of people who were most vulnerable and in danger. The helicopter pilots in the places where they were stationed had a really hard life—I'm not saying that other types of posting were not difficult too. But, they performed the evacuations of the wounded from active conflict zones. As well as this, they airlifted the parachutists and the mail to remote areas. They worked with the paramedic nurses, who were women of immense courage, admired by everyone. In Guinea, all the helicopters worked with these nurses. My husband never spoke to me about what he had been through or what he had seen. He only told me about the nice things. Even today. The other day, we were talking about those days, and he even said to me that he really had to stop talking about the overseas provinces the way he did, because when he talks about them it is only to say good things: to reminisce about the parties, the fun, the sunny side of our stay in Africa, giving the impression to those who are listening that it was all a big jamboree. And it certainly was not. Not at all. But, at the time, we had to cling to the positive things, since the harder life became, the more important it was that we were united and that we got along. I think he never told me about his missions, because they were really hard, and he wanted to spare me, he did not want to add to my anxiety. I think that the fact that I was over there, at his side, was fundamental, a determining factor that allowed life to retain some degree of normality. There were battles, there were bullets, there were dead and injured. One killed or one died. We were at war. I saw from the commendations that my husband received that he really was in high-risk situations. I went with him to receive his awards, and so I saw via the commendations the horror of war. I went twice with him to the June 10 celebrations, to receive his honors.

The June 10 ceremony was very well organized and a bit of a drag. I understood that my husband's commendations were very well deserved. They were the public recognition of him as someone who was professionally competent. They were the recognition of someone who had put his life in danger. But this is all very contradictory: I still thought that that land belonged to the Africans, but, on the other hand, my husband had been in very dangerous situations, and I thought it was appropriate that this should be publicly recognized, even if I disagreed with the war, and was not favourably disposed to the regime that promoted it, and that, in essence, clung to the war as its only means of survival.

With regard to this monument that they recently erected to commemorate the dead from the colonial war, I don't want to comment.[2] I am not nostalgic: I really don't think that land was ours, nor that it should be ours, and I never thought it should have been. Theoretically, decolonisation should have been handled better, but for that to have happened, it would have had to have been prepared properly by politicians. They should have conducted it in a different way. Given that no preparation was made for decolonisation, I really am not sure that it could have been done any differently.

Even today, I have the experience of that period I lived in Africa firmly shut in my unconscious. I have never spoken about it with my children or my relatives.

When you asked me to do this interview, I said yes straight away without thinking that reliving those times would be so difficult for me, which it has been.

In retrospect, I'm sure that I haven't changed how I viewed my time over there, although the consequences of decolonisation are, even today, so negative. The situation in the countries that gained independence really hasn't improved as much as we had expected. In some cases, it is even worse, with wars that have broken out. In fact, independence is not everything. What is essential still needs to be done: education, health care, and development, things that should be so easy for such rich countries….

Notes

1 Caxias was a prison where many political prisoners were detained by the Salazar/Caetano regime.

2 This refers to a monument inaugurated in 2002 in Lisbon, in which those who died in the so-called "Guerra do Ultramar" [Overseas War] rather than the "Guerra Colonial" [Colonial War] were supposedly honored. As well as the whole issue of the monument itself, there is the problem of its designation and how we term the war itself.

Margarida Calafate Ribeiro is author of *Uma História de Regresso: Império, Guerra Colonial e Pós-colonialismo* and co-editor of both *Fantasmas e Fantasias Imperiais no Imaginário Português Contemporâneo* and *A Primavera Toda para Ti.* Email: margaridacr@mail.telepac.pt

The Literary Memory of the Colonial War in Angola

Isabel Moutinho

Abstract: This study examines two Portuguese novels about the colonial war in Angola, unusual in that they do not present a personal, but a collective view of that war, from two perspectives: the Portuguese side (reevaluating the rhetoric of colonialism) and the Angolan side (including tentative representations of African oral history and agency).

Many Portuguese novelists make the colonial war in Angola (1961-1974) the focus of their narrative fiction from the mid-1970s onwards. Most of these novels have a strong autobiographical component, aiming simultaneously at the recovery and exorcising of personal and traumatic memories of the war.[1] Some, however, go one step further and strive to recall the memory of that war in broader, collective terms, attempting to include also a view from the other side, namely, the Angolan side. Such is the case with the two novels I propose to examine here: João de Melo's *Autópsia de Um Mar de Ruínas* (1984) [*Autopsy of a Sea in Ruins*] and Manuel Alegre's *Jornada de África* (1989) [*Expedition to Africa*].[2]

Unlike most other Portuguese novels of the colonial war, which move between one of the colonial war settings and Portugal, *Autópsia de Um Mar de Ruínas* is set solely in Angola. Its chapters focus alternately on the daily routine of a unit of Portuguese soldiers serving at the front in northern

Portuguese Literary & Cultural Studies 15/16 (2010): 127-50.

Angola, and on that of indigenous Angolans living in a nearby enclosed village (*sanzala*) under the surveillance of the Portuguese military. The story of the Portuguese battalion and that of the Angolan *sanzala* people are presented in parallel, the Portuguese side of the plot unfolding in the odd-numbered chapters, and the Angolan in the even-numbered ones.

It is never exactly clear who the narrator of each chapter is, and this ambiguity is maintained as an effective technique for widening the scope of the narrative.[3] On the Portuguese side, it could be the night sentry, or the captain, the quartermaster nurse, one particular soldier (Renato), or all of the soldiers. This deliberately misleading narrative technique unambiguously establishes the essential clue for reading the novel: *Autópsia* claims as its narrative impulse a collective voice, and one that is epic and poetic. The voice of this collective soldier at war ("eu aqui, soldado ocidental," 24) is "occidental" because it is loaded with echoes of the history and epic of the country that Camões described as "ocidental praia lusitana" (I.1.2) [the occidental Lusitanian seashore]. It is a voice embodied by a collectively "forgotten" soldier ("esquecido" 24), one who sets himself a double task: first, to record the memory of his fellow soldiers, because private memory is fragile; and second, to prod the memory of their forgetful countrymen who did not go to war, because a country's collective memory is even shorter than that of its soldiers individually: "sentei-me na noite, em Calambata, (…) e de lá vos mandei escrito de *toda a memória que há* sobre os dias desta guerra" (25) [I sat down at night in Calambata, (…) and from there I sent you (*plural*) the record of *all the memory there is* of the days of this war] (emphasis added).

This impression of a collective effort is achieved essentially through the use of variable internal focalisation. The reader continues being put off the track as to the identity of the narrator throughout the book. The narrative voice of the army chapters goes to extremes to confuse the reader as to its identity. Chapter 5 is told in the first person, and this first person insists on his stature as an eyewitness to the events he narrates: "Vi…vi…vi" (I saw). This, however, suddenly becomes: "Renato viu" (Renato saw). Chapter 7 puts more emphasis on the collective aspect of the narration by using the first person plural, but all of a sudden it throws the reader off the track again: "Eu vou endoidecer, pensou. (…) tenho medo do deus N'Zambi" (88) (I am going to go crazy, he thought. (…) I am afraid of the god N'Zambi). This sentence is doubly confusing because the character about whom we have been told that he is disturbed to the point of illness is the quartermaster nurse, not the soldier Renato; but the character who thinks of the Angolan god N'Zambi is the unnamed sentry of the first chapter. Could this be an African soldier? It is not until chapter 21 that it is explained that the sentry of chapter 1 was Renato too.

We must, then, take it as fictionally true that the narrator of *Autópsia de Um Mar de Ruínas* is Private Renato. His is an extremely self-effacing narrative voice. In any case, the narrative seems to follow most closely the point of view of the quartermaster nurse, who is the most frequent subject of focalisation. Renato and the nurse form a kind of inseparable double, the one doing the (ostensible) thinking and writing, the other taking the most active role in attending to the war-wounded. Disconcertingly, though, it is the nurse and not Renato who is described within the novel as being a writer himself, although apparently not of this book; and Renato is only presented as writing letters to his wife. Renato is meditative, the nurse, at the front, is exhaustingly busy. And yet it could be argued that, of the two, the nurse is the one best equipped and most inclined to think, ponder, and question ("tem a mania que é filósofo, faz literatura, vai ser génio um dia" (174) [he is convinced that he is a philosopher, he writes literature, he's going to be a genius one day]).

In any case, the novel's narrator multiplies himself not just into a double, but into many voices. The process is too complex not to be regarded as a deliberate strategy. To try to disentangle all the characters involved in this multiplication of the narrative voice would be to impoverish the reading of the novel, which itself at times underlines the importance of its collective aspect: "pensávamos nós em coro" (110), "responderam, à uma, os meninos do coro" (111), "sabiam que só era possível pensar em coro, todos à uma" (202) [we thought in chorus; they answered, in unison, (*like*) choir boys; they knew that it was only possible to think in chorus, all at once]. Although initially disconcerting, this is a very effective literary device in that it allows these chapters to be read as a collective narrative, the record of the entwined lives of a group of men thrown together by war.

In the chapters focusing on the Angolans, the focalisation is also internal and variable, appearing to be most often inside Natália's head, but also closely following Mamã Josefa, Vavó Katuela, Anica, and the women (all together) who need to rescue their husbands from their blind drunkenness. Sometimes the focalisation seems more external, particularly when it first follows Romeu, Natália's husband, or Cavungi, Josefa's husband, as if the narrative voice could not follow a man's point of view as effortlessly as a woman's. But it becomes internal again when it follows *soba* Mussunga, the local chief, and the elder Loneque, as well as Romeu in later chapters. Here again, then, plurality is the dominant note. It is when Romeu is the subject of focalisation that we learn more of his connections with the guerrillas who fight the Portuguese army from beyond Angola's northern border.[4] Romeu is very outspoken, he dares to vent feelings of revolt against the Portuguese that the others are too afraid to express. Nevertheless, when the narrative becomes truly engaged in the revelation of the Angolan people's profound aspirations for liberty and independence, it does so—as in the Portuguese chapters—in the first person plural:

> Quase sempre, combatentes escondiam-se no meio do povo. Traziam notícias de outros combatentes para a família, levavam informações sobre a tropa. (...) passavam nas lagoas mansas da noite, nos ninhos quentes e nas sepulturas sem nome, onde que *a guerra, a guerra dos nossos*, esperava ainda a voz ausente e a respiração única deste povo. (157; emphasis added)

> [Almost always the fighters would hide among the people. They brought news of other fighters to their families, they carried information about the army. (...) they'd pass by the quiet lagoons at night, the warm nests, and the tombs without names, to where *the war, the war of our people*, still awaited the absent voice and the breathing together of this people]

Thus the colonial war of the army chapters becomes "a guerra dos nossos" ("our war" or "the war of our people") in the *sanzala* chapters. The entanglement of narrative voices, so carefully interwoven, becomes the principal strategy for achieving the impression of a collective account of the war: that of the Portuguese soldiers and that of the Angolan civilians, the latter adding echoes of another two involved parties, the guerrillas and the white settlers.

Furthermore, the role of the voice(s) we hear in the Angolan chapters is clearly presented as different from that of the army chapters: "Ih!, esses acontecimentos estão ter lugar na minha história, é porquê então?" (102) [Eh! those happenings are taking place in my story, why is that then?]. Here, someone is telling a story. And the oral aspect of this story is emphasised throughout the novel by its being punctuated with phrases normally used to catch listeners' attention in a situation of oral communication: "sabias?" (32), "Eu conto" (81), "Vê só" (181), "vou te contar" (103), "estou-te falar" (207), and so on [did you know?; I'll tell you; Look here; I'm going to tell you; I'm telling you]. As such, in view of the predominantly oral character of the story told in the *sanzala* chapters of the novel and the emphasis on the telling, the narrator(s) of these should more properly be referred to as the storyteller(s).

Independently from just how many voices contribute to one or the other sections of the novel, there is the question of how far these voices engage in dialogue. To be sure, the voices of the Angolans are much more present here than in most Portuguese fictions of the colonial war, in which they are only very occasionally audible. Here, instead, they constitute a full half of a novel that gives equal weight to them and to the Portuguese soldiers' voices.

In fact, the very language of *Autópsia de Um Mar de Ruínas* changes as the narrative alternates between military and indigenous chapters. Those relating to the Portuguese soldiers are in standard Portuguese; those by the Angolan storyteller(s) are told in the local variety of Portuguese, with its "ungrammatical" traits ("um português desgramaticado" 71), which to a Portuguese reader immediately give an impression of foreignness. Naturally, the novel being by a Portuguese author, the language presented as Angolan Portuguese must remain an imitation, a literary re-creation of what the author perceives as the language of the Angolans living in the *sanzala*. Nevertheless, *Autópsia* does attempt to adopt the Angolan variety of Portuguese (or what a Portuguese speaker perceives as such) consistently, side by side with the European standard. This is a radical linguistic, even political choice in that it attributes the same literary prestige to both languages, rather than simply using the African variety to give exotic flavour to the speech of African characters included in a white person's narrative.

What *Autópsia de Um Mar de Ruínas* does very strikingly, which other Portuguese colonial war novels do not, is to remove the quotation marks from around the reported speech of the Other, thus much reducing the distance between Portuguese selfhood and Angolan alterity. Most of all, the inclusion on an equal footing of the chapters in Angolan Portuguese very successfully serves the purpose of rendering this novel a collective account of the colonial war, which to be truly "collective" must include the point of view of the Other. There would after all have been no colonial war if it were not for that indispensable Other. Admittedly, though, the only African voices we can hear in this novel are the ones that have learned a variety of Portuguese. By allowing the Angolan characters to express themselves in their own (albeit second) language, i.e., *as their own selves*, *Autópsia* transforms that alterity into a selfhood that becomes less and less unfamiliar to the reader as the novel progresses.

Intertextuality in *Autópsia de Um Mar de Ruínas* is yet another strategy by which collective memory finds expression. While the polyphony of the novel allows for the inclusion of synchronically co-existing accounts of the war, intertextuality brings forth another type of collective voice, a diachronic memory shaped by numerous previous literary texts dealing with Portugal's history, which inform the present-day view of the war: Camões's *Os Lusíadas*, Fernão Lopes's *Crónica de Dom João I*, and the *História Trágico-Marítima* are the most obvious ones. But *Autópsia* also engages with contemporary, censored representations of the war in the Portuguese media.

The most subtle instance of intertextual dialogue in *Autópsia* is perhaps the one the novel establishes with the poetry of Fernando Pessoa (1888-1935). Especially relevant here is the poem "O Menino de Sua Mãe." The poem's title is quoted directly, though not identified as a title (169), or with alterations ("à pobre mãe do seu menino" (134), "todos os meninos de suas mães," (167) three or four times in the novel. It is worth quoting a good translation of the poem's opening and final lines:

> On the plain left alone / Where the breeze now softens, / With bullets in his brain– / Two, once and once again– / He lies there dead, and stiffens. // His tunic is bloodstained. (…) // (O nets the Empire knots!) / He lies there dead, and rots, / His mother's little boy. ("His Mother's" 36)

The situation in *Autópsia* corresponds closely to that portrayed by Pessoa fifty years earlier, and Pessoa's language is a point of departure for the shocking, gory imagery of the novel. For its thematic parallels with the war fatalities presented in *Autópsia*, this poem is mentioned above all in chapter 13, where there lie the nine corpses of young soldiers who had, until not long ago, also been their mothers' little boys. Many echoes of this and other poems by Fernando Pessoa can be traced at various points in the novel (including the fact that there are bells also in poems by one of his heteronyms, Alberto Caeiro), but such direct quotations and indirect resonances are not the most important form of intertextual dialogue with the poet's work in *Autópsia*.

One of Pessoa's most striking contributions to Portuguese culture was his creation of various heteronyms, characters he brought into literary existence with a life and a poetical style of their own. Pessoa even determined the time of death of some of his heteronyms. The entangled double that the narrators of the army chapters in *Autópsia* seem to constitute (i.e., Renato, as the acknowledged and named narrator, and the quartermaster nurse, whose actions Renato can describe as separate from his own, but whose thoughts, feelings, and hopes have become inextricably fused with Renato's) could well be seen as a new heteronymous pair. Heteronymity was as essential to Pessoa's poetic universe as the doubling up, even the multiplication, of the narrator(s) is in *Autópsia* as a strategy for the gathering of a collective memory of the colonial war. The comparison appears all the more pertinent as the quartermaster nurse is often described as possessed by a madness ("loucura") very similar to that attributed by Pessoa to King Sebastian in *Mensagem*.[5] As António Cirurgião points out, "King Sebastian's legacy to his people is his madness," a madness that was "the dream of an empire without frontiers and without sunset" (117). The quartermaster nurse's "madness" is his hope for the children of Angola; he appears repeatedly referred to as "the man whose hope were the children of Angola" (47-49, 92, 99, etc.). The nurse's madness, then, corresponds to a further historical development, which will only become possible *after* what already appears here as the inevitable collapse of the empire of which Sebastian first dreamt. His madness begins where King Sebastian's ends, but both share the same visionary, dreamy quality: one, that of the emergence of Empire; the other, that of the future of Africa (its children) beyond it.

Nevertheless, what leads us to see in the doubleness of Renato and the nurse a case of heteronymity created in the mould of Pessoa's heteronyms is the fact that Renato is killed at the end of the novel ("No dia em que eu morri na guerra" [283] [The day I died in the war]). The fact that the narrative continues in the first person (after "I died") confirms that someone else has to be writing the story that has so far been attributed to the named, narrating I that finally explains the deliberate entanglements of Renato and the quartermaster nurse. The two are, then, not strictly heteronyms in the Pessoan sense (though it is appropriate to keep in mind that Pessoa provided dates of death for some of his heteronyms, thus also "killing" them), but they certainly fall well within the imaginative realm of Pessoa's creations. And they can well be viewed as the King Sebastian who got killed in North Africa and the madness that survived him.

Furthermore, the doubling up of Portuguese narrator/Angolan storyteller presents itself as a more substantial case of creative heteronymity in the Pessoan model—more explicitly so when it involves the structure of the whole novel. While Pessoa created his heteronyms perhaps to be able to give expression to different styles that did not ring true within his own voice, João de Melo appears to have devised a similar sort of heteronymity as a way to bring the voices of (some of the) Angolan Others into mainstream Portuguese literature, which has never otherwise seriously engaged with African cultures or given them more than a fleeting voice in its texts.[6]

Does *Autópsia* succeed in giving voice to the Angolans? Do the *sanzala* sections of the novel amount to a faithful representation of the life of a certain section of the Angolan population during the colonial war? We could only argue in the positive for a Portuguese readership. An Angolan reader would no doubt find that even this representation is merely external and flawed, or that it still perpetuates stereotypes. As Isabel Allegro de Magalhães underlines, "as suas vozes são sempre, porém, *traduzidas*, filtradas *portuguêsmente*" (*Capelas Imperfeitas* 187) [the (Africans') voices are always *translated*, filtered *through a Portuguese mind*] in these narratives. Nor indeed could it be otherwise. First of all, there is the question of the language used in the *sanzala* sections. For a Portuguese audience, it is distinctly different from standard Portuguese, but only an Angolan could judge of its authenticity. But it is important to point out that the language used does not attempt to emulate the standard Angolan variety of Portuguese, as spoken and written by the educated Angolan classes, particularly the country's intellectuals. It tries to represent the language of the partly acculturated Angolans living in the artificial conditions of a *sanzala* created for displaced civilians. And the novel makes no secret of the fact that this language could only be that of a small percentage of that population (for example, the acculturated *soba* must act as interpreter between the Angolan coffee-growers and the Portuguese colonists who come to buy the coffee). With these limitations then, yes, this is a case in which the African is heard speaking.

Furthermore, *Autópsia* attempts to validate African history by explicitly referring to its different mode. There are repeated references to the people's memory of the war: "O povo sabia e guardava na memória o testemunho dessas histórias que todos os dias ficavam escritas na terra-mãe, nossa pátria bem-amada" (119) [The people knew and kept in their memory the testimony of those histories which every day were written in the mother-earth, our beloved homeland]. African history is oral; it has not been written in European-style chronicles, but it nevertheless remains recorded in people's memories, which are transmitted orally, by the women and by the elders, with their special kind of wisdom: "são muito sábios, os mais-velhos, mentira? Ciência da vida está neles" (150) [they're very wise, the elders, a lie? Science of life is in them].

It is certainly true that the *sanzala* chapters cannot in the end represent an authentically African voice, even though they attempt to present the story (and the history) from the point of view of the Angolans, and in (an imitation of) their language. The novel endeavours to represent the traditional orality of African culture by inserting marks of oral communication throughout, but the genuine "initial and final formulas" (Moser 43) that punctuate Angolan storytelling are missing. So too are the most genuinely African elements of those stories: folk and animal tales, myths, legends, songs, riddles, proverbs. Also, the more externally focused chapters, those dealing most extensively with the Angolan view of the war, sound in a way least authentic, because they become less oral in texture. The reader becomes aware that they are still part of a fictional written text, so that they are the least successful chapters in the novel—in the sense, as Homi Bhabha would say, that they "historicise the colonial experience" (115). They make it read as a master narrative, which is a European, not an African genre. This is perhaps simply because the perspective of the army chapters begins to pervade the *sanzala* chapters too, making us forget that elsewhere the novel also tries to give voice to the validity of an alternative form of history, and an alternative way of telling stories.

Nevertheless, the *sanzala* chapters of *Autópsia de Um Mar de Ruínas* do give expression at least to the inauthentic, lives of "mimicry" that the Angolans lived under the colonial war. One good example here is the party described as taking place in the *sanzala* on a Sunday afternoon. A traditional party in Angola, a *sunguilamento*, would have occurred in the evening, when the cool hours invite relaxation and entertainment. Such a *sunguilamento* would then culminate in storytelling, generally by the elder women (see Moser 43). The *sanzala* party in *Autópsia* is but a pale imitation: a joyless, adulterated occasion in the afternoon heat, with drums and Portuguese music playing from a portable radio. The point is that the *sanzala* chapters of *Autópsia* cannot, indeed should not, be expected to represent the diversity of authentic Angolan cultures; they must settle for an overview of the life of a displaced and semi-acculturated population, which has been robbed of its real cultures by the colonial presence itself. Indeed, how could the *sanzala* people hold a *sunguilamento* when there is a war curfew on?

In the final analysis, though, *Autópsia* is reasonably successful in portraying the lives of Angolans in those altered conditions that the colonial war imposed, and also in representing the obscure, intricate ways in which the Portuguese monologue and the Angolan monologue in the end do engage in, albeit tentative, dialogue. In the initial chapters of the book, the reader may worry that the novel still perpetuates an imperialistic view of the world in Portuguese terms. Even the intertextual echoes reinforce such an impression, taken as they are from Portuguese epic and from the mythology that has shaped the Portuguese view of themselves for centuries. More worryingly, the fact that the *sanzala* chapters initially come from a female voice and concentrate on a collective memory of rape seems to perpetuate an imperialist view of Angola (or any colony) raped by (and powerlessly accepting or enduring the rape of) Portuguese colonialism, which the army is there to defend and uphold. This would amount to what Laura Chrisman has called "imperialism as sexual allegory" (501).

However, there is a radical change precisely as the *sanzala* chapters become more collective and follow the point of view of male as well as female characters. The inclusion of male voices brings with it a shift from the impotent endurance of imperial rape to an indictment of the practices of the capitalist economy that went together with colonialism (specifically in the final chapters, where the whole community is forced to sell the product of a year's work for miserable amounts to the wealthy, obese Portuguese colonists). Here there is no question of any Portuguese civilising mission any more. Here the finger is unequivocally pointed at the political economy that accompanies colonialism, the practical side of imperialism. What the army now sees in Angola is that they are there to defend, not the elevated notion of an imperial fatherland, but the capitalist interests of the colonists (in this case cheap labour and cheap coffee).

Autópsia de Um Mar de Ruínas uses heteronymity as the basis for its narrative structure, precisely because it opens up the possibility of representing in literature that fundamental split in Portuguese culture: the encounter with the African Other that made Others of the Portuguese too. But the dual narrative structure, and the "heteronymous," split/doubled/multiplied voices within each part do not remain impervious to each other: their "inter-illumination" is there to be detected, though it could only take place with great risks, in times of war, between an army and its "enemy."

Bakhtin's concept of dialogism implies interrelation between two different views of the world, as expressed by their respective "social languages." Monologue, in his terms, is typical of authoritarian regimes, which always want to have "the last word" (250). One could argue that in this novel nobody has the last word. Renato has already been killed in the penultimate chapter. Romeu, the most active guerrilla-sympathiser amongst the *sanzala* characters, is on his way to being finished off, already almost beaten to death in the novel's last page. Nevertheless, Renato's voice continues to be heard, via an obscure, alternative (heteronymous) narrator, though fictionally still in his own words, from beyond death. And so too do the voices of the *sanzala* people continue to be heard. Each and all of the characters has a *lasting* word, which becomes more important than having the last one—words that will last as part of two nations' collective memory.

What this novel achieves most successfully is the summoning and recording of the various voices that make up a collective memory of war, voices of the dead and voices still alive. Included too, therefore, must be the echoes of important milestones of Portuguese literary heritage with which the novel establishes its intertextual dialogue, as well as an attempt at representing the orality of the other side of the story, the marks of the Angolan cultural heritage, because the collective memory of a nation is inextricably bound up with the texts (written or oral) that record it. In this novel of dual structure and double/multiple narrators and storytellers, memory too has a double role: first, to record the personal experiences of not one, but multiple soldiers, who made the war and either were killed or survived. The novel's narrative time is contemporary with the war, so that such experiences are narrated as in a chronicle (i.e., as if not yet a memory). The second role is to preserve the memory of those experiences for future generations, thus aiming to become a new epic—one that rebuts the rhetoric of the old texts with which it engages and therefore brings closure to the discourse that gave rise to the earlier epics. And memory in this novel works in yet another double way: it recalls a Portuguese literary canon that is written and has maintained its prestige throughout and after the colonial war; but it becomes also the repository of moments of an Angolan history that had not yet been institutionalised in writing. *Autópsia de Um Mar de Ruínas* thus becomes a collective memory of the colonial war in Angola.

Manuel Alegre, too, constructs a collective memory of the colonial war in Angola in *Jornada de África*. As with *Autópsia de Um Mar de Ruínas*, poetry plays a major role in the composition of this novel, many pages of which directly quote lines by Portuguese and other European, as well as African poets. In the first chapter, for example, there appear passages from poems by the Portuguese Herberto Hélder and by the Angolan Agostinho Neto (who, like Manuel Alegre himself, was both a poet and a politician in his country). Nevertheless, of the three epigraphs placed at the opening of the novel, only one is taken from a poet, from Rilke's prose-poem *Die Weise von Liebe und Tod des Cornets Christoph Rilke* [*The Lay of Love and Death of Lieutenant Christoph Rilke*], quoted from a Portuguese version. The other two epigraphs are taken from prose works, one by René Char, alluding to a war in which political considerations are at stake, and the last from Jerónimo de Mendonça's homonymous sixteenth-century chronicle *Jornada de África*, which records the expedition undertaken by King Sebastian in 1578 against the Moors at Alcácer-Quibir (now Ksar-al-Kebir, in Morocco), where the visionary young king lost his life, leaving the way open to Spain's sixty-year rule of Portugal.

Some of the novel's most illuminating studies read it as an attempt to redefine Portuguese identity after the loss of the colonial empire.[7] Other scholars have seen *Jornada de África* as an anti-epic and as a work that engages in profound intertextual dialogue with Portugal's literary heritage. Following the lead of the novel's blurb, Clara Rocha calls it an "anti-epic of the colonial war" as well as "a novel of action." Margarida Ribeiro sees it (in 1999) as "the story of the personal and collective anti-epic which the colonial war was" ("Percursos" 210), although she had earlier (in 1998) considered the novel to be "a 'modern epic.'"[8] Likewise, despite actually pointing to several aspects of the novel that seem to contradict the claim, Rui de Azevedo Teixeira concludes his analysis with remarks about "the time of the anti-heroes" and "the colonial war [as] anti-epic" (328). Both Rocha and Azevedo Teixeira also address questions of metanarrativity and intertextuality as narrative strategies in the novel, establishing extensive lists of the authors directly or indirectly quoted in *Jornada de África*, with some important omissions.

The novel's first chapter indicates precise locations (London, Lisbon, Mexico, Coimbra, Luanda), where various events relating to the beginning of the colonial war in Angola are taking place at a precise historical moment: 1960. Given that the second chapter begins on a more specific date two years later (19 June 1962), and that the plot of the novel develops from that date on, following NCO Sebastião's commission at the front in Angola, it is fair to see the first chapter as a brief historical introduction to the events upon which the novel concentrates.

Soon the narrative presents a quick survey of contemporary political events, disclosing real names and locations: in London, in the House of

Commons, the first international press conference of the MPLA, the PAIGC, and the CPG takes place, where the names of the Angolan activist Agostinho Neto and of the Portuguese Prime Minister, Salazar, are freely used. In Lisbon, the activities of the political figures who attempted to introduce democratic reforms in Salazar's regime are described. In Mexico, there is a hint at the preparations by Henrique Galvão, another historical figure, which led to his 1961 seizing of the luxury cruise ship *Santa Maria*, a hijacking that captured the attention of the Portuguese public for weeks, since it was one of the few overt acts of political dissent in the country in decades. And in Lisbon, in the Aljube prison, the political prisoner Agostinho Neto writes poetry. All these political facts are presented as taking place behind the scenes of the novel's plot. And these characters, which can be described as historical in the sense that they are real-life figures summoned into the novel's universe, are above all political figures.

Simultaneously, the reader briefly follows the actions, in Luanda, of Domingos Da Luta, a semi-literate Angolan who has been a political prisoner but is now free and continues to hope for opportunities for political action. The story of this character is clearly set apart in that it is told in long parentheses and in italics, as if it were merely an aside. The parentheses thus reflect graphically the only possibility that there would have been in the Portugal of the early 1960s to pay attention to the point of view of the African. This character's status is not exactly clear; his story is full of historical details, including the fact that he, too, has met Agostinho Neto, but his name, Domingos Da Luta [Domingos of the Fight], endows him with an allegoric dimension, so that we can see him as the epitome of the Angolan (MPLA) independence fighter.[9]

Most of all, the inclusion both of extensive details about the political lobbying that aimed at bringing about the end of Portuguese colonialism (taking place in various locations) and of the political activities of one MPLA fighter taken as the epitome of his country's pro-independence guerrillas serves one particular purpose in the novel: to emphasise the extent and importance of the agency of the Angolans, which certainly is unusual in the Portuguese novels of the colonial war. Written almost fifteen years after the end of the armed conflict, and also written by an author who in real life has had a long career as a politician and parliamentarian, *Jornada de África* widens the portrayal of the African independence wars in contemporary Portuguese narrative to include a strong political edge and, above all, to attribute a dimension of real agency to the actions of Angolans. It is appropriate to point out here that Domingos Da Luta is famous (in the novel) not for indiscriminately killing large numbers of Portuguese troops with unerring rifle shots, but specifically for killing Portuguese army officers only, so that not only his guerrilla skill is stressed, but above all his political determination and purpose.

This specific emphasis on the agency of the Angolans is a new element in the genre, where the presence of the Africans is not necessarily erased, as we have seen, but where they are mostly presented as beings who elicit either distant compassion (for example, in António Lobo Antunes's *Os Cus de Judas*, 1979, also set in Angola), or fear derived from lack of direct contact or lack of understanding (in José Martins Garcia's *Lugar de Massacre*, 1975, or in Álamo Oliveira's *Até Hoje*, 1988, for instance, both set in Guinea-Bissau). The same is true even of *Autópsia de Um Mar de Ruínas*, where Africans have a much stronger presence than in any other of these novels, but are nevertheless not really portrayed as agents of their own historical change, except for the echoes of the guerrilla fighters' activities that reach the *sanzala* people. It is for this reason that *Jornada de África* is much more a political novel than an action novel. It appears that, as time progresses from the date of the end of the conflict, Portuguese narrative becomes more capable of presenting the colonial war in a different perspective, finally encompassing the political agency of the Other.

Historical and fictional characters cross paths in this novel. Some are "real," contemporary, political, or military figures transfigured, either renamed (with recognisable names) or unnamed (the Chief—Salazar; the General—the then commander-in-chief in Angola—General Venâncio Deslandes; the Colonel—António Spínola). Others are the real-life sixteenth-century expeditionists who accompanied King Sebastian to Alcácer-Quibir, now brought back to life in literature as the group of military men around this latter-day Sebastião: Jorge Albuquerque Coelho, who loses his legs like his earlier namesake; Leandro, the first one to lose his life in both *Jornadas*; Luís de Brito, the last one to see (one and the other) Sebastião alive; João Gomes Cabral, Duarte de Meneses, Miguel Noronha, Vasco da Silveira, Alvito, who share names and vicissitudes. The first group is contemporary with the novel's setting; the second is made up of historical figures rescued from time's oblivion by Jerónimo de Mendonça's chronicle.

This re-appropriation of names of previous historical and/or literary characters is part of a more general strategy for the re-interpretation of the country's collective memory of its imperial past, intricately bound up as it is with the colonial war to which it eventually led. The summoning forth of a whole literary tradition (which dealt with, informed, and glorified Portugal's imperial venture) amounts not just to a rereading of that canon, but indeed a rewriting of it in a new light. What Manuel Alegre does in *Jornada de África* is to test his readers' literary memory to the limit, by transcribing, quoting, misquoting, rewriting, or simply alluding to a whole array of texts of the Portuguese literary tradition, including its ramifications in Brazil and Africa. By this means he constructs something similar to what Kristeva calls a "mosaic of quotations" (though quotation is here too restrictive a term), in which "any text is the absorption and transformation of another" (66). Such a mosaic makes use of the European canon too,[10] which is important also as a strategy for the building of a novel type of epic; *Jornada de África* is thus inserted into a long, illustrious European tradition, not because the European authors with whom it engages are necessarily epic but because their inclusion heightens the general tone of the novel.

Pessoa's is a case in point here, precisely because, together with Camões, he is one of the poets most used in *Jornada de África*'s "ventriloquism." However, while Pessoa fragments the notion of authorship by creating his heteronyms, the narrator of *Jornada de África* emphatically undermines the notion of individual authorship by parodically pushing it to the limit in the opposite direction: who is the author of *Jornada de África*? "O A.?" (216)—"the A.?" Alegre? The chronicler Jerónimo de Mendonça, whose work is, so to speak, repeated in this novel? The poet Rilke, whose *Cornet* determines the form and to some extent the contents of this new *Romance de Amor e Morte*? The other Jerónimo de Mendonça, "the Writer," who is a character in the novel? So the author of *Jornada de África* becomes a collective author, built up from a vast cultural memory.

The reader soon realises that this Sebastião must disappear at the end of the novel, as did the other, more illustrious Sebastião. Whatever end the novel's narrator might like to give to its plot, he cannot escape the necessity of that disappearance. "Estava escrito" (174) [it was written], says Bárbara with all the irony and ambiguity of something having been written in the stars, or written by a previous author, or simply being indelibly inscribed in our collective memory. Fate or intertextuality, the possibilities are humorously left open to interpretation. Is it possible for a literary work to escape its predestined conclusion? Is it possible for a country to escape the notion of its historical destiny as written by its epic poets, perpetuated by its governments, and engraved in its cultural memory?

The irony implied in the possibility that events are written by fate is particularly strong in a book that rewrites Sebastião's story. The disappearance of the earlier Sebastião, presumed dead at Alcácer-Quibir, was the starting point for the long-standing belief that the sixteenth-century king would one day return to Portugal to restore the country to its former glory, the basis for the Sebastianist myth that has repeatedly found literary expression and popular support among sections of the Portuguese population. The myth that King Sebastian will one day return and rescue the Portuguese from the mediocrity of a present that does not match the glory of their past is of course responsible for an attitude of generalised "desviver" [unliving] (to use the term coined by Manuel Alegre), that is, a morbid attachment to the past with consequential avoidance of responsibility in the present.

The narrator of *Jornada* begins by questioning Pessoa's attitude of detachment from the world:

> Repugnava-lhe essa festa do avesso, o narcisismo da renúncia e a tão portuguesa autoternura da derrota. Agora procura escapar ao império tutelar e totalitário daquele heterónimo de si mesmo. (...) Nem Ode Marítima sem viagem, nem Mensagem sem acção. Não ao escrever-se desvivendo. O poeta, o narrador, sabe-se lá quem, quer outra vida, outra escrita. (21)
>
> [He loathed that inside-out celebration, that narcissistic renunciation, and that oh-so-Portuguese self-pity in defeat. Now he tries to escape the protective and totalitarian empire of that heteronym of himself. (...) Away with a Maritime Ode without voyage, away with a Message without action. Away with writing while unliving. The poet, the narrator, who knows who, wants a different life, a different writing.]

Here for the first time we come across two notions that become very significant in the whole novel: that of an "inside-out" reality and that of "desviver" [to unlive], as an accusation directed by the narrator at Fernando Pessoa, but also more generally at the sort of lifestyle imposed by Salazar's regime on the Portugal of the sixties. The statement can almost be read as programmatic for the whole book. The narrator has just declared that Pessoa has already said everything (20) and that his own path is like that of an inside-out Pessoa ("Pessoa do avesso" 21). This, then, is a novel preoccupied both with turning inside out Pessoa's work and with reversing a generalised attitude of non-engagement with the present in Portuguese society. For this narrator, there is a clear need to find novel ways of expression: "outra escrita," a different kind of writing.

Jornada de África attempts the different kind of writing that its narrator desires, and it also engages intertextually with the whole mythology of a country obsessed with its glorious maritime past, with the voyages of discovery, with magnificent military expeditions and the conquest of other peoples and territories. But it chooses to draw attention to the first such expedition that went wrong, that of King Sebastian to Alcácer-Quibir. His was the first defeat in the history of Portuguese overseas expansion, ominously spelling out an eventual, much larger defeat, which would mark the end of Portuguese colonialism. In this novel in which nothing is innocent, in the sense in which Umberto Eco refers to the loss of literary innocence in postmodern literature, the defeat thus foretold can be seen as fate (history repeating itself) or as a point of departure for new ventures. While the loss at Alcácer-Quibir gave rise to "that oh-so-Portuguese self-pity in defeat," which has led the Portuguese to Sebastianism and nostalgia for the past, it has also spurred others, such as the narrator of *Jornada de África*, to try to find new ways forward, even new kinds of writing. The poet-narrator finds himself at a particularly interesting confluence in time, simultaneously pulled towards the past (the yearning) and towards the future (the desire to create that which is lacking). This tension underlies the very original voice of the narrator of *Jornada de África*, whose love of Portuguese culture makes him engage with the authors of the past, but whose desire for new directions in literature (as in life) leads him to search for new ways of writing. Consequently, in order to be faithful to its purpose of engaging with the present, that search must also include contemporary literary works.

While Camões's *Os Lusíadas* can be said to have given rise to and simultaneously to have embodied a love for the epic in the Portuguese, the contemporary novels of the colonial war are in a way creating a similar epic interest among the post-revolutionary Portuguese reading public. These novels keep alive the memory of the lost colonial wars, which the country would perhaps prefer collectively to forget. *Jornada de África* does so in a more literary self-conscious way than most other novels of this sub-genre, by engaging in unobtrusive but powerful intertextual dialogue with the very novels of the colonial war that are shaping the country's re-imagining of itself in the present. Curiously, while critics have so far brought to light the extensive interplay between *Jornada de África* and the more or less canonical Portuguese literary heritage, its important intertextual engagement with other novels of the colonial war appears not to have been noticed.

First of all there is the name by which Bárbara affectionately refers to Sebastião: Olhos-Azuis [Blue-Eyes], which is exactly what the flight-attendant in Lobo Antunes's *Os Cus de Judas* (120) calls the protagonist of that novel. Even the fact that both female characters are flight-attendants cannot be coincidental. In *Os Cus de Judas*, the narrative situation requires her to be a flight-attendant; in *Jornada*, the fact that Bárbara is a flight-attendant seems almost an afterthought in the portrayal of a character who is fundamentally an Angolan political activist and an avid reader of Angolan poetry. In chapter 7, there is an unusual expression directly lifted from Lídia Jorge's *A Costa dos Murmúrios* (a 1988 novel dealing with the colonial war in Mozambique): the military who have seen action and developed a taste for cruelty are described as "gente que já fez o gosto ao dedo" (*Jornada* 58), Lídia Jorge's own striking formulation (*Costa* 49). Nor can the scars displayed by Miguel Noronha in *Jornada* ("uma grande cicatriz no braço esquerdo, outra no peito, vê-se através da camisa aberta," 98 [a large scar on his left arm, another one on his chest, you can see it through the open shirt]) fail to remind us of Captain Forza Leal's magnificent specimen of a scar proudly displayed through equally open and deliberately transparent shirts, on which the narrator of *A Costa dos Murmúrios* lavishes her ironical attention more than once.

In chapter 12, the unusually detailed physical description of the military men sitting around the table appears to be a send-up of the group of men that the protagonist of Álamo Oliveira's *Até Hoje* first encounters in Binta, Guinea. The insistence on the physical beauty of the latter is as initially surprising in *Até Hoje* (62) as the detailed physical description of the former is unexpected in *Jornada* (98), a novel that does not otherwise devote much time to such descriptions.

The words with which the commander captain signals his readiness to attack, "Vamos a eles" (*Jornada* 101), while not unusual in colloquial Portuguese, nevertheless sound very much like the imaginary title that the narrator of *Autópsia de Um Mar de Ruínas* invents for the war memoirs that one of the characters in that novel may one day write. The fact that four pages later (in *Jornada*) there is a sentence using exactly the same mock medieval language that appears in *Autópsia* confirms that there is a real intertextual intention.

It is no doubt also from *Autópsia* that the narrator of *Jornada* gets the model for the format he uses in this novel: the separation of the passages and chapters dealing with the Angolan Other. In *Autópsia,* the chapters are totally independent; in *Jornada* there are sometimes independent chapters, sometimes independent sections separated by parentheses. And, as in *Autópsia, Jornada's* narrative voice also emphasises the oral character of Angolan culture when, in chapter 17, which deals with the victory the guerrilla fighters have just scored, it is the telling of the story and the process of transmission of oral history that come to the fore: "cada um conta à sua maneira" (139), "desde menino os mais velhos lhe contaram," and "ainda se fala da grande vitória de 1907" (140) [each tells it in his own way; the elders have told him since he was a child; they still talk about the great victory of 1907].

Likewise, Sebastião's thoughts about "o racismo de uma gente que se desforra aqui das frustrações vividas em Portugal" (219) [the racism of people who avenge themselves here for the frustrations they once endured in Portugal] may simply describe a situation that various writers encountered in colonial Angola, but it does sound remarkably close to Wanda Ramos's formulation of the same phenomenon in *Percursos* (46-47), another novel dealing with the colonial war in Angola.

Furthermore, while blue eyes are not uncommon in Portugal, blond hair is rather more unusual. Nevertheless, both NCO Roque in chapter 7 and Captain Garcia in chapter 8 are extremely blond, perhaps recalling the fact that the most sinister characters in José Martins Garcia's *Lugar de Massacre* are surprisingly blond. Much more clearly reminiscent of *Lugar de Massacre* is the use of prolepses initiated by the phrase "within a few years:" "Daqui a uns largos, largos anos" (*Jornada* 100) is a very frequent line in Martins Garcia's novel (151, 153, 155, 156, 159, etc.). Moreover, I should also like to suggest that the spelling of Domingos Da Luta's surname with the uncharacteristic capital D is an intertextual response to the equally uncharacteristic d' spelling of Count d'Avince's surname, the aristocratic character in *Lugar de Massacre.*

On the other hand, there is a strong possibility that the choice of this name for the MPLA fighter amounts especially to an homage to the work of the Angolan novelist (and political activist) José Luandino Vieira, the best-known writer of his generation. Not only are some of Luandino's memorable black characters motor-mechanics like Domingos Da Luta, but this independence fighter's name also can be seen as a direct reference to another of

Luandino's characters, Domingos Xavier, the political activist brutally killed by the PIDE in his first novel, *A Vida Verdadeira de Domingos Xavier.*

There is yet another very likely echo of Luandino's work in the passage where Sebastião recalls his childhood in Coimbra. The activities of the group of four young boys growing up in the Portuguese city are very reminiscent of the activities of the four young boys (white, black, and mulatto) in Luandino's novel *Nós, os do Makulusu.* As if to confirm the literary homage to Luandino, the narrator mentions a few pages later the "negros, mestiços, brancos de Angola" (*Jornada* 87) [blacks, mulattoes, and whites of Angola].

Attention to all these details may seem excessive, but they are important in the definition of what *Jornada de África* attempts to do: to recover a country's collective memory of its most recent war, and to search for a new way of doing so, one which no longer looks only towards the past for models but must learn to engage with the present and find models in contemporary literature too. To build a new epic must not mean destroying the old epic tradition, because part of a country's epic sense of itself comes indeed from a feeling of continuity and collective identity, which epic tradition both constructs and reinforces. Rather, the fashioning of a new epic must imply engaging with and transforming the tradition, or, as Margarida Ribeiro suggests, metaphorically "revisiting Alcácer Quibir," the complex process that constitutes the very fabric of *Jornada de África.* But the narrator of the novel also explores new possibilities. Perhaps a new epic mode must now be found in prose, not in poetry, given that it is in narrative fiction that most contemporary authors are dealing with the colonial wars. As such, even though the text is interspersed with a myriad of echoes from poetic works, it also calls forth a vast number of narratives dealing with the same theme both from Portugal and from Angola.

The inclusion of Angolan literary works in the corpus that *Jornada de África* erects as canonical for a new kind of epic takes on special significance towards the end of the novel. The Angolan and the Portuguese literatures are presented side by side as fulfilling different functions, both connected with the memory of the colonial war. On the Portuguese army side, what we see is a fear that the country will forget its soldiers: "os mortos serão esquecidos. Mais tarde ninguém contará" (124), "ninguém nos cantará" (186) [The dead will be forgotten. Later nobody will tell; nobody will sing of us]. This novel and many others dealing with the colonial war are the actual proof that this is not the case, but the formulation of such a fear appears always in very pessimistic terms, and grammatically in the negative. Curiously, the need for keeping the memory intact appears in more positive words at the end of chapter 28, when Sebastião's disenchantment with the war is at its highest. The narrative voice suddenly turns away from military concerns to speculate about two African writers. The Angolan Mário de Andrade is probably writing his anthology of African poetry in Portuguese at that very moment; or else he is reading the work of Senegalese author David Diopp.[11] A passage from Diopp is quoted, which finishes with the mention of the role of poetry in "preserving the memory of Africa" (209). In a statement that shows that the optimistic, self-affirming attitude of postcolonial writers applies not only to their writing but even to their confidence in history's memory, the African positively affirms that poetry will preserve the memory of his continent, a sharp contrast with the depressing fear on the Portuguese side that they will be forgotten by their country.

Thus, towards the end, *Jornada de África* gathers lusophone pace again by contrasting Portuguese fear of collective oblivion and Angolan confidence in collective, literary remembrance. It does so also by means of a further literary quotation taken from Agostinho Neto, in which the Angolan author and politician claims: "Nós somos uma encruzilhada de civilizações e ambientes culturais" (220) [We are a cross-roads of civilisations and cultural environments]. Perhaps the lesson that *Jornada de África* suggests should be drawn is that the memory of the colonial war will best be kept alive in the literature not only of Portugal but also of the (now independent) Portuguese-speaking African countries, so that once bitterly opposed political enemies in the future can find a common ground that transcends their past political differences. This will be achieved by the various literatures that inextricably share the common linguistic and cultural heritage once imposed by colonialism, which both sides may one day come to see as a mutual source of cultural enrichment.

Both *Autópsia de Um Mar de Ruínas* and *Jornada de África* show considerable empathy with Angolans, so that their narrators include, to some extent at least, the other side of their stories, that is, Angolans' view of the colonial situation, or what the narrators perceive as possibly being their view. *Autópsia de Um Mar de Ruínas* gives equal weight to the memory of the war by certain members of the Portuguese army and by some members of the Angolan community living in the *sanzala*, even by some of the guerrilla fighters. *Jornada de África* expresses such empathy not only through the inclusion of the point of view of one particular independence fighter, but also through the attention it pays to the literatures of various African countries, especially Angola itself. Limited as this may be, still it gives these books a very distinctive character, rarely found in the narrative fiction of any war.

Notes

[1] However, not all novelists of the colonial wars in Africa actually participated in them.

[2] Citations throughout this article are from the editions listed in the Works Cited, and translations are my own unless otherwise stated.

[3] Margarida Ribeiro, in "Percursos Africanos," makes the very interesting point that "the elaborate narrative construction" of this novel "contains in itself a structure that absolves the Portuguese narrator" (144). I agree to a large extent with her observation but believe that there is more at stake here. It is not simply a question of absolving the Portuguese narrator, it is an attempt to multiply him, to make him a collective voice; and then also to absolve him, in the sense that there is safety in numbers, that if we are all implicated, we are more likely to all be absolved.

[4] The connection with the guerrillas is not necessarily the prerogative of the males. Anica, too, is described as having been the wife of a guerrilla fighter who left her to join the MPLA army. The storyteller herself is privy to much information that reveals close contact with the insurgents.

[5] "D. Sebastião, Rei de Portugal" is the fifth poem in the third section of *Mensagem*'s first part ("As Quinas").

[6] On this subject, see Isabel Allegro de Magalhães, "The Last Big Voyage Out": "Our literature about the colonial wars is almost entirely bereft of African characters [...] rarely do we hear a person-to-person dialogue. [...] Blacks become invisible to the Portuguese soldiers [...]. The African Other is almost not seen" (398-400); see also her later, more in-depth study, "Narrativas da Guerra Colonial."

[7] See in particular Vecchi.

[8] See "Revisiting Alcacer Quibir." In fact, this article presents a more cohesive study of the novel than the segments included in "Percursos Africanos." Given the vagaries of the publication process, it is not impossible that the 1999 essay was written before the 1998 one.

[9] His name is always spelt with a capital D, Da Luta, uncharacteristic as it is of Portuguese surnames. Azevedo Teixeira, 255, uses lower case and identifies him as Pedro Afamado, better known as "o Mata-Alferes," an ex-soldier of the Portuguese army.

[10] Euripides, Sophocles, Cervantes, Shakespeare, Mallarmé, Rimbaud, Pound, Tolstoy, Dostoevsky, Camus, and Pirandello are all there, more or less disguised.

[11] The standard spelling of the French West African author's surname is Diop.

Works Cited

Alegre, Manuel. *Jornada de África: Romance de Amor e Morte do Alferes Sebastião.* 2nd ed. Lisbon: Dom Quixote/Círculo de Leitores, 1989.

Allegro de Magalhães, Isabel. "The Last Big Voyage Out." *The Paths of Multiculturalism.* Ed. M. A. Seixo, et al. Lisbon: Cosmos, 2000. 391-403.

———. "Narrativas da Guerra Colonial: Imagens Fragmentadas da Nação." *Capelas Imperfeitas.* Lisbon: Livros Horizonte, 2002.

Azevedo Teixeira, Rui de. *A Guerra Colonial e o Romance Português: Agonia e Catarse.* Lisbon: Notícias, 1998.

Bakhtin, M. *The Bakhtin Reader: Selected Writings of Bakhtin, Medvedev, and Voloshinov.* Ed. Pam Morris, with a glossary compiled by Graham Roberts. London: Edward Arnold, 1994.

Bhabha, Homi. "Foreword." *Black Skin, White Masks.* By Frantz Fanon. London: Pluto, 1986. vii-xxvi. Rpt. in *Colonial Discourse and Post-Colonial Theory: A Reader.* Ed. and intro. by Patrick Williams and Laura Chrismam. New York: Harvester Wheatsheaf, 1994. 112-23.

Camões, Luís de. *Os Lusíadas.* Ed., intro., and notes by Frank Pierce. Oxford: Oxford UP, 1973.

Chrisman, Laura. "The Imperial Unconscious? Representations of Imperial Discourse." *Colonial Discourse and Post-Colonial Theory: A Reader.* Ed. Patrick Williams and Laura Chrisman. New York: Harvester Wheatsheaf, 1993. 498-516.

Cirurgião, António. *O 'Olhar Esfíngico' da* Mensagem *de Fernando Pessoa e a Concordância.* Lisbon: Ministério da Educação/ICLP, 1990.

Eco, Umberto. "Postcript." *The Name of the Rose.* Trans. William Weaver. San Diego: Harcourt Brace Jovanovich, 1983.

Gomes de Brito, Bernardo. *Quadros da História Trágico-Marítima.* Selecção, prefácio, e notas de Rodrigues Lapa. 4th ed. Lisbon: [Gráfica Santelmo], 1963.

Jorge, Lídia. *A Costa dos Murmúrios.* 5th ed. Lisbon: Dom Quixote, 1988.

Kristeva, Julia. *Desire in Language: A Semiotic Approach to Literature and Art.* Ed. Leon S. Roudiez. Trans. T. Gora, A. Jardine, and L. S. Roudiez. Oxford: Blackwell, [c. 1980].

Lobo Antunes, António. *Os Cus de Judas.* 14th ed. Lisbon: Dom Quixote. 1986.

Lopes, Fernão. *Crónica de Dom João I.* 1st part. *Presença da Literatura Portuguesa: 1. Era Medieval.* Ed. Antônio Soares Amora. 3rd ed. rev. São Paulo: Difusão Européia do Livro, 1969.

Luandino Vieira, José. *Nós, os do Makulusu.* Lisbon: Sá da Costa, [1967] 1975.

———. *A Vida Verdadeira de Domingos Xavier.* Lisbon: Edições 70, [1961] 1974.

Martins Garcia, José. *Lugar de Massacre.* 3rd ed. Lisbon: Salamandra, 1996.

Melo, João de. *Autópsia de Um Mar de Ruínas.* 4th ed. Lisbon: Dom Quixote, 1992.

Moser, Gerald M. "Oral Traditions in Angolan Story Writing." *World Literature Today* 53.1 (1979): 40-45.

Oliveira, Álamo. *Até Hoje (Memórias de Cão).* N.p. [Angra, Azores?]: Signo, 1988.

Pessoa, Fernando. "His Mother's Little Boy." Trans. Keith Bosley. *A Centenary Pessoa.* Ed. Eugénio Lisboa with L. C. Taylor. Manchester: Carcanet, 1997.

———. *Poesia de Fernando Pessoa.* Ed. Adolfo Casais Monteiro. Lisbon: Confluência, 1942. 2 vols.

Ramos, Wanda. *Percursos (do Luachimo ao Luena).* Lisbon: Presença, [c.1980].

Ribeiro, Margarida. "Percursos Africanos: A Guerra Colonial na Literatura Pós-25 de Abril." *Portuguese Literary & Cultural Studies* 1 (1998): 125-52.

———. "Revisiting Alcacer Quibir: History, Myth and War in Manuel Alegre's *Jornada de África.*" *Portuguese Studies* 14 (1998): 242-54.

Rocha, Clara. Rev. of *Jornada de África. Colóquio/Letras* 115-116 (1990): 187-88.

Vecchi, Roberto. "La guerra coloniale tra genere e tema: *Jornada de África* di Manuel Alegre." *Dalle armi ai garofani: studi sulla letteratura della guerra coloniale.* Ed. Manuel G. Simões and Roberto Vecchi. Roma: Bulzoni, 1995. 51-58.

Isabel Moutinho lectures in Spanish and Portuguese in the School of Historical and European Studies, La Trobe University, Australia. Her main research area is contemporary Portuguese literature, particularly fiction dealing with the colonial wars in Africa. Other research interests include comparative literature (contemporary European) and the literatures of other Portuguese-speaking countries. She is author of *The Colonial Wars in Contemporary Portuguese Fiction* (Tamesis, 2008). Email: I.Moutinho@latrobe.edu.au

Jorge Arrimar's Long Journey Back to Angola: The Return of a Native Son

David Brookshaw

Abstract: There is a long tradition of Angolan writers who have recalled their native land from exile, the most emblematic example of this condition being that of the founder of the nation, and many would argue, of modern Angolan poetry: Agostinho Neto. The independence of Angola in 1975, which brought Neto home from exile, in its turn produced another generation of "refugee" writers fleeing the ensuing civil war, whose work reflects a sense of "angolanidade" both on the move and rooted in memory. Possibly the most extreme example of this is Jorge Arrimar. This article will survey the work of Arrimar, paying particular attention to the themes of de-racination and the depiction of a regional Angola seen through the prism of memory and of history—the hallmarks of this particular writer.

An inevitable result of the great inter-continental movements of people, deriving first from European colonial expansion and then from decolonization and postcolonial migration, has been the proliferation of diasporas far from their countries and continents of origin. The global dimension of these movements of population is a phenomenon associated with what we have learned to call modernity, which is why literary themes linked to or deriving from the disaporic condition—exile, social and cultural alienation, displacement, a concern with so-called cultural "authenticity" (or otherwise with "hybridisation")—is part and parcel of what we understand to be the anguish

Portuguese Literary & Cultural Studies 15/16 (2010): 151-61.

of modernity. An example from the lusophone world at the turn of the nineteenth and twentieth centuries was Camilo Pessanha, whose identification with Portugal, the country he abandoned as a young man, was most acutely expressed from his Chinese exile, but who yearned to return to the East on the few visits he made to Portugal. Indeed, in a letter written to a friend while on passage back to Macau, Pessanha manifested a desire for the journey never to end.[1] The idea of continuous movement, of a journey without end, is a theme to which I shall return later in relation to the work of Jorge Arrimar.

In the case of Angolan literature—not to mention the other literatures from lusophone Africa—the African consciousness of a whole generation began to be expressed as a consequence of exile and/or imprisonment. Here, the most obvious example is that of Agostinho Neto, most of whose poetry was written when he was a student and political activist in Portugal, or when he was in prison in Portugal or banished by the Portuguese dictatorship to Cape Verde. In spite of this, Neto was conscious that he belonged to a generation of African intellectuals profoundly convinced of their role as leaders in an irreversible political and historical process that would put an end to their situation of exiles. The very process that would lead eventually to the return of Neto and his fellow nationalists to Angola produced a rupture within the heart of the colonial population, which would lead to other exiles. While there were clearly many colonials who lent their unreserved support to the old regime and were unable to envisage any other type of political arrangement, there were others who abandoned the country on the eve of its independence for sudden practical reasons, among which, the very real threat of renewed war, or the impossibility of continuing studies thrown into upheaval by the mass departure of teachers and other skilled personnel. Some left, hoping to return, but ended up staying in their host countries, becoming permanent exiles. Many considered themselves Angolans, albeit Angolans in exile, Angolans on the move.

At this point it is important to stress that the Angolan roots of Jorge Arrimar lie in the highlands of Huíla, around the town of São Pedro da Chibia, where this author was born in 1953 and where he lived until the age of twenty-one. Huíla is therefore the geographical context for Arrimar's Angolan identity, for he is the product of a community present in the region for at least a century and a half, and which originated in the early colonial settlement of Atlantic islanders from Madeira and the Azores, surrounded by African ethnic groups with distinct cultures, and whose social organization was based on pastoral activity. On the other hand, some aspects of this regional society, possibly as a result of the influence of Brazilians, who settled in the region after the independence of Brazil, or because of the activities of Portuguese and *mestiço* traders known as *pombeiros*, who penetrated the interior in search of slaves, led to some degree of miscegenation, albeit not to the extent that occurred in and around Luanda. Arrimar's strong identification with his region was evident in his first collection of poems, *Ovatyilongo* (1975), in which he demonstrated profound ethnographic and linguistic knowledge of the indigenous cultures of the southern highlands. These poems seem to illustrate the intentions of the group to which he belonged, explicitly expressed in an article in the cultural section of the regional paper, which spoke of the need to create a literature that was openly directed towards the specificity of Angola. The proponents of this type of literary and cultural aspiration attracted the attention of the Portuguese political police, who kept them under close supervision, but there was the added difficulty of their being unable to obtain any of the texts of the 1948 generation, whose main literary figures, poets like Neto himself, António Jacinto, António Cardoso, not to mention Luandino Vieira, were in prison or on parole in Lisbon after long periods of incarceration, while others, such as Viriato da Cruz and Mário Pinto de Andrade, were in exile. It was no doubt for this reason that they had to resort to older, and perhaps less controversial sources of inspiration: the article, "Literatura sem ambiente," originally written by F. Morais Sarmento, and published in the newspaper, *A Província de Angola* in 1941, was rediscovered by Arrimar, who transcribed the article with his own commentary. Sarmento's words seemed as relevant to Angola at the beginning of the 1970s as they had three decades earlier. He had criticized the literature produced in Angola for its portrayal of whites as not being attached to the land, while at the same time lamenting the absence of a literature that unequivocally declared itself to be Angolan, following the example of Brazilian literature, still under the influence of the modernist and regionalist movements, or of Cape Verdean writers who had launched the "Claridade" movement but a few years previously. Sarmento, reproduced by Arrimar, had concluded:

> Não se julgue (...) que este caso é um caso literariamente circunscrito aos escritores brancos de Angola. Não. Os pretos e os mestiços não descobriram por enquanto, como aconteceu já aos cabo-verdianos, o sentido angolano da sua mensagem literária. Nos seus escritos, quer sejam prosa ou verso, eles ainda não nos deram, como diria Sílvio Romero e João Ribeiro dos mestiços e pretos brasileiros.[2]

In writing this in 1973, Arrimar could not (or perhaps chose not to) predict the speed with which his vision of an authentically Angolan literature would be swept away, or perhaps better emerge with a vengeance as a result of political developments in the following year.

In October 1975, a month before the formal independence of Angola, with war already flaring up in the south, Arrimar abandoned his homeland. He completed a degree in history in Portugal and went into secondary school teaching in the Azores before eventually leaving for Macau in 1985. He lived there for the next thirteen years, publishing various collections of poetry, as well as organizing anthologies of poetry devoted to Macau. While it is not the purpose of this article to discuss his poetry in detail, suffice to say that each collection he published during those years focuses on a particular stage in the evolution of his consciousness as an exiled Angolan, and on the cultural fissures produced by his sense of dislocation.[3] In *Murilaonde* (1990), his efforts to rekindle memories of his native land are still strong. This sentiment is maintained in *Fonte do Lilau* (1990), in which there is a limited attempt to identify, as the title of the collection suggests, with the land of his exile, while at the same time acknowledging the failure of his ability to integrate emotionally into the world of Macau. In *Secretos Sinais* (1992), the poet is still influenced by his Chinese surroundings, but there are now more fluid, maritime images that seem to draw him back towards his more remote ancestral Portuguese roots. Since his return to Europe in 1998, Arrimar has entered another phase in his evolution as a writer, switching literary genres and publishing mainly fiction. This phase has also marked his gradual return to Angolan themes. His two novels, *Viagem de Memória às Ilhas* and *O Planalto dos Pássaros*, were both published in 2002 and to some extent complete the author's long journey back to his native land.

Viagem de Memória às Ilhas tells the histories of personalities brought to light by Alberto Meneses, the author's *alter ego*, during his research in the archives in Funchal. Like Arrimar, Alberto is a dislocated Angolan, a descendant of Madeirans who had established themselves in Huíla in the nineteenth century. In 1975, his family fled to South Africa and then to Australia, but Alberto later decided to leave for Europe in order to discover his ancestral roots. However, his nomadic instincts had caused him to leave again, this time to a post in the Portuguese Embassy in Bangkok, mirroring the Asian experience of Arrimar himself. Alberto's trajectory thus seems to illustrate the following spiritual anguish: the greater the rupture with one's roots, the more intense the urge to wander, the longer the period of wandering, the greater the desire to return to one's origins, the greater the importance of memory:

> A vida tinha-o desassossegado demais para que ele agora conseguisse ficar calmo e tranquilo para sempre no mesmo sítio. A sua memória continuava ancorada a uma terra que ele precisava de reencontrar, para se encontrar de vez com ele próprio, ou então... perder-se inevitavelmente! (*Viagem* 12)

For Alberto, the greatest problem is his realization that memory is focused as much on people, acquaintances or family, as it is on place. The absence of this crucial element means that a return can never be complete, but merely another stage in an "incessante procura." Alberto's anguish seems to coincide with that of the migrant as defined by Iain Chambers:

> To return, rather than simply to re-visit or re-view, that is, to apparently turn back and return "fully," to African, Caribbean or Indian roots in pursuit of a displaced and dispersed authenticity today hardly seems feasible. The impossible mission that seeks to preserve the singularity of a culture must paradoxically negate its fundamental element: its historical dynamic. (74)

Perhaps Arrimar himself was conscious of this condition when he revisited his native region in 2002 for the first time in nearly thirty years. In an article on his journey, Arrimar recalls participating in a dance—the *etanda*—that marks the passage from adolescence to adulthood:

> Senti um apelo antigo e levantei bem alto o bastão bifurcado dos dançarinos, saltei a vedação do tempo e bati com força os pés no chão ao som compassado de palmas e cânticos... e eu dancei pela última vez a etanda sob os céus da Huíla.[4]

The reference to "última vez" not only suggests that the dance is unrepeatable, given that one does undergo this rite of passage twice in one's life, but perhaps indicates that the visit was necessary in order that he should leave again, for, as Chambers points out, revisiting is not the same as returning.

In *Viagem de Memória às Ilhas*, Alberto's restless spirit, his psychological instability, are partly due to the lack of any historical consciousness, and it is worth recalling here that Arrimar is a graduate in history who was responsible for the historical archive in Macau as well as for its national library. The community to which Alberto belonged only had vague, fragmented notions of the origins of its presence in Angola:

> Os primeiros descendentes angolanos desses ilhéus de oitocentos quiseram acreditar que eram de geração espontânea, como se aquele pedaço de terra africana sempre lhes tivesse pertencido. (*Viagem* 21)

It is as a researcher that Alberto is attracted to the documents in the Funchal archives, but as he reads between their lines, his imagination blurs the division between history and fiction, and so the book becomes a series of inter-related stories that explore the origins of the family in Madeira, with particular emphasis given to the Bettencourts, one of the oldest island family names, with ramifications in the Azores and the Canaries, and from whom Arrimar claims ancestry on his mother's side. The stories narrated correspond, for the most part, to episodes of love, and in most cases culminate in a journey, when the lovers are obliged to leave their place of residence, or their homeland, with the implied consequence that they will never be able to return to their point of origin. Thus, the orphan girl from Lisbon is given a king's dowry to marry the first *donatário* of Porto Santo; a disapproved marriage forces José António Bettencourt and his wife to leave for Angola; a Macanese, the son of the Azorean *Ouvidor*, or Chief Magistrate of Macau, Miguel de Arriaga,[5] tires of the intrigues in Lisbon and leaves for the islands, where he falls in love and puts down roots—a *retornado* over a century before the term was first coined; the colonization of Lanzarote by the Frenchman Jean de Bethancourt, his love affair with a Guanche princess, ends with the withdrawal of this pioneer to Madeira, following the agreement between Portugal and Castile, which transferred sovereignty of the Canaries to the latter. Once again, an adventurer becomes the victim of *realpolitik*. Just as in his poetry, then, Arrimar seems to wish to reclaim his origins in a whole process of inter-oceanic migration that began with Portuguese maritime expansion. Apart from this, it is also clear that his concept of travel involves both a physical and temporal space, for while he sits in the archive, his research leads him on a journey into history:

> foi como se tivesse feito uma viagem aos confins dos tempos e tivesse regressado ao porto do presente. (*Viagem* 169)

Equally important is the metaphorical role played by these islands in Arrimar's work: they are frontier zones, crossroads for generations of travellers and migrants, settlers and colonizers. At the same time, these spaces both are and are not Portugal. Without being strictly colonies, they are nevertheless peripheries. Hence to some extent their function as symbolic representations of isolation, fragmentation, and dispersed roots: the islands are physical embodiments of psychological states, confirming the cliché "every man is an island." Alberto leaves Porto Santo carrying in his luggage a tiny sachet of sand by way of a souvenir of his passage through his ancestral land, but also as a recollection of his rootlessness and angst:

> Mas era apenas um punhado de areia... areia daquela ilha, onde ele havia tentado encontrar, ali também, alguns dos sulcos que as suas longínquas raízes islenhas haviam deixado gravados. Mais uma ilha, mais raízes soltas ao vento. (*Viagem* 208)

Finally, we can surely see some parallels between the archipelagos of Madeira and the Azores and the colonial archipelago that Arrimar inhabited in the south of Angola. While the presence of the surrounding ocean is fundamental to our understanding of the cultural sensibilities of the islanders—the symbiosis of sea and soil being a constant theme in the literatures of the Portuguese islands—the sea that Arrimar, as a boy and young man, contemplated, observed, and respected from his island of Huíla, contained the African cultures that first inspired his poetry. For Arrimar was a member of a community whose own cultural roots were, after all, alien to the region, just as islands are within the domain of the ocean, and, like the Portuguese Atlantic islands, Arrimar's Angolan community was not prototypically colonial in the sense that it had to some extent become Africanized, nor did it belong to the mass of the colonized population.

O Planalto dos Pássaros was published simultaneously in Portugal and Angola and marked a new phase in Arrimar's reintegration in Angola. Its launch was the occasion for his first visit to his native land since he had left it nearly thirty years before. Moreover, his acceptance as a member of the Angolan Writers' Union reflected a formal, institutional reconciliation with his past, while also indicating how Angola itself was opening up as peace was re-established in the country. The novel is very clearly fictionalized history complete with footnotes. The story opens and closes with the flight of a young man from Huíla in 1975. He is the descendant of one of the first

Portuguese families to settle in the southern highlands at the end of the eighteenth century. Through a series of flashbacks, it narrates the story of this family, the arrival of the first *capitão-mor*, the Madeiran António Jardim, nominated by the governor in Luanda in 1784. Much of the plot focuses on the relationship between Jardim and Huilana, the daughter of João Pilarte, a Portuguese *pombeiro* and backwoodsman who has long been resident in the region. The death of the local African chieftain, Kanina Gonga, who had protected Portuguese settlers in his domains, signals the end of a period of stability. The whites and their African allies (the so-called *guerra preta*) are defeated and obliged to take refuge in Benguela, bringing to an end the first attempt to establish a Portuguese administrative presence in the southern Angolan interior. The attempt would only be repeated some sixty years later, when a grandson of the first *capitão-mor* would join an expedition that would once again make for the Huíla highlands. But by relating the events of the late eighteenth century with those of the late twentieth, Arrimar is presenting us with a cyclical view of history, as if he were seeking to legitimize the long period of colonial settlement in the area and reclaim roots in this particular region of Angola. The introduction of two love stories, that of Feliciana and João Pilarte, the founding members of the family, and that of Jardim and Huilana, would seem to indicate some similarity with the foundational romances of Brazilian literature, except that here, the community disintegrates once it is established, and while it returns and lasts for over a century until its final rupture in 1975, Arrimar's Huíla is, in the final analysis, no more than a lost paradise.

When we speak of a foundational literature, and the concept of a national identity supported by a literary canon, we should not forget that such a literature is often the product of a profound sense of loss. It seeks out a future in the past. The great Brazilian romantic, José de Alencar, set a number of his novels during what he and his generation considered the heroic age of Brazil's construction as a nation, an edenic, rural Brazil prior to the technological advances and negative urban influences that the author felt typified his own age. His Indians were idealized, mythological figures, incorporated into literature at a time when the Indian presence had been almost totally eradicated from the Brazilian littoral and the vicinity of its coastal cities where most of the population lived. In the fiction of Mia Couto and of Pepetela, the attempt to reunite the divided self—a favourite theme of the romantics—is focused on a tale of love. Hence, Couto's *Terra Sonâmbula* is about love between two individuals of a lost, transitional, or threshold generation, not born at independence and which did not die out with the end of colonialism. In Pepetela's *A Geração da Utopia*, the two main male and female protagonists, Aníbal and Sara sacrifice their love in order to create a nation. In Arrimar's *Viagem de Memória às Ilhas*, the relationship between Alberto and his Azorean lover, Mariana Arriaga (a descendant perhaps of the "Ouvidor" of Macau), is sacrificed in order that the "hero" may continue his journey and complete his story. But the quest to reunite the divided self, just as it was for the romantics, would lead us to agree with the philosopher Karl Popper, namely, that the self is an emergent and not an absolute entity, which means of course that identity is an unfolding process and not a fixed state waiting to be found or recuperated (Eakin 195). Travel, dislocation, and exile are, for Arrimar, just as they were indeed for Pessanha, a consequence of this process. The quest for his roots is, paradoxically, a cause of his deracination—or better, the author put down roots in exile and in a type of pluralism of identity based on his life's experience. The young refugees from Huíla (both in 1790 and in 1975) take with them one token of their African cultural inheritance: a *quissange* or thumb piano. When he leaves Madeira at the end of the twentieth century, Alberto sets off in search of the black metal effigy of Christ the child that belonged to the young wife who left for Huíla almost two hundred years before. Arrimar's travelling Angolan identity is no more than an attempt to reconcile these two extremes of his cultural inheritance.

Arrimar's reinscription into the literature of Angola does not, however, stop here. In 2003, he published a short story in Angola that seems to contain within its plot, its social archetypes, and its language, resonances of an earlier, pioneering literary age. *Os Infortúnios de Juvêncio* is set firmly within postwar Angola, but the scenario is remarkably similar to that depicted by Luandino Vieira in his story "Vavó Xixi e seu neto Neca Santos," which featured in the classic of Angolan fiction of the 1960s, *Luuanda*. Like Luandino's unemployed youth, Juvêncio has been brought up by his grandmother after his parents are lost in the war. Dreaming of a better life, he decides to go and seek work at an orphanage run by a nun, who has become well known in the hinterland of Luanda for her work among abandoned children. However, on his way to the town where this orphanage is situated, Juvêncio is caught stealing a banana and thrown into jail, where he remains without trial. In due course, he and other prisoners are let out of their cell to go and labour as contract workers. The story ends with a quote from António Jacinto's well-known poem "Monangamba," which had evoked the exploitation and plight of Angolan contract workers in the interior of Angola in the 1940s and 50s. Arrimar's language, replete with *kimbundu* words and expressive dialogue, is very different from that employed in his historical fiction. It is as if the cycle has turned and we are back in the Angola of the late colonial period, and, indeed, this is no doubt the author's intention: to suggest how the pattern of social inequalities and arbitrary justice is being repeated once again five decades after an earlier generation of writers focused on them. Once again, Arrimar presents us with a cyclical view of history, and this idea of an eternal return perhaps further serves to re-legitimize Arrimar as a literary voice within the social, political, and cultural mainstream of post-revolutionary and postwar Angola.

Notes

[1] Letter to Carlos Amaro, dated 26 January 1909, and written aboard a ship in the Mediterranean, during his fourth return to Macau. See Pessanha 93-95.

[2] "Literatura sem ambiente," in "Grucuhuíla" 5, 9 August 1973, a cultural page run by a group of students known as the Grupo Cultural da Huíla, and published in the newspaper *Jornal da Huíla.*

[3] For a study of Arrimar's poetry, see Brookshaw.

[4] Jorge Arrimar wrote a report on his return to Angola: "Eu dancei a etanda na minha terra," *Seixo Review*, <http://www3.telus.net/eduardo-b-pinto/arrimar_regresso.html>.

[5] Miguel de Arriaga Brum Silveira was Chief Magistrate in Macau in the first half of the nineteenth century. Arrimar, the historian and archivist, took part in an international seminar entitled "O Município no Mundo Português," held in Funchal in 1998, and presented a paper entitled, "O Leal Senado de Macau e Miguel de Arriaga na Primeira Metade do Século XIX."

Works Cited

Arrimar, Jorge. *Fonte do Lilau.* Macau: Livros do Oriente, 1990.

———. *Os Infortúnios de Juvêncio.* Luanda: Chá de Caxinde, 2003.

———. *Murilaonde.* Macau: Edição do Autor, 1990.

———. *Ovatyilongo.* Angola: Edição do Autor, 1975. (With a preface by Pe. Carlos Esterman.)

———. *O Planalto dos Pássaros.* Porto: Campo das Letras, 2002.

———. *Secretos Sinais.* Macau: n.p., 1992.

———. *Viagem à Memória das Ilhas.* Lisbon: Salamandra, 2002.

Brookshaw, David. *Voices from Lusophone Borderlands: the Angolan Identities of António Agostinho Neto, Jorge Arrimar and José Eduardo Agualusa.* [National University of Ireland] *Maynooth Papers in Spanish, Portuguese and Latin American Studies* 4 (March 2002).

Chambers, Iain, *Migrancy, Culture, Identity.* London/New York: Routledge, 1994.

Eakin, Paul John, *Fictions in Autobiography: Studies in the Art of Self-Invention.* Princeton:

Princeton UP, 1985.
Luandino Vieira, José. *Luuanda: Estórias*. 4th ed. Lisbon: Edições 70, 1974.
Pessanha, Camilo. *Obras de Camilo Pessanha II*. Mem Martins: Europa-América, n.d.

David Brookshaw is Professor of Luso-Brazilian Studies at Bristol University. His publications include *Visions of China: Stories from Macau* (2002); *Voices from Lusophone Borderlands: the Angolan Identities of António Agostinho Neto, Jorge Arrimar and José Eduardo Agualusa* (2002); and *Perceptions of China in Modern Portuguese Literature–Border Gates* (2002). He is also the translator of Mia Couto's fiction. Email: D.R.Brookshaw@bristol.ac.uk

Subjects on a Voyage through Alterity

Laura Cavalcante Padilha
Translated by Phillip Rothwell

Abstract: In this article, Laura Padilha offers a voyage through alterity. Angolan authors are read as products and producers of a culture that fuses tradition and modernity, oral and written. Their main purpose on this journey, in which we as readers participate, is to locate their own culture in difference, and to know themselves by knowing their own Others.

> Ouvi dizer que as teorias viajam e, quando chegam aos lugares, são transformadas, transculturadas (...). Algumas vezes, entretanto, as teorias não viajam. E, quando isso acontece, a diferença colonial as torna invisíveis para as teorias dominantes e universais que podem viajar e têm passaporte para atravessar a diferença colonial.
> —Walter Mignolo

The process of colonization and, more generally, colonialism, often begins with a maritime voyage. Indeed, the voyage was regally inscribed in our imaginations as readers in the very fabric of the Portuguese language by the most important sixteenth-century poetic voice, who, after decanting some of the names of the "barões assinalados," addressed himself to his king, in *Os Lusíadas*, as follows:

> E enquanto eu estes canto, e a vós não posso,
> Sublime Rei, que não me atrevo a tanto,

Portuguese Literary & Cultural Studies 15/16 (2010): 163-73.

Tomai as rédeas vós do Reino vosso:
Dareis matéria a nunca ouvido canto.
Comecem a sentir o peso grosso
(Que polo mundo todo faça espanto)
De exércitos e feitos singulares
De África as terras e do Oriente os mares. (I.15)

In contrast, the desire for decolonization, when it surfaced with urgency in the then Portuguese colonies of Africa, found one of its strongest symbolic paradigms in the fictionalization of travel through land. Such a journey through the "inside" aims to connect the Self to its own Others, and no longer to think of and through Others brought from over the endless sea, in an act of Western expansionism. With this in mind, I return to Camões, remembering his perception of expansion: "Os Portugueses somos do Ocidente / Imos buscando as terras do Oriente" (I.50).

Through their new journey, or counter-voyage through alterity, here thought of as the relation formed between the Self and one's own Others, African writers, and I intend to refer principally to the case of Angola, somehow respond to the questions raised by Camões's navigators, who found "gente estranha" of a "cor (...) verdadeira / Que Faeton, nas terras acendidas; / Ao mundo deu, de ousado e não prudente" (I.49, 46). They ask:

Que gente será esta? (em si deziam)
Que costumes, que Lei, que Rei teriam? (I.45)

The search for a reply to such a fundamental question cannot but draw on another type of cultural archive where other customs reside, other "leis" are kept, and whence springs the force of other "reis." A principal part of the African cultural archive is, beyond a shadow of a doubt, oral tradition. As is well known, such tradition is one of the most important elements when one considers African ancestral culture.

The power and prominence of oral tradition should not be confused with the opinion that African peoples cannot write. Rather, it means insisting on the force of a whole semiotic set that finds other ways of signifying beyond letters on a page, as Simon Battestini has amply demonstrated in his *Écriture et texte: contribution africaine* (1997). At the end of the day, these modes of identification give a people the contours of its identity. Through them, alterity is affirmed as difference, allowing us to know, along the lines of Homi Bhabha, *a priori* cultural contents and customs. These have little or nothing to do with those used by white-European Western culture as it moulds its symbolic and cultural roots.

To voyage through oral texts implies an attempt to know this Other archive, an archive governed by an Other logic. Such an archive, always silenced in the game of obliteration intrinsic to the process of colonization, ends up offering to the producers of African symbolic goods an opportunity to reactivate the legacy of their ancestral memory, something that they do frequently and compellingly.

I believe that revisiting the corpus of oral texts means looking for the imagistic traces or threads they continue to produce in the fictional web to this day. One such element through which new meanings are negotiated in the Angolan novel is the depiction of subjects on a journey. In fact, this journey has nothing to do with that other journey that was at the origin of the colonizing process. These subjects frequently seek to reinforce their own location of culture, in order to demarcate the limits of their difference, as I shall now explore.

The Ritual Power of Naming

I will begin by remembering that the journey is an intrinsic part of the rites of initiation. In order to complete such rites, the neophyte must leave behind his or her known world—family, village, slave quarters, *quimbo*—in order to undertake his or her passage into a new social condition in other locations such as the forest, the river side, the savannah, or even distant villages where their future initiators live. On their return, the now initiated youth gains at the rites of puberty a new and definitive name, ceasing to be a mere walk-on part in the life of the community, as Honorat Aguessy points out.

The gesture of naming and/or being named means, in the words of another scholar of African cultures, Alassane Ndaw, "the act through which a man concludes a true pact of peace and fraternity" (163). In this sense, and digressing a little from Angola in the direction of Mozambique, I am reminded of the saying of the old grandmother in Paulina Chiziane's *O sétimo juramento*. In a given scene, she declares in her wisdom: "Nome é testemunho da existência e delimitação da fronteira de todas as coisas" (59).

The power of naming is a recurrent trait in modern lusophone African fiction. Significantly, in Pepetela's *As aventuras de Ngunga*, the child protagonist, on ending his journey into knowledge, inverts the order of the ancient rites, in which the initiated would receive his name, and names himself. He shares his secret—that is his new name—only with Uassamba, the object of his affection. Thus, the last stage of his initiation is completed. His name is a type of temple of being.

As a palpable object capable of being known, through its very materiality, the African novel also performs a naming pact. Through its words, it tells of the cultural diversity that engendered it. Through its very texture, it engenders that cultural diversity. It becomes an initiation rite, a type of return journey, with its reader participating as a special subject in a ritualistic ceremony through which, to repeat the phrase of Alassane Ndaw, "a true pact of peace and fraternity" is sealed.

Such an invitation to the reader to participate, in the sense of becoming a companion on the text's voyage of initiation, takes concrete form in the narrative wrapping of Ruy Duarte de Carvalho's *Vou lá visitar pastores*. In this novel, the narration is the result of a tape recording of what the narrator lived through in his dislocation to the Cuvale territory. In other words, it is a concrete attempt to know, as the Angolan that he is, a little about his own Others, in this case, the pastoral Cuvale people.

At a diegetic level, the recording objectifies the recuperation of everything that the narrator saw, heard, and experienced, for a friend, who does not appear to accompany him on his voyage. At the level of enunciation, however, it is a way of including the reader in the "telling" of the text and in the journey this very text triggers, so that one can get to know more closely the Cuvale shepherds and by extension the Angolan land itself. This land of necessity can only be conceived of in its dense cultural multiplicity. The enunciator, through the voice of his narrator, tells us:

> Era a maneira de tentar ajudá-lo (...) a alargar o contacto com o que buscava. Não chegou a aparecer e mais tarde transcrevi essas cassetes. Divulgo agora os salvados, são a viagem do texto. (11)

The transcription referred to by the narrator should be read as a way of translating the Other, in this case, a way of organizing the Cuvale world. At a deeper level, what is translated is Angola, in one of its many ethnic versions. It is not by chance that, at the end of the first paragraph of the work, the narrator enounces his intention to give "o sentido da colocação geográfica (...) para fazer sentido" (15). In this demarcating action, he seeks a way of strengthening the very act of naming a culture that was always elided in the reductive gaze of the Other. This quest answers in some way the question of Camões's navigators who did not know who those people were. Nor did they know their fundamental cultural codes, as becomes clear in those verses that talk of "costumes," "Lei," and "Rei," in a game of allegorizing capital letters.

Journeys at Various Times

Given what I have already discussed, I do not think it a fluke that so many Angolan writers have tried and continue to try to find new modes of representing the culture that they have formed, and which has formed them. Mohamadou Kane points out that the originality of African works resides precisely in the fact that their writers always end up mimicking their dual legacy. They draw on both the traditional and the modern, but nearly always with an emphasis on the former. This is what happens, for example—and here I am making a necessary temporal leap—with António de Assis Júnior, in his enigmatic novel *O segredo da morta.* For him, the novelist invites his reader to journey in his company, evidently through the voice of his narrator. They journey through the lands of Dondo, Pungo Andongo, Cambo Camana, and elsewhere, where not a king, but a mythical queen, Jinga, or Nzinga Mbandi, imposed her laws and left her mark. That impression overcame the corpus of history and created a myth that could not be extinguished. Inverting the colonial paradigm, the imaginary of Assis Júnior substitutes the River Kuanza for the sea, and its ships become the little steamboat where, in mid-voyage, one of the novel's protagonists, Elmira, is born. In the name of the land, Kapaxi, she represents a fictional bringing-up-to-date of the Jinga myth. It is equally not by chance that the timeframe chosen by the novelist is the end of the nineteenth century and the beginning of the twentieth century, when a desire for "angolanness" began to gain currency and the voice of the "naturais de Angola" made itself heard, echoing the desire for emancipation in the then colony, as has been widely pointed out by scholars of the history and culture of Angola.

Proposing such an inversion in the Western paradigm may be read in another form not just at the diegetic level, with the many journeys that authors have enacted, but also as a discursive solution that brings up to date the entire source of Angolan oral tradition. It becomes a kind of narrative game—a creative hide-and-seek in the literary history of the nation. The novel is a camouflage for *missossos, makas, malundas,* and riddles—every type of traditional narrative that thus, through its compass, travels from the oral to the written, donning new and surprising clothes.

In an echo of *O segredo da morta*, another Angolan, Arnaldo Santos, seventy years later, in *A casa velha das margens*, brings up to date the thematic tapestry of the earlier novel, inviting the reader to accompany Emídio Mendonça, a mulatto, on his voyage as he returns to Angola and is almost killed as his Portuguese father had been. The scene of both novels is, in principal, the same—Dondo, which also represents the region of Massangano, as well as several populations on the banks of the River Kuanza, with incursions into the lands of the Quissamas, namely, Songo. In the words of the text, they are lands "áridas e sem vegetação," where "estranhos mitos" took place that rendered those who lived there beings with a "feitio (...) belicoso e exaltado" (110). The mother of the protagonist, who comes from there, is called Kissama.

The time setting of the novel is also towards the end of the nineteenth century, with all its historical importance to Angola. It is no coincidence that the poet Cordeiro da Matta, one of the icons of voyages through alterity, becomes one of the characters in Santos's novel, and is presented as "chefe da primeira divisão de Calumbo," in 1889. This year is very significant when we remember that the canonical texts of the poet, "Kicôla" and "Uma quissama," were from 1888 and 1891 respectively.

The ends of the nineteenth and twentieth centuries are interlaced when Arnaldo Santos's novel echoes the work of Assis Júnior. It revisits Angolan society from the time in which the Generation of 1880 came to prominence, exactly the generation of Cordeiro da Matta. That generation embodied a movement that challenged the prior politico-cultural consensus and envisioned "angolanidade" as an ideal that could be realized. With Santos, on his voyage undertaken over both time and space, the doors of the old house which was Angola at that historical juncture are opened. Thitherto, Angola had always been put at the margin of reductive westernization. Nowadays, in our new era of so-called globalization—the new buttress of westernization—it remains marginalized by the globalization process that opens the new avenues of neocolonization. Today there is a new collision, like the one of old, against what is classified as the periphery. There is a certain effort to elide differences, branding that same margin—where we place everything we are incapable of understanding—as a non-place, which is utterly archaic and without any cultural or ontologic value.

The novel *A casa velha das margens*—precisely because of the suggestion of its title as something *old*, *marginal*, and related to a *place*—draws on African cultural roots in their Angolan manifestation, and has the ethical dimension of an Other. It provides a counter-discourse that exalts difference and practices inclusiveness, effectively erasing the gaps and silences imposed historically by the agents of cultural domination. It attempts to translate voices long buried in a move that gives them new life through the gesture of artistic creation, which does not avoid ways of bringing oral tradition up to date. With this modernization, the whole foundation of the modern novel is shaken. The *missossos*, the *makas*, and the *malundas* all reappear, while riddles are sown into the very fabric of fiction.

In this collision, what Boaventura de Sousa Santos has called a "sociology of absences" abounds. Through such an inclusive gesture, "os silêncios e as ignorâncias que definem as incompletudes das culturas, da experiência e dos saberes" are denounced, to quote João Arriscado Nunes (26). Thus reconfigured, "a casa velha das margens" offers itself as a shelter of Other imaginaries alongside the identity maps that sustain them.

There are many novels that narrate journeys through alterity, or subjects in search of recognition of their own body of cultural difference and, as such, the very body that signifies for them. However, cultural difference should not be taken as a synonym for an essence nurtured on the lap of first principles. Following Bhabha, we know that such a difference is always a construction of systems of cultural identification and should be understood as a process of signification through which the affirmations *of* culture *about* culture differentiate, discriminate, and authorize the production of fields of power, reference, applicability, and ability. As Bhabha alerts us, it becomes about the recognition of *a priori* cultural contents and customs.

Ruy Duarte de Carvalho reinforces Bhabha's critical position in his *Vou lá visitar pastores*, considered by many to be a non-novel, to be situated in an interstitial zone, crossed by anthropology, ethnography, and the history of ideas, among other disciplines. His book becomes a generic hybrid and, for many critics, a work that defies categorization. He affirms at a given moment in the novel through the voice of his narrator that, by staging the pastoral world of the Cuvale, he wanted to undertake:

> (...) uma aventura pessoal que me situa, em plena recta final do século XX, a pouco mais de dois anos da viragem do milênio e cercado pelo rumor histórico da globalização, empenhado mas é em decifrar os termos da resolução—rigorosamente situados no tempo e no espaço (...) —de uma cultura milenar que todos os dias se reafirma actualizando, desenvolvendo, no presente, uma estratégia

> de integração total entre o meio que lhe assiste, as pessoas que a compõem e o "impalpável" que a envolve, sem no entanto poder descurar nunca a relação com um exterior que a nega e a longo termo acabará por inviabilizá-la? (357-58)

The desire to reaffirm culture artistically, through a fictionalization in difference that attempts to give a voice to "uma estratégia de integração total entre o meio que lhe assiste, as pessoas que a compõem e o 'impalpável' que a envolve," leads the novelist to excavate the terrain where the pillars of the very genre of the novel were planted. The narrative paradigms of an oral tradition and the discursive model baptized by the West with the name of novel refind each other as if they were river and sea. The bustle of the waters of knowledge creates a hybridity of expression that assails the bulwarks of genre. In Brazil, João Guimarães Rosa did the same thing when he recreated the pathways of the hinterland of Minas Gerais, through which the speech of an Other walks in difference: it is the speech of nature; of men; of myths and social rituals. *Grande sertão: veredas* emerges as a landmark in Brazilian literature. In it, the voice of Riobaldo unravels his "causos" to a mute interlocutor—the mask of all of us, his readers. In his words, "lugar sertão se divulga: é onde pastos carecem de fechos (...). O gerais corre em volta. Esses gerais são sem tamanho" (7). Voice and the written word contaminate each other, embodying what has no limit or size.

In the African cultural universe to which we will now return, narrators frequently clothe the skins of ancestral storytellers in the written word. In so doing, they de-immobilize the rigidity of the written word captive on the page, so to speak. They travel through the pathways of orality, as if the text unleashed its own voice. A voyage of the written word, which is a gesture of naming difference, thus becomes a rite of initiation.

There are many novels that revolve around voyages. Listing them all would be a futile exercise. Among the many I could mention, think of Boaventura Cardoso's *Mãe, materno mar*, an incredible contemporary *missosso*, as Carmem Lúcia Tindó Secco points out in her preface to the work. In this novel, the character of Manecas undertakes a voyage—a rite of initiation in the culture of his land—that takes fifteen years, leaving from Malanje and reaching Luanda, where he will glimpse the sea of which he has so often dreamed.

Another novel I would like to mention is *Rioseco*, by Manuel Rui Monteiro, in which we accompany the encounter of river dwellers—Noíto and Zacaria—with those from the sea—Mateus and his son, who is purposefully called

Kuanza. In the work, whose main protagonist is an old woman, Noíto, ancient tradition is rewoven and controlled by the body of an elderly woman with the heart and the mind of a mere girl. Manuel Rui draws on tradition, with the memory of ancient knowledge impregnating the present and recreating Angola, as Lourentinho, one of Luandino Vieira's creations might say. In this novel, the multiple is inscribed and the meeting of the Selves—those from the river—with their own Others—those from the sea—shows this very well.

Conclusion

By way of a conclusion, I would like to cite the words of the Argentinian writer Ricardo Piglia, taken from an email discussion he had with a Chilean writer, Roberto Bolaño, that was published in *El País* in Argentina and republished by the Brazilian newspaper *Folha de São Paulo* in its supplement "Mais!" [12 September 2004]. The two writers discuss Latin American literature and its reception. What interests me is a section in which Piglia argues for the importance of conceptualizing beyond the contingency of his own territoriality as a Latin American subject. He says: "Penso que há novas constelações em formação e que são essas constelações o que avistamos do nosso laboratório quando apontamos o telescópio para a noite estrelada" (4).

This pointing of "o telescópio para a noite estrelada," where there are various nodes in difference, or new identity constellations, if they can be glimpsed, is a gesture that repeats itself in the body of new African fiction. This literature not only tackles the global, in which it cannot avoid being inscribed, it also reinforces the local where it was born and which it cannot and will not avoid seeing and sensing. Rivers, islands, forests, distant villages, mountains, savannahs, *quimbos*, and even ancient cities and their dwellers gain new meanings. Other identity mappings are elaborated in this process, which are moulded "nas margens das representações e através de um movimento que vai das margens para o centro," to quote Boaventura de Sousa Santos (33). In such a projected space, other narratives are born, as I have tried to show. According to Walter Mignolo, such narratives "não são (ou, pelo menos não apenas) nem narrativas revisionistas nem narrativas que pretendam contar uma verdade diferente, mas, sim, narrativas acionadas por uma lógica diferente" (47).

I wanted to walk through one of these spaces where an Other logic is offered to us. I have tried to reread certain stories and open up some maps that Angolan authors have offered to us. By opening its windows and doors, they try to air the house that another culture said or deemed to be hegemonic, both domestically and abroad, tried so hard, and still tries, to seal. Those of us who are foreign people, whose colour was "imposed" on us by the error of Phaethon, and who reside in the south of the south, have embarked on a journey through our own alterity. In many cases, it has been through literary texts being written in this south. In other cases, it is through the act of reading what has been written there. In all cases, we try and answer the question that was asked of us so long ago:

> Que gente será esta? (em si deziam)
> Que costumes, que Lei, que Rei teriam?

Works Cited

Aguessy, Honorat. "Visões e percepções tradicionais." *Introdução à cultura africana.* Ed. Sow, Alpha, *et al.* Lisbon: Edições 70, 1997. 95-136.

Assis Júnior, António de. *O segredo da morta: romance de costumes angolenses.* 2nd ed. Lisbon: Edições 70, 1979.

Battestini, Simon. *Écriture et texte: contribution africaine.* Paris: Les Presses de L'Université Laval, 1997.

Bhabha, Homi. *O local da cultura.* Belo Horizonte: Editora da Universidade Federal de Minas Gerais, 1998.

Camões, Luís Vaz de. *Os Lusíadas.* Porto: Porto, 1980.

Cardoso, Boaventura. *Mãe, materno mar.* Porto: Campo das Letras, 2001.

Carvalho, Ruy Duarte de. *Vou lá visitar pastores: exploração epistolar de um percurso angolano em território cuvale (1992-1997).* Rio de Janeiro: Gryphus, 2000.

Chiziane, Paulina. *O sétimo juramento.* Lisbon: Caminho, 2000.

Kane, Mohamadou. *Roman africain et traditions.* Dakar: Les Nouvelles Éditions Africaines, 1982.

Matta, Joaquim Dias Cordeiro da. *Delírios.* Lisbon: Imprensa Nacional/Casa da Moeda, 2001.

Mignolo, Walter D. *Histórias locais/Projetos globais: colonialidade, saberes subalternos e pensamento liminar.* Belo Horizonte: Editora da Universidade Federal de Minas Gerais, 2003.

Monteiro, Manuel Rui. *Rioseco.* Lisbon: Cotovia, 1997.

Ndaw, Alassane. *La pensée africaine: recherches sur les fondements de la pensée négro-africaine.* Dakar: Les Nouvelles Éditions Africaines, 1983.

Pepetela [Pestana, Arthur]. *As aventuras de Ngunga.* São Paulo: Ática, 1980.

Piglia, Ricardo, and Roberto Bolaño. "Histórias extraordinárias." Supplement Mais! *Folha de São Paulo* (12 September 2004): 4-7.

Rosa, João Guimarães. *Grande sertão: veredas.* São Paulo: Círculo do Livro, n.d.

Santos, Boaventura de Sousa. "Entre Próspero e Caliban: colonialismo, pós-colonialismo e inter-identidade." *Entre ser e estar: raízes, percursos e discursos da identidade.* Ed. Maria Irene

Ramalho and António Sousa Ribeiro. Porto: Afrontamento, 2002. 23-85.

Santos, Boaventura de Sousa, and João Arriscado Nunes. "Introdução: para ampliar o cânone do reconhecimento, da diferença e da igualdade." *Reconhecer para libertar: os caminhos do cosmopolitismo multicultural.* Rio de Janeiro: Civilização Brasileira, 2003.

Vieira, Luandino. *Lourentinho, dona Antónia de Sousa Neto & eu.* Lisbon: Edições 70, 1981.

Laura Cavalcante Padilha is Professor Emerita at the Universidade Federal Fluminense. Among many other works, she is the author of *Entre Voz e Letra* and *Novos Pactos, Outras Ficções.* Email: edufflau@vm.uff.br

Revisitação do *Orientalismo* através da Literatura Angolana

Ana Maria Mão-de-Ferro Martinho

Resumo: Neste texto procuro recuperar o conceito de Orientalismo para a leitura crítica da Literatura Angolana. Partindo da actualidade dos seus pressupostos, seleccionei três autores: José da Silva Maia Ferreira (poeta oitocentista, cultor de uma poesia orientada por modelos convencionais de leitura da identidade), António Jacinto (autor de uma poesia de edificação ideológica anti-colonial) e Ruy Duarte de Carvalho (que nos propõe a revisão da identidade angolana por meio do conhecimento de tradições de resistência cultural activa).

A edição portuguesa de *Orientalismo* em 2004

Este texto foi-nos inspirado pela leitura recente de uma edição portuguesa de *Orientalismo*, nomeadamente o Prefácio do Autor, nela incluído e datado de 2003. Aí, Said interroga-se, com surpresa, sobre a forma como este conceito se mostrou resistente ao tempo, tendo continuado ininterruptamente, desde os anos 70, a inspirar comentários, actualizações e traduções. As razões para este fenómeno estarão certamente na dimensão pan-cultural que facilmente nele se percebe, mas também no modo como a sua associação à própria ideia de Imperialismo mostrou ser de grande eficácia epistemológica.

Por outro lado, a negação de uma justificação ontológica para a ideia de Ocidente e de Oriente veio trazer à leitura do Outro a hipótese desconstrutiva de um dos clichés mais duradouros de sempre. E, de facto, ao ouvirmos o

Portuguese Literary & Cultural Studies 15/16 (2010): 175-82.

modo como os meios de comunicação social fazem o relato das notícias internacionais, percebemos que o critério de leitura das realidades externas é regularmente marcado pelo comentário que é também avaliação da diferença a partir de uma matriz de auto-referência. São por vezes muito imperceptíveis os sinais dessa leitura, mas suficientemente resistentes para merecerem uma leitura crítica e atenta.

"Nós, os Ocidentais," parece ser a medida mais comum para definir o olhar que se adopta sobre o exterior. Curiosamente, quando fazemos com os nossos alunos um exercício de pesquisa sobre a localização do Ocidente, eles são rápidos a associá-lo à Europa e aos Estados Unidos da América, mais indecisos na inclusão de países como o Canadá ou a Austrália, como se construissem pouco a pouco a consciência do Oriente como tudo o que fica para lá de uma dimensão do Mundo lida a partir de uma identidade difusa e de uma diáspora de matriz europeia.

Este é um tópico que se relaciona também com o modo como as identidades colectivas têm sido sucessivamente reinventadas para servir propósitos de modalização civilizacional e como diferentes formas de conflitualidade são geradas por essa dinâmica. Não será talvez possível dizer se esses problemas começam por ser culturais ou políticos, se as guerras de hoje são estrategicamente eficazes na medida em que afectam, por fragmentação, as heranças culturais. Talvez as guerras que na actualidade são justificadas por intervencionismos de raiz moral não sejam mais que a mimetização de uma forma de expansionismo que Said situa na invasão do Egipto por Napoleão. Ou seja, continuam a partir de uma realidade que tem uma componente material efectiva. Como refere este autor, o "Oriente" não é um lugar que existe só na imaginação, ele constitui-se como elemento real da civilização e culturas europeias. A sua adjacência histórica e simbólica em relação à Europa tem levado a que o "Ocidente" se redefina ele próprio como espaço de mobilidade recorrente de significados provisórios, mas estruturalmente dependente de uma matriz civilizacional presa à alegação da sua supremacia.

Revisão e actualização do conceito

O Orientalismo deve ser visto como um discurso que se impôs através diferentes perspectivas, doutrinas académicas e políticas, que fixaram a leitura colectiva de um mundo representado a partir de imagens de dominação e reestruturação tal como o Ocidente as foi concebendo. Durante todo o século XIX, nomeadamente, esta ideia viu-se concretizada através de diferentes projectos de inversão das realidades colonizadas, numa estratégia de criação de modernidade a partir do pressuposto de um vazio civilizacional e de uma desordem intrínseca nas culturas de contacto.

No fundo são três os princípios que consubstanciam esta hipótese: distribuição (da consciência destes princípios em textos de estética, filosofia, história), elaboração (de conjuntos de interesses), vontade e intenção (de compreender para controlar e incorporar, mundos diferentes). Se a modernidade se construiu com base em grandes meta-narrativas, a pós-modernidade há-de traduzir o princípio da incredulidade face a tais textos. E aí pode residir eventualmente um dos argumentos centrais de rejeição das diferentes formas de pré-textualização e pré-interpretação que o Imperialismo, enquanto teoria, impôs ao Colonialismo enquanto prática.

Como Said sugere, será necessário, no sentido de inverter esta realidade, intensificar a prática activa de um discurso racional e secular, bem como criar condições para um Novo Humanismo que não se baseie numa autoridade reconhecida e aclamada.

O texto de T. Serequeberhan: "The critique of Eurocentrism and the practice of African Philosophy"

Para este filósofo, mais do que através da força física, a "Euro-América" domina na actualidade através de uma hegemonia de ideias e de modelos de desenvolvimento de adopção universal. Como ilustração desta tese, Serequeberhan lembra Fanon que, em *Les damnés de la Terre*, chama a atenção dos "Orientais" para a necessidade de abandonarem a "velha" Europa e assumirem a invenção de novas historicidades. Este pressuposto não será suficiente para inverter a situação a não ser que seja antecedido da desconstrução de todo o quadro de especulação metafísica que estrutura e dá fundamento ao Eurocentrismo.

O discurso contemporâneo da filosofia africana há-de então basear-se na libertação primeira desta realidade e na construção sistemática de um discurso que faça a crítica a todos os modelos de pensamento de base kantiana. A associação desta área de estudos àquilo que tem sido a profícua experiência de escrita literária em África, nomeadamente através da revisitação das culturas tradicionais, pode ser a resposta que muitos procuram para a construção de uma textualidade que, decisivamente, rompa com a dependência epistemológica e histórica que o Orientalismo gerou e mantém.

A literatura angolana à luz destas diferentes hipóteses

A questão que colocamos neste ponto é a seguinte: de que forma podemos aplicar as ideias acima expostas à Literatura Angolana? Por que razão pensamos fazer sentido essa aproximação? No contexto das literaturas dos países que passaram pela colonização portuguesa, Angola ocupa um lugar decisivo para interrogação dos limites da experiência imperial. Primeiro, porque foi palco de um intervencionismo de séculos, depois porque marcou ao longo desse tempo a imagem de Portugal no Mundo, ou a imagem que Portugal queria que o resto do Mundo tivesse de si como lugar de progresso e vanguarda. Ícone do regime, cresceu durante todo o século XX como espaço de afirmação utópica do seu ocupante. Serviu múltiplas formas de idealização política e cultural e recebeu e adaptou sucessivos modelos de desenvolvimento. A projecção de Portugal sobre Angola, nomeadamente durante o Estado Novo, é tanto mais relevante quanto a construção da sua própria identidade foi baseada numa forma de leitura "salvífica" que pretendia mobilizar toda a sociedade.

É também Angola o país que mais tem sido mitificado em termos de contactos inter-raciais.[1] A alegação de existência de uma "crioulidade" racial e cultural com génese na cultura portuguesa levada para a África Ocidental, tem marcado, até hoje, uma forte incomodidade nas relações entre os críticos, nomeadamente os literários. Em nosso entender, a ambos os grupos faltam argumentos suficientemente validáveis. Não é verdade que a cultura angolana se reduza a uma imagem de dependência histórica e cultural de Portugal (os Kwanyama teriam muitos motivos para rir se lhes chamassem "lusófonos" ou "crioulos"). Também não é verdade que os fenómenos de contacto não sejam relevantes ao ponto de terem gerado, entre outras consequências culturais, uma literatura escrita em português que reflecte uma das representações mais significativas da cultura angolana, sem que isso a diminua na sua dimensão africana, ou tão-pouco lhe permita reclamar a representação dominante do sentido da angolanidade.

Durante a guerrilha, as elites angolanas procuraram, em grande medida, idealizar uma sociedade em que a dimensão do Outro, pela sua multiplicidade étnica, justificasse uma sociedade multicultural representativa de todas as diferenças e viável em termos de pacificação da sociedade. O essencialismo desta hipótese de leitura da identidade veio a revelar-se insuficiente como resposta à complexidade de um sistema de desigualdade social e participativa.

Para ilustrar alguns dos tópicos acima expostos seleccionámos três escritores angolanos: José da Silva Maia Ferreira, autor do século XIX e ícone de uma sociedade marcada por convenções literárias e culturais de dimensão atlântica; António Jacinto, protagonista do período revolucionário e poeta militante; Ruy Duarte de Carvalho, escritor das transições entre a utopia revolucionária e as heterotopias culturais pós-coloniais.

José da Silva Maia Ferreira

Sendo natural de Angola e tendo publicado o muito lido e comentado volume de poemas *Espontaneidades da Minha Alma—Às Senhoras Africanas*, editado em Luanda em 1849, é o intelectual típico da segunda metade do século XIX em África: poeta, político, funcionário público. A sua poesia tem um traço que merece ser destacado neste contexto: o de ser participante de um paradigma, instituído por toda uma geração de poetas e intelectuais, de dimensão atlântica e enquadrado por convenções literárias típicas do período romântico. O ambiente literário que se vivia em Angola não era muito distinto do dos salões da sociedade brasileira ou portuguesa. Faz sentido, quanto a nós, falar desse período como o de uma realidade geracional mobilizadora de uma identidade colectiva de natureza atlântica, como dizíamos antes, mas sobretudo de classe.

Em que ponto é relevante invocar o Orientalismo como traço de leitura desta realidade? No sentido em que todas as imagens reproduzidas na poesia de Maia Ferreira são marcadas por um olhar do Outro que parece provir de um lugar de dimensão cultural eurocêntrica. Maia Ferreira fala do "Sóba de tribu selvagem," das "Virgens (sem) faces de neve," para amplificar o lado mais exótico da cultura umbundu, nomeadamente. Ao fazê-lo, inscreve nesse processo significados que resultam sempre de comparações com a cultura europeia (tanto por imitação de procedimentos formais como por aposição de conteúdos em que à cultura africana é atribuído o lugar de uma infância estética e moral).

Com profusas dedicatórias, percebemos no texto deste autor a existência de uma rede de relações literárias e culturais que são a confirmação exacta da dimensão estruturante da realidade colonial: como espelho duplicado, Angola revia-se em Portugal e no Brasil e em ambos encontrava afinidades fundamentais. Portugal é a matriz não discutida, o Brasil a representação de um Outro mais próximo pela selecção de traços convencionais da identidade (de um lado o índio, do outro o africano, ambos revelando as mesmas qualidades básicas—ingenuidade, felicidade, beleza intocada, provindo de culturas marcadas pela contingência temporal e às quais faltaria uma dimensão civilizadora).

Dir-se-á que estamos perante traços culturais que são de época, que não poderiam ser outros ao tempo. Para nós o importante não é essa questão: antes a de que, para todos os efeitos, há por detrás da intervenção cultural dos intelectuais angolanos da segunda metade do século XIX um discurso civilizador e um olhar que tende a corrigir uma realidade vista e lida como imperfeita. Este facto é dos mais resistentes, até hoje, em muito do que se escreve e diz sobre África.

António Jacinto

Nascido nos anos 20, António Jacinto é um dos muitos angolanos de ascendência portuguesa que se juntou às forças de resistência em Angola, tendo colaborado com o MPLA e participado na transição para a independência e na actividade política que se lhe seguiu. Do ponto de vista literário, insere-se numa geração responsável pela concretização de um discurso político baseado em estratégias que poderiamos classificar genericamente como meta-narrativas. Ou seja, a partir da construção de uma identidade colectiva, o discurso da resistência e o da libertação prepararam a re-interpretação das culturas angolanas. Os efeitos de pré-textualização, responsáveis pelo revisionismo da resistência à colonização, faziam da utopia angolana uma História de dimensão exemplar e generalizável.

Ao escrever uma poesia com marcas linguísticas importadas do kimbundu, com intensa oralização e reiteração de um léxico relacionado com fenómenos de opressão, Jacinto mimetiza os comportamentos de resistência quotidiana e amplifica os seus significados ideológicos.

No seu famoso poema "Monangamba," por exemplo, assume a voz dos trabalhadores e dos oprimidos e afirma simultaneamente a raça como responsável pela estratificação social. A sua poética é marcada por uma linguagem radical de afirmação da afinidade absoluta entre a literatura, a raça e a acção política: "(...) o meu poema sou eu-branco / montado em mim-preto / a cavalgar pela vida" (135-6).

É no ponto em que estas características se convertem em dados generalizáveis a toda uma geração, e na medida em que essa geração se ocupa em olhar para a cultura angolana como um objecto susceptível de revisão histórica, que voltamos a aproximar-nos do *Orientalismo* de Said. O modo como as elites angolanas organizaram o seu projecto de mudança partiu de um efeito de edificação ideológica que sacrificou a representação das culturas angolanas na sua diversidade para as conduzir a um projecto com estabilidade e homogeneidade ontológica. Nesse sentido, Angola edificou no seu espaço um Oriente e um Ocidente que ainda hoje coexistem.

Ruy Duarte de Carvalho

Ruy Duarte de Carvalho é talvez dos autores angolanos aquele que, de modo mais claro, pode suscitar a discussão das formas de aplicação de um discurso pós-colonial à literatura angolana. Faz parte de uma geração que passou pelo período colonial, pela pós-independência, e manteve-se ligado aos processos de evolução social e política do país até hoje. Correspondendo à diversidade da sua própria formação, os seus textos apresentam uma significativa quantidade de discursos e géneros de notável originalidade. Uma das obras em que culmina esta característica é, nomeadamente, *Vou lá Visitar Pastores*. De natureza epistolar, este texto é um exercício heterotópico que, através de um percurso em terras dos pastores kuvale se apresenta como narrativa de viagens, digressão lírica, estudo antropológico. Partindo do "lugar que são" os kuvale, implica o leitor nas suas narrativas pluralizadas em todas as instâncias da fala e cria a ilusão de representações históricas coerentes na sua descontinuidade.

A aceitação dos caos existenciais, as de-totalizações do espaço reconhecível, permitem sugerir a existência de um discurso da pós-colonialidade, no sentido em que se ligam às narrativas pré-coloniais e as reconstroem por via de uma estratégia de leitura-escrita dos lugares e dos sujeitos em simultâneo. A selecção, para estudo, de uma das nações mais representativas de uma cultura de excepção e sobrevivência, dá também a ver a dimensão resistente dos universos de configuração pré-colonial. Neste sentido, é fácil perceber que estamos perante um exercício ideológico de revisão dos modelos de ocupação e desenvolvimento imperiais, até pela negação de uma linguagem que explicite cronotopias contínuas ou identidades singularizadas.

Esta dimensão colectiva é muito distinta das presentes nos autores que antes referimos. É, aliás, contrária. Não se baseia num Orientalismo de continuidade, tão-pouco em um de substituição, antes inscreve a identidade pós-colonial no centro dos mundos mais antigos, marcados por tradições únicas de resistência cultural.

Nota

[1] Excluímos intencionalmente neste caso Cabo Verde, dado que a sua cultura crioula e mestiça assume contornos excepcionais no contexto colonial português. Não só pela forma como nasceu, sem culturas precedentes às de colonização, mas também por ter tido ocupação colonial sem uma guerra de guerrilha.

Obras Citadas

Duarte de Carvalho, Ruy. *Vou lá Visitar Pastores.* Lisboa: Cotovia, 1999.

Fanon, Frantz. *Les damnés de la Terre.* Paris: Maspero, 1962.

Ferreira, Manuel. *No reino de Caliban.* Lisboa: Seara Nova, 1976.

Jacinto, António. "Monangamba." *No reino de Caliban.* Lisboa: Seara Nova, 1976. 135-6.

Said, Edward W. *Orientalismo.* Trad. Pedro Serra. Lisboa: Cotovia, 2004.

Serequeberhan T. "The critique of Eurocentrism and the practice of African Philosophy." *The African Philosophy Reader.* Ed. P.H. Coetzee e A.P.J. Roux. 2ª ed. New York: Routledge, 2002. 74 ss.

Silva Maia Ferreira, José da. *Espontaneidades da Minha Alma—Às Senhoras Africanas.* [1849]. Luanda: Edições 70, 1980.

Ana Maria Mão-de-Ferro Martinho é Professora do Departamento de Língua, Literatura e Cultura Portuguesas da Universidade Nova de Lisboa; Docente de Literaturas Africanas em Língua Portuguesa, de Literaturas Africanas Comparadas e de Ensino do Português L2/LE; Coordenadora dos Mestrados em Ensino do Português como L2 e LE e em Estudos Africanos; e Co-Coordenadora do Mestrado em Ensino do Português na Universidade Agostinho Neto (Lubango-Angola). Email: ana.martinho@gmail.com

Telling the Nation: The Case of Angolan Literature via History and Geography

Livia Apa

Abstract: The classical concept of "literary history" has instilled in us a notion whereby each individual literature acts as a kind of magnifying glass through which it is possible to view the world in its particular mode of self-representation. Not surprisingly, this "notion" becomes especially interesting in the context of postcolonial literatures, which have a necessary though ambivalent relationship with the tradition but also an urgent need to settle accounts with their own past. This article analyzes the case of post-independence Angolan literature, which bifurcates in two directions: the "historical tendency" and the "geographical tendency." It traces the evolution of both tendencies and how they have contributed to the definition of a national canon.

La parola è in chi resta / nella volgente era [...] / da lui a te e a me [...] in me / miserere —Eugenio de Signoribus, "September," in *Ronda dei conversi,* 2005

An image to guide us: that of a war survivor, or of someone who survived a life marked by violence, and who finally goes home and searches among the rubble for the bell tower of the church, a house, his neighbor's shop, a street—in an effort to recover his personal geography and thereby return to himself. It is a necessary reconnaissance, the reinsertion of himself in a network of familiar objects that can restore his sense of affective roots and, in so doing, his sense of belonging.

Portuguese Literary & Cultural Studies 15/16 (2010): 183-90.

This image contains for me, at a gut level, many of the elements characterizing the specific case of Angola, a context where traumatic violence knows no "after"; there is, rather, an endless "during" that compels artisans of the word to a twofold negotiation (which is also a necessary and inevitable "struggle") between constructing and conserving the memory of an identity rooted in a bygone, negated time.

If it is true that at the origin of every trajectory leading to the creation of national values there is always a momentous act, a break whose violence is relegated to a mythic past, a "primordial wound" that is at the same time the foundation of a "we," an almost hygienic and cathartic experience absolutely necessary for the growth of a collective project, in Angola, because of the unceasing war, those who write must witness and record a kind of "past that doesn't pass," a "before" that can't be reached, an excess of the present, which cannot tell the tragedy since it cannot point to an end that would render it explainable and interpretable. Perhaps the particularity of Angolan literature in general, therefore, is precisely the act of telling through writing, since there is normally no talking in wartime, there are only positions, and the face of the enemy—perhaps all the more so in a fratricidal war—should not and cannot be known, much less interpreted. And yet the literature of Angola is known for being fertile and varied; it is the word that insists on telling so as to ground itself in the immensely confused present.

From the time of the colonial war through national independence and up to 2002, when the hostilities officially ended, the enduring conflict has been the only shared national memory possible, and to write of that memory, of how it influences daily life, is to speak about Angola as an emotive space. To paraphrase Pedro Rosa Mendes, those who write are working on a torn fabric, reconstructing or inventing a linearity in the filigree of the fragments (68). They must situate their writing and their own selves in a context where there is no more network, and where constructing a narrative map is the means for being in contact with all the possible "others" that make Angola what it is. Ruy Duarte de Carvalho, who has meditated long and hard on the relationship between national identity and national literature, asks: "How many 'others,' then, are needed to make a 'we'? And how many points of view, logical arguments and reasons must be woven into the task we must confront and out of which will finally emerge our possibility as a nation?" (*Actas* 221).

During the fight for independence and the national revolution, time and space were still definite terms, such that the war-torn present contained in a certain way the future, and Angola was a country discernible in the distance. But during the years of civil war and the resumption of the conflict, the categories of space and time lost their defining coordinates. Space was lost in the devastation that comes with all wars, and time stagnated in a seemingly endless present, without the limits of past and future. This broke the synthesis between politics and literature that had characterized the emergence of Angola's national literature, and it became difficult to read texts produced in recent years in the light of broad literary movements and trends or even within the narrower confines of a specific genre's development. Each author became, to a certain extent, a unique universe. The shared discourse became individualized, but without ever falling into mannerist autobiography. The feeling of belonging to one's own nation, understood as a "condition to pursue" [condição a perseguir], resorting once more to the words of Ruy Duarte de Carvalho, no longer needed to be demonstrated, but the failure of that feeling to be realized made it necessary to bear witness to the existence of that nation and to tell it in writing. This need to tell, when the maps had been forever annulled by war, gave rise to a common effort to (re)construct the idea of a nation and to reinstate in the void—in the universe of destruction where the nation plays out its role in terms of absence and lack—the memory of a country that in its intimate geography could resist the horror of the destruction. The question that emerged was: "Where are we? What is the common ground that makes the Angolans a nation?" In the case of Angola we can perhaps apply, albeit with caution, the notion of genocide understood as the uprooting of people from their own time and space.[1]

I am not sure if we can define this literature, in its recent manifestations, as one of "reconnaissance," but it is undoubtedly marked by a sense of subtraction from a space, from history, from memory. Or it is as if space, history, and memory had been subtracted. The writing attempts to offer a response, and the postcolonial Angolan space—this "new world"—attempts a possible (impossible insofar as it is utopian?) synthesis of past and present, upon which a future identity can be erected and negotiated. This follows the suggestion of the critic Robert Young, who stresses the need to reflect on the role assumed by all anticolonial thought within the postcolonial context.[2]

The insightful book by Ruy Duarte de Carvalho that has already been cited, *Actas da Maianga*, skillfully guides us through all these issues.[3] In the volume's various essays, which span the most critical moments of contemporary Angolan history, in part following up on an article published in the journal *Lusotopie*, the writer insists on the need to distinguish between political practice and literary practice and to consider the project of a formative national canon as well as the project of the nation itself.[4] Literature thus faces the obvious but complicated task of "telling," as proposed by Homi Bhabha, to achieve the ambitious goal of postcolonial thought—namely, that of escaping the endogenously produced globalized logic that thwarts the functioning of that "new world" just referred to.[5] This naturally opens up a wide range of possible solutions and trajectories (as there also was in the past). The other great merit of Ruy Duarte de Carvalho's book is that it reintroduces a complex notion of identity, even in its formative stage, insofar as it can accommodate the nation's many endogenous cultural differences.

Given these premises of subtraction (which can be considered the guiding concept of this brief study) of the individual from his or her time and space, we can identify two corresponding thematic (i.e., content-based) threads—one "historical" and the other "geographical." Both contribute to the constitution of a canon distinguished by its projective character and by its continual dialogue with the notion of collective memory.

The first "lens" I propose—the historical one—negates (in the specific case of Angola as well as in many other African contexts) the Hegelian notion of Africa as a timeless space. Works about the war for independence, such as Manuel Santos Lima's *As Lágrimas e o Vento* (1975) and Pepetela's *Mayombe* (1978, but written in 1969), represent the attempt to tell history beginning from the moment when "the dreamed future begins"; they try to reset the starting point for when the future will resume. Despite their undeniable differences, both are foundational novels. This new narrative space, especially in the case of Pepetela, is committed to the forging of an identity, and it has the virtue of recording an epic moment, a point after which the authors undertake to reconstruct a historical trajectory, recovering the precolonial period or the period prior to de facto occupation of national territory by the Portuguese. It is almost like picking up the thread of a discourse, passing across five centuries of colonial occupation. *Mayombe* inherits much of its essence from the pre-independence, engagée literature that greatly contributed to the cause of independence, and it aspires to help build and to be recognized within a space of shared identity. Pepetela's subsequent novels, on the other hand, present a past that can include the colonial experience but that may at the same time signify the search for a new direction, a new criterion for building an aesthetic canon, independent from the one imposed by the old colonial relationship.

As in other contexts, African or otherwise, to affirm what was is an act that implies redefining the present. To narrate history also means to traverse a porous terrain that joins a narrative plot to historical research. This is the recipe for much of the literature written by Pepetela, who attempts to respond to the negation of the nation's existence, which colonialism to a large extent represented. This model, which reaches its highest expression in novels such as *Yaka* (1985) and *A Geração da Utopia* (1994), sees literature as an explanation of the nation's internal events, and it will be followed, in successive generations, by writers such as José Eduardo Agualusa, at least in his early phase, in novels such as *A Conjura* (1989) and *A Estação das Chuvas* (1997). The reconstruction undertaken by Agualusa in his first novel is concerned to rebuild and reappropriate Angola's protonationalist movements, in which are woven stories—or rather, *estórias*—whose purpose is to characterize the narrative facts but also to anchor them in a definite geographic space. The case of Agualusa is interesting, because the writing in his subsequent books, which open up to other Portuguese-speaking regions, also seems to open up to the sort of writing that was urgently invoked up until the 1960s—a writing that resorts to *estórias*, a term dear to Luandino Vieira, whose stories about contemporary daily life in specific geographical spaces helped Angolan literature to break with the colonial canon, which had tended to describe those spaces with the colors of a facile exoticism. It was in fact the perfect balance that Luandino, in his fictions, was able to achieve between language and content that brought about that break and the birth of a new world, since language finally becomes the dreamed nation, opening up the way to that contemporary sense of Angola that no longer eludes a precise placement in time and space. Luandino's work is, in a certain way, an implied canon for whoever writes in Angola, as demonstrated by novels such as Ondjaki's *Quantas Madrugadas tem a Noite* (2004).

Literature, like historical research, is a voluntary act from the perspective of the practitioner, and the genesis of Angolan literature—like pre-independence history—is, as it were, decoded for us in its critical moments of rupture, when the interactive relationship it maintains between language and society is laid bare. Interesting contributions in this respect have been made by researchers not strictly connected with the literary domain. As an example, we may cite the Angolan anthropologist António Tomás, who in his considerations about the literature of his country stresses precisely the importance, in terms of identity and rupture, of a literary canon that follows the path forged by Luandino, with the work of writers such as Manuel Rui being mentioned in this connection.[6]

This descriptive capacity, which resorts to a precise linguistic form capable of expressing once more a "we," corresponds to the need of inventing a territory through words, understood yet again as a foundational act, namely that of founding the land, the common *chão* [ground] itself.[7]

Looking through my second, geographical "lens," we find works by authors such as Ruy Duarte de Carvalho and Ana Paula Tavares. Both writers, in my view, respond to the need of renaming, subverting a certain type of canon represented by ethnographic writing. If it is true that the term "ethnography" has two meanings, indicating a particular mode of research as well as the results of that research, thereby guaranteeing in its own duality the transmission of the "knowledge" acquired during field work,[8] the above-mentioned authors pursue an exercise in which geography coincides with a process of renaming in an attempt to restore names to things. The literary project of Ruy Duarte de Carvalho is characterized by an impressive internal coherence and a keen sense of purpose, which is evident even in the titles of his works: *Chão de Oferta* (1972), *Como se o Mundo não tivesse Leste* (1977), *Vou lá Visitar Pastores* (1999), *Observação Directa* (2000), and the very recent *Paisagens Propícias* (2005). His pseudo-ethnography of other Angolas, such as that of the Kuvale people or of the Axilunada (on the Island of Luanda), maps out the loci of the nation,[9] making it possible—through the apparently ethnographic description of their complexity, considered as a moment of alterity—to revisit the very canon of ethnographic writing. Thus divested, from within, of its ideological apparatus, it takes on a different character, overcoming whatever implicit relationship it had with the colonial experience. Perhaps the profound intent of Ruy Duarte's research, of his endeavor to describe so as to name, is to restore voice to the "words" of the people, against the "language" of laws, cancelling their rigid boundaries so as to make the border between ethics and aesthetics porous again. The same concern informs the writing of Ana Paula Tavares. In both her poetry and prose, the fruit of the land, the rituals, and the wisdom of tradition are not stock images or pretexts but the flesh and blood of a relentless project of telling and preserving.

What is needed, then, is to reconstruct the maps and the most intimate geographies, with full awareness of the ongoing negotiation between the individual and the collective. War and blood cannot found a country, but the word that is restored through time and space to its full dimension in memory—as occurs in the poetry of authors such as Arlindo Barbeitos, Maria Alexandre Dáskalos, and José Luís Mendonça, or in the work of the artist Fernando Alvim, as well as the writers I have discussed—is perhaps a personal exercise capable of inventing "we" ourselves.

Notes

[1] The term "genocide" was used at the Angola and São Tomé Bishops' Conference during a visit by Madeleine Albright to Angola in the 1990s.

[2] See his *Postcolonialism. A Very Short Introduction.*

[3] The volume is significantly subtitled "[...dizer da(s) guerra(s) (,) em Angola(?)...]."

[4] See "Sobre a expressão literária angolana."

[5] See "DissemiNation: Time, Narrative, and Margins of the Modern Nation," in *Nation and Narration.*

[6] See his essay "Letteratura angolana: decolonizzazione o ricolonizzazione?"

[7] Ruy Duarte de Carvalho also addressed the issue of language during the launch of his latest book, *As Paisagens Propícias*, in Coimbra, on 28 February 2005.

[8] See Matera, 23.

[9] See my "Aulas de geografia: cartografias, mapas e local da nação. Construção e desconstrução do cânone em Ruy Duarte de Carvalho," in *5 Povos, 5 Nações* (Lisboa: Novo Imbondeiro, 2007), ed. Pires Laranjeira, Lola Geraldes Xavier and Maria João Simões.

Works Cited

Agualusa, José Eduardo. *A Conjura.* Lisbon: Caminho, 1989.

———. *A Estação das Chuvas.* Lisbon: Dom Quixote, 1997.

Barbeitos, Arlindo. *Angola, Angolê, Angolema.* Lisbon: Sá da Costa, 1976.

———. *Na Leveza do Luar Crescente*, Lisbon: Caminho, 1998.

———. *Nzoji.* Lisbon: Sá da Costa, 1979.

Bhabha, Homi. "DissemiNation: Time, Narrative, and Margins of the Modern Nation." *Nation and Narration.* London: Routledge, 1990.

Carvalho, Ruy Duarte de. *Actas da Maianga.* Lisbon: Cotovia, 2003.

———. *Chão de Oferta.* Luanda: n.p., 1972.

———. *Como se o Mundo não Tivesse Leste.* Lisbon: Cotovia, 2003 [1977].

———. *Observação Directa.* Lisbon: Cotovia, 2000.

———. *As Paisagens Propícias.* Lisbon: Cotovia, 2005.

———. "Sobre a Expressão Literária Angolana," *Lusotopie* (2000): 646-51.

———. *Vou lá Visitar Pastores.* Lisbon: Cotovia, 1999.

Dáskalos, Maria Alexandre. *Do Tempo Suspenso.* Lisbon: Caminho, 1998.

———. *Jardim das Delicias.* Luanda: Ler & Escrever, 1991.

———. *Lágrimas e Laranjas.* Lisbon: Caminho, 2001.

Luandino Vieira, José. *A Cidade e a Infância: Contos.* Lisbon: Casa dos Estudantes do Império, [1960].

———. *Duas Histórias de Pequenos Burgueses.* [Luanda: Sá da Bandeira, 1961].

———. *Luuanda.* Belo Horizonte: Eros, 1965.

Matera, Vincenzo. *La scrittura etnografica.* Rome: Meltemi, 2004.

Mendonça, José Luís. *Um Canto para Mussuemba.* Lisbon: INCM, 2002.

Ondjaki. *Quantas Madrugadas Tem a Noite.* Lisbon: Caminho, 2004.

Pepetela. *Mayombe.* Lisbon: Edições 70, 1980.

———. *Yaka.* Lisbon: Dom Quixote, 1985.

———. *A Geração da Utopia.* Lisbon: Dom Quixote, 1994.

Rosa Mendes, Pedro. "Gli uccelli e l'infinita mutezza." *Lo Straniero* [Rome] 44 (Feb. 2004).

Rui, Manuel. *Quem Me Dera Ser Onda.* Luanda: n.p., 1982.

———. *Rioseco.* Lisbon: Cotovia, 1997.

Santos Lima, Manuel. *As Lágrimas e o Vento.* N.p.: n.p., 1975.

Tavares, Ana Paula. *Diz-me Coisas Amargas como Frutos.* Lisbon: Caminho, 1999.

———. *Ex–votos.* Lisbon: Caminho, 2003.

———. *O Lago da Lua.* Lisbon: Caminho, 1998.

———. *Ritos de Passagem.* Luanda: UEA, 1985.

Tomás, António. "Letteratura angolana: decolonizzazione o ricolonizzazione?" *Il colore rosso della jacaranda.* San Marino: Aiep, 2005.

Young, Robert. *Postcolonialism. A Very Short Introduction.* Oxford: Oxford UP, 2003.

Livia Apa teaches Portuguese at the Univerisità degli Studi di Napoli "L'Orientale." Currently, she is writing her doctoral dissertation on the representation of war in Angolan poetry. Email: liviaapa@hotmail.com

A função catártica da memória na actual literatura angolana: *O caso de Botelho de Vasconcelos*

Inocência Mata

Resumo: *Tábua* (2004), o sétimo livro do poeta Adriano Botelho de Vasconcelos, é, tal como o fora o livro *Os Limites da Luz* (2003), de E. Bonavena (aliás, Nelson Pestana), um livro que *evoca* e *provoca*: *evoca* as crises e os afectos destroçados, conseqüência da repressão pós-27 de Maio de 1977; *provoca* pela temática que passa pela ideia de que é preciso falar-se dos *dissensos* para os sanear, na contramão da "doutrina nacionalista" de uniformização totalizante. As duas posturas enunciativas vêem-se na ritualização do luto, na homenagem aos mortos e na expiação da dor que a poesia de ambos os livros actualiza para que, pela exposição das fracturas e das fissuras individuais e segmentais, a purificação colectiva se processe. Eles próprios vítimas de prisão no período do regime monopartidário, é como se os dois poetas se insurgissem contra o muro de frases feitas do discurso da reconciliação. No entanto, essa postura de confrontação com o passado não pressupõe o seu culto, pelo que a nostalgia que daí resulta não é regressiva, mas projectiva, a direccionar ao futuro. Nada há de mais construtivo do que organizar as ruínas do passado, na contramão do anjo de Paul Klee, reinterpretado por Walter Benjamim. Na verdade, as "ruínas" dos poetas—pessoais e pátrias—não se amontoam para se dispersarem a seus pés: os poetas arranja(ra)m-lhes um lugar, para que cada uma funcione no corpo pátrio que se pretende reconstruído e liberto dos *dissensos* de um passado demasiado recente para não provocar angústia pela sua nomeação.

É a perda da memória, e não o seu culto, que fará os homens prisioneiros do passado.
Paolo Portoghesi

Portuguese Literary & Cultural Studies 15/16 (2010): 191-202.

Publicado em 2004, *Tábua*, de Adriano Botelho de Vasconcelos, é, juntamente com *Os Limites da Luz*, de E. Bonavena (aliás, Nelson Pestana), um livro que vem tornando explícita uma tendência na literatura angolana: a da reinvenção do vivido a fim de que ele signifique no tempo da História. Na verdade, esta não é, em rigor, senão em poesia, uma novidade na literatura angolana, na medida em a prosa de ficção vinha ensaiando esta tendência há já algum tempo: pense-se em *Crónica de um Tempo de Silêncio* (1988), de António Fonseca; em *A Geração da Utopia* (1992), de Pepetela; em *O Signo do Fogo* (1992), de Boaventura Cardoso ou ainda em *Maio, Mês de Maria* (1997), do mesmo Boaventura Cardoso; e na recente colectânea de contos de João Tala, *Os Dias e os Tumulto* (2004), distinguida com o Grande Prémio de Ficção da UEA, edição de 2004—só para citar alguns exemplos.

Tábua é o sétimo livro do poeta Adriano Botelho de Vasconcelos, distinguido com o Prémio Sonangol de Literatura, na sua edição de 2003, em *ex-aequo* com outro original de ficção, *A Candidata* (2004), da (até então apenas poetisa) cabo-verdiana Vera Duarte, autora de *Amanhã Amadrugada* (1993) e de *O Arquipélago da Paixão* (2001). Depois de *Voz da Terra* (1974), *Vidas de Só Revoltar* (1975), *Células de Ilusão Armada* (1983), *Emoções* (1988), *Anamnese* (1989) e *Abismos de Silêncio* (1996), Botelho de Vasconcelos surpreende duplamente os seus leitores: em termos técnico-compositivos, com um procedimento formal novo na sua bibliografia e no sistema de que faz parte, actualizado numa inclassificável poemática (serão dezassete poemas em *voltas* ou um só poema que se desenvolve em dezassete andamentos?), de irregular composição estrófica e versificatória, mas que retoma uma forma poética antiga, diria ate clássica, que é a composição em mote e glosa; em termos semântico-pragmáticos, com uma nova temática que passa pela recomposição psicocultural individual e colectiva, após situação de (o)pressão pós-ditatorial e conflito pós-bélico.

Estas obras redimensionam, pela sua intencionalidade, as premissas do projecto literário da construção da Nação, instaurando outras coordenadas como liberdade, responsabilização e cidadania, considerada esta enquanto efectivo exercício de direitos cívicos (e políticos) e desempenho de deveres, o que requer, neste contexto literário pós-colonial, constante questionamento e revisitação crítica do passado.

Transmutações da alma na poesia de Botelho de Vasconcelos

"Os heróis são as memórias das nossas / tragédias" (92)

Disse uma vez o escritor brasileiro Manoel de Barros que não gostava de "palavra costumada" (71)—palavra de efeito previsível, conhecido, consensualmente partilhado; palavra de efeito consensual e não problematizante; palavra que, mesmo que nomeie a realidade, não a interrogue e a invective; enfim, palavra que não produza efeito ético e performativo, isto é, que não leve a acção. Parece que Botelho de Vasconcelos também não. A hesitação do autor entre *Tábua*, título que foi a concurso da Sonangol, em 2003, e *Olímias*, título por que o autor pensara optar para depois abandonar em privilégio do primeiro, revela uma dupla intenção: reter a dor para fazer o luto e, simultaneamente, por esse *gesto de purificação*, enveredar pelo rumo da luz, para o que remete a palavra *olímias*—inventada, diga-se, sendo que, como se verá mais adiante, a sua primeira remissão é para a luz, para a vitória sobre a sombra e o silêncio para o que remete o seu livro anterior, *Abismos de Silêncio*, acima referido.

Esse caminho visa buscar a reconciliação e o apaziguamento pessoal, familiar, social e político, após cerca de três décadas de uma dor contida, devido ao facto de o próprio e alguns de seus irmãos terem sido vítimas da repressão da DISA (a polícia política do regime monopartidário, responsável por torturas e valas comuns após a tentativa de golpe de estado de 27 de Maio de 1977). Não é despiciendo o facto, como já tive a oportunidade de assinalar no prefácio deste artigo, de o autor ter concorrido ao Prémio Sonangol sob o pseudónimo Aires, precisamente o nome de um dos irmãos então mortos, o mais velho. Neste contexto, é muito significativa a opção final pelo título original, *Tábua*, a remeter semanticamente para o continente de um corpo inerte, sem vida—o caixão. No momento em que relia o livro para registar em forma definitiva estas linhas, estava a ler o livro *Não Tenhas Medo de Saber*, da ruandesa Yolande Mukagasana, recentemente lançado em tradução portuguesa. Trata-se de um depoimento testemunhal pungente de quem perdeu a família (marido, três filhos, irmãos, amigos) na louca voragem de ódio entre tutsis e hutus que varreu o seu país, o Ruanda, em 1994. Apesar de a autora afirmar a sua convicção na impunidade dos verdadeiros responsáveis (a França, por exemplo, que, aliás, acusa, explicitamente), este livro—que, segundo notícias, será filme—não é de silêncios contidos: "Os heróis são o que os nossos olhos escondem / dos túmulos" (91) ou "Os heróis são as memórias das nossas / tragédias" (92)—diz-nos o poeta Botelho de Vasconcelos, estabelecendo interlocução com Yolande Mukagasana e com os seus confrades Boaventura Cardoso, o de *Maio, Mês de Maria* (romance publicado em 1997, significativamente 20 anos depois dos eventos que se seguiram a esse fatídico 27 de Maio de 1977, que ficaram silenciados no discurso oficial, mas não—vê-se na escrita dos escritores—na memória histórica dos angolanos e que Botelho de Vasconcelos transpõe agora para a *fala*!) e com Bonavena, o de *Os Limites da Luz* (2003).

Oiçamos Bonavena, que, evocando os seus amigos Kimpwanza e Wadalika, conclui: "Apenas me legaram / este dever de memória" (24). Antes, pelo contrário, trata-se, o livro de Yolande Mukagasana, de uma homenagem à Paz (nem é despiciendo o facto de a sua autora ter sido agraciada com a Menção Honrosa do Prémio UNESCO de Educação para a Paz, na sua edição de 2003). Por seu turno, pelo elogio da vida, apesar da dor, que este livro de Adriano Botelho de Vasconcelos faz, parece-me que ele se aproxima, salvaguardadas as diferenças de intenção e genológicas, do de Yolande Mukagasana e de E. Bonavena. A reconciliação com o Mundo—isto é, com a pátria e o "eu"—começa a desenhar-se com o reencontro com a dor, com a ritualização do luto, que é necessário fazer-se para que a purificação se processe, pela exposição das fracturas e das fissuras individuais:"*O luto leva os velhos a apagarem* os silêncios que foram úteis para que a palavra não tivesse outras ousadias" (64) e pátrias: "Encontrei o meu morto vou dar-lhe banho com as pátrias e pétalas do meu quintal." (82)

O que *Tábua* propõe é uma discussão sobre as feridas dos anos da guerra—guerra de todos os tipos: também aquela que tem um contendor identificado internamente, que resulta da repressão, por discordâncias político-ideológicas e até culturais, como essa de que terão sido vítimas os entes queridos dos escritores em diálogo, os chamados *fraccionistas*. *Tábua* significa, assim, na contramão do que tem vindo a ser ideia comum para a reconciliação e o encontro com a Pátria. E essa ideia, supostamente apaziguadora, alia a reconciliação pós-bélica, ou pós-ditatorial, à necessidade de perdão e de esquecimento, porque se tem a presunção de que a sociedade se pacifica pelo silenciamento dos horrores, físicos ou psicológicos. E é aqui que ambos, a ruandesa e o angolano (ou melhor, os angolanos citados), dialogam com o arquitecto italiano Paolo Portoghesi, que resgato da epígrafe, para quem é a perda da memória, e não o seu culto, que fará os homens prisioneiros do passado. É neste contexto de desvelamento dos lugares comuns oficiais que significa o seguinte mote: "*Quem faz o discurso para os heróis precisa* de muitos vazios onde Deus não tenha espaçopara recordar que toda a linha e esquadroé o que o homem não pode fazerde si próprio" (88).

Muito mais adiante, a meio da caminhada catártica, o sujeito enunciador dirá, de forma sentenciosa: "Às vezes não se sabe que a cabeça é a montanha de uma insónia, uma força distante do corpo que chama os criminosos pelos seus nomes numa ferida por onde circulam já bêbados os homens" (54).

"Porquê que se vê através do poema / o modelo da terra?" (90):

Nem, de outra parte, deve ter sido por acaso que me lembrei de Manoel de Barros—e precisamente de *Livro sobre Nada*, é que, tal como este, *Tábua* também não me parece ser um livro comum: nem pelo género (será poesia em prosa? Prosa poética?), nem pela mancha gráfica, pelas linhas impressas (versos?), pelas imagens, enfim, pela sequência de pensamentos apresentados em fragmentos. Outrossim, a "instintiva" associação ao livro de Manoel de Barros também me surgiu da recepção desta colectânea como resultado de um exercício metapoético, como se a palavra pudesse conter o âmago do Mundo, como neste excerto: "Em cada boca existe a delicada palavra que vem de um nó que foi parte da confusão dos deuses e pode parecer uma nave que cintila no próprio fogo" (43) e "*Em cada boca que recita a palavra* em pele se sublinha o poder da manhã" (78).

Estas são palavras editadas no poema-mote e que se reeditam, em amplificação, no poema-glosa—como nos outros trinta e quatro poemas da colectânea. De facto, parece existir uma filosofia de contaminação clássica neste procedimento de construção estrófica adoptado pelo poeta, em que recorre a uma ideia-base, ora sentenciosa ora proverbial, marcada graficamente em negrito, para, na(s) estrofe(s) seguinte(s), se amplificar a ideia em intermediações metafóricas e alegóricas.

Desde o Formalismo russo que sabemos que uma das funções construtivas do literário é o estranhamento, isto é, a *desfamiliarização*. É por essa função que uma obra literária entra em correlação com os outros elementos do sistema (autoral e literário) e significa na sua originalidade. E o estranhamento que este novo livro de Botelho de Vasconcelos suscita começa pelo duplo título: "Tábua" e "Olímias."[1] Ao título, *Tábua*, por causa da sua dimensão tão visceralmente pungente, o autor tem dado melhor explicação e significação, designadamente na entrevista que acompanha, em publicação anexa, o livro de poemas (Cristóvão s.p.).

Mas porquê "Olímias"?, perguntei eu ao poeta. Por nada: simples exercício lúdico a partir de um antropónimo—Límia—a que, num jogo sonoro, o poeta recorreu à derivação prefixal, com flexão do plural, dando origem à palavra "Olímias," que remete, em termos de associação fónica, a luz, luminosidade, aurora... E os poemas deste livro, diferentemente dessoutros de *Abismos de Silêncio*, são lunares e, até, solares. Isto é, poemas que convocam à Luz—que é, de facto, a palavra que percorre este texto, tanto em termos quantitativos quanto em termos isotópicos (que formam campos semânticos afins), considerando os trinta e cinco poemas como um só texto que desenvolve um movimento de pura revitalização psicossocial e afectiva—individual e colectiva: "A sanzala regressou sem poder contaras ausências. É como se tivéssemos medo de reconhecer a falta dos jovens. O fundo do espelhodo lago é o que advinha na alma a distância entre a vida e o monstro" (93).

"Uma utopia na corrente de um panfleto" (92)

Todo o (macro)poema é um percurso de subjugação, pela Luz, da Noite—e todas as remissões semânticas que sugestionam a ambiência nocturna (guerra, repressão, morte, caos, sofrimento, tristeza, desagregação identitária, fragmentação psicossocial, miséria de corpo e de espírito). Esta poesia aponta, assim, para uma reconstrução, uma desfribilação em relação aos anos da repressão e da guerra e seus corolários, como seja a fragmentação sociocultural de que o livro anterior, *Abismos de Silêncio*, dá testemunho. Aqui, neste livro, *Tábua*, há sinais de outro universo bem diferente, com lexemas e expressões recorrentes que apontam para campos semânticos menos elegíacos e mais *cosmogonizantes*, como em: "Uma mão pode fazer a duração do sonho se tiver no seu barro o que se pode adiantar como preço dos erros de Deus quando o trigo não fazia ainda sorrir a terra e separe do seu húmus os mortos que fazem ouvir as queixas" (41).

Um deus que também erra, luz, fogo, mão, trigo, terra, barro, húmus, mortos que (já) podem "falar," numa insistência na imagética revitalizante e de reconversão do desencanto e do desfazer das incertezas. Aliás, os elementos primordiais—Luz (Ar), Fogo, Terra, Água nas suas versões metonímicas—são o *leitmotiv* deste "relato da revitalização"—qual, antes, "relato de nação"—em inúmeros poemas, como, por exemplo, neste "Oh! luz que foi descansar na lagoa para fazer o espelho" ou essoutro "Oh! luz que veio por detrás do teu corpo como," entre muitos outros... O poema também labora, no seu percurso de significação, contra o monolitismo ideológico e identitário da utopia que se constituiu sob imperativos nacionalistas e, por urgência performativa, se fez panfletária, com palavras desempregadas de tertúlias e poetas sem cais—e assim vigorou durante o período de consolidação da nacionalidade política: "Na catedral as gaivotas fizeram durar os mares até as pátrias ficarem sob o domínio de uma única razão. Perdido o seu tesouro—uma utopia na corrente de um panfleto—os velhos tentam fugir das confissões até as suas palavras desempregarem nas tertúlias e cais os poetas" (92).

"Toda a existência / é uma tentativa de réguas" (94)

A revitalização individual e colectiva acima referida solapa o movimento do reconhecimento das perdas e da fragmentação psicossocial, afectiva e espiritual e tem alicerces no processo de recuperação psicossocial e de reconciliação da comunidade. A retórica da reconciliação sobrepõe-se, doravante, à do silêncio que vigorou, a fim de que se altere a "senha" da oficialidade: "As frases ficaram simples para que através de uma senha se entenda como fomos hábeis em usar das cobrasas sombras até para nas gavetas anularmos o nome dos irmãos" (94).

É como se poeta se insurgisse contra o muro de frases feitas do discurso da reconciliação. No entanto, essa postura de confrontação com o passado não pressupõe o seu culto (como, aliás, "desaconselha" Portoghesi), pelo que a nostalgia que daqui resulta não é regressiva, mas projectiva, a direccionar ao futuro. Nada há de mais construtivo do que organizar as ruínas do passado, na contramão do anjo de Paul Klee, reinterpretado por Walter Benjamim. Nas verdade, as "ruínas" do poeta—pessoais, afectivas, ideológicas, pátrias—não se amontoam para se dispersarem a seus pés: o poeta arranja-lhes um *lugar* e um *sentido*, qual "velho Kinga [que] entrega à velha Ngonga o osso dos espíritos" (52), para que cada uma (ruína, segundo Klee, ou osso, segundo o Velho Kinga) funcione no corpo reconstituído do passado: "Recomece então a nova identidade como a única estreia do mundo e prova-o um barco que estique a sua vela para que se abra o mar. Tantos têm sido os caminhos à procura de um lugar para o corpo" (53).

"No húmus a mais longa perda / do nome faz a defesa do epitáfio" (95)

Com a fala do enunciante—também ele actor, pois refere, logo no início, e por duas vezes, a sua condição discipular nesse processo de aprendizagem e de reconciliação com o Mundo—a ganhar uma conotação projectiva, aqui começa novo trecho nesse percurso de *humuficação* do solo da memória, que já começara com a convocação da afectividade familiar. Na verdade, já a meio do percurso, entre o poema-mote "Ó, meus sangues! Não foram as minhas vidas" e a poema-glosa correspondente, "Esse é o sabre que empunho diante de ti," os pilares da identidade psicossocial, individual e comunitária, começam a emergir, com a nomeação da família, afinal seguro porto de afectos. E será por ela, a família, que vão entreabrir-se os postigos e se erigir "a catedral das ideias," onde se refaz o bálsamo da memória. É que esse processo de rememoração funciona como bálsamo: "a memória das pessoas"—ensina-nos Ecléa Bosi—"também depende desse longo e amplo processo pelo qual sempre *fica* o que *significa*" (32). Esse húmus, que é a radicação afectiva, toma forma na explicitude fistular—no sentido cirúrgico do termo, em que fístula se pensa canal com finalidade terapêutica (outro sentido deste termo no texto, ao lado do seu significado como marca ou ferida moral e psicológica). Diz o enunciador, explicitamente: "Foi através da luz que refiz os signos para que as palavras que nos guiam através das fístulas e feiras mantenham as partes finais que celebram nos cristaiso sono que se descobre nas salivas das cobras" (44).

Intermezzo... Que fazer com esta dor?

Depois... o percurso se nos baralha: o poeta parece regredir na dor, tão crespuscular se torna a semântica do universo poético. Entre "O corpo [que] ficou entre as lianas repetindo / em seus erros a dor que a outros fez durar" (96) e a vergonha que nos está próxima do coração—o mote do poema seguinte (97)—o poeta volta à interioridade (pessoal e colectiva) do sofrimento e busca a voz dos mortos. Mas talvez seja, apenas, um regresso purgativo. Porventura mais dionisíaco que elegíaco, como se fosse uma pausa para a recomposição final, uma libertação orgíaca da memória e uma catarse da dor: "Os mortos de outras guerras mais antigas estavam tontos nas poças de vinho." (98)

Do sal das lágrimas à flor na Primavera

"Kanjala com o seu tempo perfeito depois / de muitas fogueiras" (124). Porque a seguir o movimento final se anuncia de reconciliação: trata-se, na verdade, de um tempo de generosidade, por que o cidadão também pugna ao afirmar, em entrevista já aqui citada: "Curemos os nossos enganos lavando os pés dos outros"! Há a proposta da reconciliação por via do luto, do desmascaramento pela palavra, pelo apelo à confissão e à contrição, pela evocação dos mortos (Joana, Ximinha, Aires)—e neste terreno Bonavena é muito mais explícito no inventário dos *seus* mortos—pela citação de mortos, enfim, pelo apelo à "denúncia das verdades" como caminho para a pacificação social e para a utopia de uma sociedade reconstruída, de que Kanjala, no texto de Botelho de Vasconcelos, é representação. A metáfora da queimada para deixar visíveis as causas (108) é bem representativa: as sombras da História desfazem-se; o Kwanza (que, em 1977, terá "acolhido" o corpo de Aires, o irmão morto) ganha outras funções, mais sublimes, que já não passam pelo encobrimento dos crimes: "apanhar a intimidade / da pátria" (116); a terra terá outra ordem: "Que chegue agora o silêncio—para que a terra tenha outra ordem: a lua mais perto do mar" (117).

A associação corpo / morte que se fazia em segmentos anteriores deste relato tem agora novas conotações, mais genesíacas, mais prospectivas: "Teu corpo dança nos anéisda música que só pode ser entendida no meioespesso e lento do meu esperma" (110). O amor substitui as sombras e as lágrimas de dor (elas são agora de amor) e se dispõem à geração, à generosidade. É amor sereno, que sobrevém a um cansaço, cuja imagem, porventura menos sublime e mais terrena e orgástica, se retém dos seguintes versos:

> quando tu sentes que falo contigo
> com uma força de ancas
> e unhas? Ó, Deus, como o amor a si próprio
> se entrega ao cansaço que faz e, no entanto,
> parecer ser outro e em nunca vivido no momento
> das humidades que untam de luas
> os teus braços poisados nas minhas
> nádegas. (122)

E o sujeito até propõe a transmudação do objecto de culto: "O poema deveria desfazer o meu nó numa estrofeque troque o meu epitáfio pelas flores" (120). (Não disse o russo Alexandre Potebnia, 1835-1891, que "não existe arte e particularmente poesia sem imagem?" (39)—postulação que tão bem "serviu" o programa simbolista, mesmo se depois se tenha chegado ao consenso de que a imagem, tal como outros recursos ditos literários, não são exclusivos da linguagem cuja função dominante é a estética?). Seja como for, a esta imagem de positividade está associada Kanjala, metáfora do milagre da Paz: Kanjala, uma vila do Sul de Angola, muito sacrificada durante a guerra civil (por ambos os contendores armados), é hoje um milagre da cicatrização das feridas da guerra, com suas extensas plantações de milho.

> Kanjala de barro que completa o que Deus deixara
> por fazer pela divisão do pão, todo o tema da vida procura o ouro numa ponta de milho.
> (...)
> Kanjala com o seu tempo perfeito depois
> de muitas fogueiras. Um milheiral levanta a terra numa mesa
> acesa que ocupa o horizonte. E primeiro levantas as dúvidas
> que feriram a inocência e depois preferes que destes braços
> se faça o cálice da utopia. (123-4)

O caos está definitivamente organizado nesta última paragem, numa relação comunicante com os elementos naturais, culturais e espirituais do Mundo. Porém, não sem antes se proceder ao desvelamento da "última" verdade, um dos aspectos mais perversos da ideologia: "Olhavas para os homens com um coração incapaz de aceitar como uma lavra pode salvar um País que decidiu pelas ideologias escolher os seus melhores filhos" (124).

É o elogio da diferença e do pluralismo; é a invectivação da intolerância que levou à repressão e à perseguição e aniquilamento dos *diferentes*. Um dos aspectos mais perversos, porém também um dos mais geradores da nova utopia, pois como aqueloutra seminal, a utopia revolucionária, esta nova utopia se constrói de palavras: "A palavra atravessa toda a ilusão como se cumprisse uma missão. Podemos apresentar-nos como vítimas das suas tábuas onde Deus acabara de jurar o repouso das manhãs" (125).

A utopia agora também através do verbo. Como antes Pepetela, que, a propósito de *A Geração da Utopia*, afirmara que a escrita seria realmente a sua última utopia... como sempre fora, aliás, acrescenta o romancista (3). Também desta feita, o poeta olhando para a memória não de modo ingénuo e sob punções teleológicas:

A cicatriz é delicada
como se tivéssemos que olhar para a memória
com uma outra escolha e astúcia.
(...)
Por isso as palavras vão compondo
numa só estrofe o que a vida mesmo atenta não pode
consagrar. (126)

Doravante, há condições para todas as celebrações, uma vez que, feita a catarse, com projecção futura, é possível escrever o poema "como uma possibilidade do amor": "Celebras tudo até a memória dos nossos dias ficar como fitas de um poema que tinhas escrito como uma possibilidade do amor" (128).

Como uma "lei" da vida, cria-se a disposição para o regresso temporário à dor. Mas contra isso, nada se pode fazer: é a marca da Vida vivida na marcha inexorável do tempo: "Todo o minuto só existe saturado por insinuação das nossas dúvidas e regressos temporários à morgue" (129). Tal como é inevitável que o poeta, pela sua flauta—não deveria ser kissanje?—continue a oferecer sonhos aos outros: "Um poeta toca a flauta da tua tarde de esperas à janela como se pedisses numa agonia que te oferecesse um gesto" (130).

Pela recepção, pela *intelligentzia*, ora reveladora de constrangimentos ora silenciosa, que obras deste teor causam na sociedade angolana (e refiro-me a *A Geração da Utopia* e a *Maio, Mês de Maria*, respectivamente), pode dizer-se que a palavra ajudará, mais uma vez, na reconstrução do corpo fracturado da nação, agora devido a conflitos internos—como antes a palavra literária fora um dos seus mais importantes artífices, pela pena dos poetas-políticos. Hoje, pela palavra—criativa e reflexiva—a nação busca agenciar as ruínas e prosseguir ainda no caminho da utopia, agora não apenas da nação, mas da pátria (que solapa, pela sua significação, a "comunidade imaginada") e da cidadania, categoria até então inexistente na configuração do *local* da cultura e da nação. Na verdade, e como acima ficou dito, a cidadania requer outros ingredientes que não se compadecem com a intenção exclusivamente celebrativa, pois, sendo de teor legalista (apesar de este ser concomitante de qualquer nação, como nos ensina Anthony Smith [147]), pressupõe uma participação e transporta outras implicações que não são necessariamente uniformizantes e centrípetas, embora ainda de unidade, implicações conducentes à construção de uma sociedade livre, justa e aprazível de se viver.

Não são estas, afinal, as coordenadas dos programas máximos dos movimentos de libertação?

Nota

[1] Quando o original deste livro me chegou às mãos para prefácio, ainda tinha como título "Olímias."

Obras Citadas

Barros, Manoel de. "Não gosto de palavra costumada." *Livro sobre Nada*. Rio de Janeiro: Editora Record, 1997.

Bonavena, E. *Os Limites da Luz*. Lisboa: Imprensa Nacional-Casa da Moeda, 2003.

Bosi, Ecléa. *Memória e Sociedade: Lembranças de Velhos*. São Paulo: T.A. Queiroz, 1979.

Cristóvão, Aguinaldo. "Vasconcelos: onde exista uma injustiça social estará sempre presente a pena dos poetas." *Discursos & Entrevistas & Ensaio*. ABV: Gráfica EAL Inserto do livro *Tábua*.

Mukagasana, Yolande. *Não Tenhas Medo de Saber*. Lisboa: Coimbra, Diocese de Coimbra, 2003.

Pepetela. "A escrita é a minha utopia." *Diário de Notícias* 9 de Agosto de 1992, ed. de Lisboa: 3.

Portoghesi, Paolo. *After Modern Architecture*. New York: Rizzoli Internat, 1982.Potebnia, Alexandre. "Notas sobre a teoria Literária." "A arte como procedimento." Vítor Chklovski. *Teoria da Literatura: Formalistas Russos*. Porto Alegre: Editora Globo, 1976.

Smith, Anthony D. *A Identidade Nacional*. Lisboa: Gradiva, 1997.

Vasconcelos, Adriano Botelho de. *Tábua*, Luanda: UEA, 2004.

Inocência Mata é professora de Literaturas Africanas, Literaturas Pós-coloniais Comparadas e Língua e Interculturalidade na Faculdade de Letras da Universidade de Lisboa. É autora de vários livros, entre os quais *Diálogo com as Ilhas: sobre Cultura e Literatura de São Tomé e Príncipe* (1998), *Literatura Angolana: Silêncios e Falas de uma Voz Inquieta* (Lisboa/Luanda, 2001) e *A Suave Pátria: Reflexões Político-culturais sobre a Sociedade São-tomense* (2004). Email: imata@netcabo.pt

The Renaissance of Angolan Cinema[1]

Fernando Arenas

Abstract: This article offers a critical review of recent Angolan films that together constitute a renaissance of cinema in Angola, thanks to the normalization that has been made possible during the post-war years. The films *The Hero* by Zézé Gamboa (2004) and *Hollow City* by Maria João Ganga (2004) are discussed within the context of the emergence of cinema in Angola, which is indissociable from the larger historical and political context since independence.

The history of Angolan cinema is closely intertwined with the political and historical scenario that involved the liberation war between 1961-75 and the civil war between 1975-2002. At the time of independence, the Portuguese left virtually no film infrastructure behind or trained technicians in their African territories. The fascist-colonialist authorities limited film output to monthly propaganda newsreels.[2] In contrast, according to Diawara (1992), the British and Belgians left production facilities in Ghana, Nigeria, and the Belgian Congo, and even trained African technicians. Thus, "national cinemas" in the case of Angola as well as Mozambique had to be built up as an integral part of the armed struggle and independence movements of the 1960s and 70s, involving initiatives by, and collaborative efforts with, foreign film directors and producers. While the reigning economic, material, and geopolitical conditions at the time of birth and subsequent development of

Portuguese Literary & Cultural Studies 15/16 (2010): 203-14.

cinema in the former Portuguese colonies were much more precarious than in the rest of Africa, the experience of armed struggle that marked the origins of cinema in Angola and Mozambique differentiates it even more dramatically from the cinema produced in other African countries in their early years of independence. Hence, the lack of training in filmmaking and infrastructure, on the one hand, and the cohesion and unity of purpose within the MPLA in Angola and FRELIMO in Mozambique, on the other hand, inspired a wave of international solidarity such that filmmakers and activists from France, Sweden, Yugoslavia, Cuba, the US, and other countries aided in the production of numerous films (mostly documentaries). They committed their talent and resources to the liberation movements' emancipatory vision, aiding in an ideologically complex strategy: the use of film as a tool or even as a strategic weapon in order to document, educate, and disseminate information about the war, making it possible to educate the African public about their own historical condition and, at the same time, informing the international community about the anti-colonial wars in Africa.[3]

The most important fiction film to emerge during the liberation war period was *Sambizanga* (1972) by director Sarah Maldoror of Guadeloupe, based on the classic 1961 novel by Angolan writer José Luandino Vieira, *A vida verdadeira de Domingos Xavier* [*The Real Life of Domingos Xavier*].[4] Both the novel and film document the first years of the struggle for independence in Angola through the story of Domingos and his family, highlighting, among other things, the tenacity of Domingo's commitment to the nascent liberation fight. The film, however, expands on Luandino's novel by stressing the politicization of women within the liberation movement through the special attention given to Maria (Domingo's wife) and her unflinching devotion to husband and family and, by extension, to the collective struggle. *Sambizanga* was made under the auspices of the MPLA in exile and the government of Congo-Brazzaville (it was filmed entirely in the Congo), with French subsidies. Critics across the board consider it one of most outstanding films of the early era of black African cinema due to its political potency, wide humanistic appeal, and artistic strengths. It is also remarkable for a relatively early African film to privilege the representation of women's experience in the struggle for national liberation from the perspective of a female director. *Sambizanga* is seldom seen even though it is revered in the context of African film history and criticism, and even more particularly so in Angola. Unfortunately, in spite of its historical importance and aesthetic merits, *Sambizanga* has not yet been released on video or DVD, even though New Yorker Films holds the rights for its distribution and exhibition in the Anglophone world.[5]

Once in power, the MPLA committed resources to film production at the service of a national cause oriented ideologically by a Marxist-nationalist ethic. Hence, dozens of documentaries for internal consumption were commissioned featuring the daily lives and colonial experiences of various types of workers in different regions throughout Angola or heroic accounts of the liberation struggles. Two film directors stand out during this period: visual artist António Ole and poet/anthropologist Ruy Duarte de Carvalho. While both directors initially made documentaries, they gradually moved beyond the mere depiction of events to a more stylized filmic production that evinces heightened aesthetic consciousness and poetic sensibility. While Ole focused on Angolan popular culture, Ruy Duarte de Carvalho problematized the relationship between history, culture, and the nation.[6] Sadly, due to the impending pressures of an escalating civil war, film production in Angola collapsed into a state of stagnation around 1982.

The year 2004, however, was marked by the renaissance of Angolan cinema with three films released: *O herói* [*The Hero*] by Zezé Gamboa, *A cidade vazia* [*Hollow City*] by Maria João Ganga, and *O comboio da Canhoca* [*The Canhoca Train*] by Orlando Fortunato.[7] All of them took between ten and fifteen years to be completed and they are a testament to the unflinching perseverance on the part of film directors working against overwhelming obstacles. Since the war ended in 2002, the Angolan Ministry of Culture and the reactivated Angolan Film and Multimedia Institute have modestly funded film production, small scale amateur and professional video and film festivals, as well as film exhibition throughout the country. Both *The Hero* and *Hollow City* focus on the topic of the civil war and its survivors struggling to refashion a tenuous existence in the frightening yet fascinating metropolis of Luanda. While *The Hero* takes place after the war, *Hollow City* situates its story during the conflict. In both cases, the utopian time of Marxist-nationalist independence is over and the people of Angola are confronted with the tragic legacy of war in a nation-state that nearly imploded. As the protagonist of *The Hero* says, "the war destroyed our country and the dreams of our entire generation."

Angolan filmmaker Zezé Gamboa is based in Lisbon but most of his films focus on Angolan reality. He received his early training while working for Angolan national television in 1974, where he directed newscasts until 1980.

After studying film sound engineering in France, he made several documentaries in the 1990s.[8] Documentary filming constituted his training ground before making his first feature film, *The Hero*, which according to Gamboa was inspired by a Reuters photograph of a wounded Angolan war veteran who was homeless. The film took ten years to be made, partly due to the war that raged until 2002 and partly due to the difficulty in securing funding for the picture. *The Hero* involved a multinational crew and cast featuring Senegalese actor Oumar Makena Diop as the title character (dubbed into Portuguese), the celebrated Brazilian actors Maria Ceiça and Neuza Borges (who, as Afro-Brazilians, are increasingly cast together with Zezé Motta in Lusophone African films, while they struggle to switch from their Brazilian accents to the Angolan or Cape Verdean ways of speaking Portuguese), in addition to numerous Angolan actors, including Milton Coelho, who plays the boy Manu. *The Hero* won the Sundance Film Festival Prize for World Cinema and had the honor of opening the 34th New Directors/New Films series in New York in 2005.

The Hero opens and closes with superb aerial shots of the city of Luanda featuring an urban geography that is saturated with shantytowns (or *musseques)* while dotted with small pockets of middle- and upper-class wealth. The early sequential shots provide the viewer with a spatial sense of the dramatic socio-economic chasm that pervades throughout the film where the various social classes intersect. *The Hero* is a multi-layered film that portrays the myriad social spheres affected by the catastrophic effects of war through its three primary characters, whose lives crisscross to a greater or lesser degree amid the cruel and violent, but also exuberant and even hospitable, urban chaos of Luanda. These characters are: Vitório, the homeless war veteran whose prosthetic leg is stolen; Maria Barbara, the bar girl who has lost her twelve-year-old son to the war; and Manu, the mischievous orphaned schoolboy who lives with his grandmother. Vitório and Maria Barbara could be long lost spouses and Manu their son, but they are not. Yet they must all forge bonds of solidarity and create new forms of sociability and ethical responsibility in order to rebuild their lives after surviving the seemingly endless cycle of war in Angola. *The Hero* can be characterized as a contemporary Angolan parable, punctuated by deep-seated tragedy, cruel irony, social criticism, along with moments of humor, tenderness, and hope. The pivotal action in the narrative that unleashes the dramatic sequence of events in this film is the tragic irony of a gang of shantytown boys stealing Vitório's prosthetic leg and war medal to be sold on the black market. In his review of *The Hero,* Rodrigo Brandão interestingly describes the junkyard where Vitório's prosthetic leg and war medal end up as a "site for trade and negotiation" that is emblematic of Gamboa's articulation of the project of postwar Angolan society, where "rebuilding the whole (…) involves uncovering, reassessing and reincorporating used (i.e. historical) parts" ("Bringing It All Home"). While such articulation entails the possibility of reconciling a fractured (or amputated) society, as occurs idealistically in *The Hero,* the junkyard can (and must) also be read as emblematic of an economy—driven by the predatory greed of the Angolan elites and foreign allies—that permeates to a degree the social interactions among the majority poor (as witnessed by the actions of the young shantytown bullies) and that also, above all, forces them to trade in "scraps" and "residues" in the black market in order to creatively survive.

While the main plot of this movie as well as the subplots are all fictional, they could easily have been extracted from the same real-life experience as the Reuters photo that inspired Zezé Gamboa to make this movie in the first place. In fact, in one of *The Hero*'s most poignant sequences, the reality of postwar Angola invades the actual filming, as Gamboa points out in interviews. The crew of *The Hero* stumbled upon an outdoor film session of the Angolan TV public service program called *Ponto de Reencontro* [*Reconnection Point*], where hundreds of men, women, and children stand in line waiting for their turn to make a plea on air in search of relatives who have disappeared during the war, in some cases, for many years. Gamboa asked the producers of this program whether one of his actors (Maria Ceiça—the Maria Barbara character) could also stand in line and make her plea in search of her twelve-year-old son, to be subsequently incorporated into the *The Hero* screenplay. This request was readily granted, adding a significant amount of texture to the film, where fiction intersects with reality.

The experience of civil war is a central point of reference in order to understand postcolonial Angola and Mozambique and this reality is vividly reflected in the films made by Zezé Gamboa, Maria João Ganga, and Brazilian-Mozambican director Licínio Azevedo.[9] In the Angolan case, the war contributed to a siege mentality that led to obstacles in the development of a truly democratic political culture in spite of the multiparty system in place since the early 1990s. Furthermore, the effects of a war that was largely fueled, especially during its final years, by the wealth produced through oil and diamond exports fostered a culture of corruption, where lack of government accountability and transparency was and continues to be an Angolan trademark.[10] In spite of the multibillion-dollar oil boom experienced by Angola in the mid- to late 2000s, there are still huge socio-economic gaps,[11] an outrageously high cost of living, dismal basic services for the majority of the population (particularly for shantytown or *musseque* dwellers), reflected in the lack of an adequate water supply and sanitation, wretched living conditions, and a vastly deficient health system, which in addition to government incompetence and inefficiency have facilitated the massive spread of preventable diseases.[12] Gamboa's *The Hero* aims to expose the lack of responsibility on the part of the Angolan government in addressing urgent social issues. There is an important narrative sequence that functions as a meta-commentary regarding the film's main problematic: the plight of war veterans. Manu's schoolteacher, a sensitive upper-class *mestiça* who stumbles upon Vitório in the hospital, is moved by his situation, while seeming to be fascinated by him. She convinces her upper-class *mestiço* boyfriend, who has just arrived from graduate school in the US and is guaranteed a job at the Ministry of Interior, to help Vitório. She conjures up a plan featuring Vitório on a radio program where he shares his tragic story with the audience. During the same program, the Minister of Interior is interviewed, and he makes a plea for solidarity as well as "Angolan hospitality" towards war victims. At the end, he promises Vitório a job. Subsequently, the minister is literally mobbed by journalists and war victims. The former bombard him with questions regarding concrete measures to help war victims, while the latter with their presence bring to bear the drama of the situation. The minister answers evasively with generalities and platitudes, revealing his political opportunism, but also the government's deficiencies in coping with the aftermath of war in its staggering human and infrastructural dimensions.

Maria João Ganga's *Hollow City* has been acclaimed by critics and has circulated worldwide at various film festivals, garnering prizes at the festivals of Paris, Milan, and Créteil (France). While *Hollow City* is her feature film debut, Ganga has directed and written for theater over a number of years. She has also worked as assistant director on several documentaries, including Abderrahmane Sissako's *Rostov-Luanda* (1998). She wrote the screenplay for *Hollow City* in the early 1990s inspired by the victimization of children as a result of armed conflict. However, due to Angola's civil war and consequent lack of funding for cinema, it took her almost fifteen years to make the film. Most of the actors in this film hail from the Angolan theater scene, while the children actors were chosen through local casting efforts. In essence, *Hollow City* offers a devastating portrayal of the effects of war on the lives of children that is at the same time tender and unsentimental. Maria João Ganga situates the story in 1991, the year in which the MPLA and UNITA signed a peace agreement that allowed for the first multi-party elections to take place in Angola in 1992 and offered a brief respite from the civil war.[13] It was a moment of hope in the history of the twenty-seven-year-old armed conflict. That hope was shattered by UNITA's refusal to accept defeat in what international observers at the time declared fair elections. It would take ten years more and the death of Jonas Savimbi for the war to truly end.

The protagonist of *Hollow City* is Ndala (played by the amazingly expressive Roldan Pinto João), a twelve-year-old orphan from the central Angolan province of Bié who has arrived in Luanda as a war refugee with a group of orphans under the supervision of a Portuguese nun. Ndala surreptitiously runs away from his group as the orphans and soldiers are leaving the aircraft shortly after landing. Suddenly, he finds himself wandering aimlessly through the menacing streets of downtown Luanda, pulling a little tin car that he has built. Early on, there are poignant scenes with Ndala exploring the city amid roaring traffic and imposing high-rises. At times, the camera provides a point-of-view shot of the city, conveying Ndala's sense of awe and fascination. In one visually arresting scene, there is a close-up image of Ndala while the overpowering traffic lights appear out of focus in the background, then suddenly, in a seamless transition towards the following scene, there is a clearly focused high-angle long shot of Ndala standing alone and vulnerable in the middle of the street with cars approaching and honking at him. Afterwards, along the way he encounters three different individuals who will provide support as well as guidance: Zé (the talented Domingos Fernandes), a fourteen-year-old school boy who plays the character of Ngunga in a school drama based on Pepetela's classic children's novel, *As aventuras de Ngunga* (1977) [*The Adventures of Ngunga*], written in 1972, which functions as a key symbolic intertext throughout the film; an old fisherman, who lives on the *Ilha de Luanda* (by the ocean, across the bay from downtown) and who may become a much-needed father figure; and Joka (played convincingly by Raúl Rosário), a lively, bragging trickster in his twenties or thirties, whose flashiness seduces little Ndala to the point of choosing him as a role model. The buddy, the father, and the older brother figures offer Ndala life-lessons as well as options that may lead the intelligent yet impressionable and immature young boy to his survival or demise. Meanwhile, the Portuguese nun spends most of the time searching frantically for Ndala all over Luanda. In fact, the climate of uncertainty regarding Ndala's fate provides the dramatic kernel of this film. In spite of its tragic premise, *Hollow City* also displays an exuberant city, bursting with life, where the dilapidated and grim quotidian reality of Luanda is tempered by a certain *joie-de-vivre*, human warmth, pulsating rhythms, in addition to the playfully melodious Portuguese spoken in Angola. In fact, it can be argued that as the setting for both films, *Hollow City* and *The Hero*, Luanda plays a significant role, given its status as a microcosm of the Angolan nation that grew exponentially in large part due to the war, which created a mass exodus from rural areas into the capital city and stretched Luanda's infrastructure to capacity as well as exacerbating socio-economic hardship for many.[14] In *Hollow City*, Luanda at times displays a militarized environment due to a strictly enforced curfew during the time period in which the film is set, lending added tension as well as meaning to its title given the desolate nocturnal urban landscape and the myriad dangers haunting its lonely and vulnerable young protagonist. Meanwhile, *The Hero* portrays a climate of uncertainty in postwar Luanda during the months immediately following the war's end, where thousands of people desperately search for loved ones who disappeared during the war. Nonetheless, *The Hero* ends with a hopeful note that is reflected in the closing scene featuring a stunning view of downtown Luanda from the *Avenida Marginal* along the bay, while playing Paulo Flores's anthem-like song *Poema do Semba*, which is a tribute to Angola's national music as well as to the people of Angola.

As mentioned earlier, the classic Angolan novel *As aventuras de Ngunga* plays a key symbolic role in Maria João Ganga's *Hollow City*. In essence, it constitutes a fable that has served an exemplary function for children in the formation of post-independence Angola under the tutelage of the Marxist-nationalist project of the triumphant MPLA. It tells the story of a thirteen-year-old orphan boy who has lost his family to the war (in this case, the liberation war against Portuguese colonialism) and ends up living in the villages controlled by the MPLA in the Angolan hinterland. Forced by the circumstances of war, he becomes a young soldier engaging in combat alongside adult soldiers as they fight against the colonialist forces. At one point, Ngunga is held captive by the Portuguese (since he is a boy soldier he is used as a servant instead of being held in prison) but he is able to outmaneuver his captors and kill a Portuguese secret police chief (or PIDE), therefore becoming a hero. Ngunga is an intelligent, curious, independent, and courageous boy, representing an archetypal figure—a heroic model to be imitated in order to build the new Angolan nation. While Ndala shares Ngunga's primary traits, he represents an archetypal young refugee victim who may or may not endure the battle to survive a war that destroyed the utopia for which Ngunga and his contemporaries so valiantly fought. The scene in which Ndala wanders the streets of Luanda while the Angolan national anthem plays in the background brilliantly projects an acute sense of irony with regard to his life. The national anthem, which is in reality the MPLA anthem, is a tribute to those who "fell" during the struggle for independence, while celebrating Angolan history and the collective aim of creating "the New Man" through dedicated work.[15] The tragic irony expressed through this scene in view of Ndala's (and Angola's) life circumstances as well as the insurmountable gap between the ideals expressed in the Marxist-nationalist anthem (now historically anachronistic), and the heartrending reality that befell Ndala and the Angolan nation as a whole cannot be more startling.

The final moments of *Hollow City* entail a sequence of cross-cutting scenes of the dramatized version of Ngunga's story and the final scenes of Ndala's odyssey. Not only does Maria João Ganga masterfully succeed in creating a highly suspenseful climate leading to the film's *dénouement*, but she also establishes a partial analogy between both interrelated stories whose outcomes are radically different. Both stories represent the socio-historical as well as human dimensions that are constitutive of Angola's postcolonial predicament: the utopia of a unified, egalitarian, and independent African nation-state and the dystopia of civil war caused by a staggering complex of internal and external factors that led to the near-implosion of the national project of Angola.

The Angolan films *The Hero* and *Hollow City* focus on the extensive "collateral damage" caused by war where lives are destroyed, families are torn apart, the ties to the ancestral lands are severed, and where infrastructural damage together with climatic misfortune lead to ecological disaster and massive human suffering. Even though the films featured here are based on the specificities of the Angolan experience of civil war, they also speak to a universal human victimization caused by the ravages of armed conflict. The psychic, social, and material aftereffects of war last a very long time, with profound consequences for those victimized. In the case of Ndala, the orphan boy featured in *Hollow City*, his chances of survival and of being afforded a dignified existence remain uncertain at best.

The renaissance of Angolan cinema with films that have been acclaimed internationally is an auspicious sign of the normalization of life in postwar Angola, with welcome effects in the realm of cultural production, more particularly for a medium as costly as cinema. The MPLA government is well aware of the symbolic capital behind cultural manifestations such as cinema, popular music, as well as soccer, as they have recently garnered prestige for Angola on the global arena. According to the director of the Angolan Film and Multimedia Institute (IACAM), Miguel Hurst, only time will tell whether Angolan cinema will continue to be an object of attention on the part of public and private institutions in order to continue developing into the future.[16] Here's for hope!

Notes

[1] This article is part of an extensive chapter focusing on Lusophone African cinema from my forthcoming book, *After Independence: Globalization, Postcolonialism, and the Cultures of Lusophone Africa.*

[2] In an interview with *Cahiers du Cinéma* published in 1977, Ruy Duarte de Carvalho mentions the advent of television during the final years of Portuguese colonialism in Angola with two broadcasters (public and private) in their early development stages. Unfortunately, there is a dearth of information regarding the development of cinema during the colonial period in former Portuguese Africa. See Manthia Diawara for limited information on this time period (1992).

[3] For more information on the history of the first years of film production in post-independence Lusophone Africa, see José Mena Abrantes, Manthia Diawara, Frank Ukadike, Claire Andrade-Watkins, José Matos da Cruz and José Mena Abrantes.

[4] The screenplay of *Sambizanga* was written by Angolan intellectual and nationalist leader Mário Pinto de Andrade.

[5] While numerous critics refer to *Sambizanga,* the most nuanced and detailed analyzes have been written by Dembrow, Moorman, and Gugler.

[6] See António Ole's documentaries on popular culture, *Carnaval da vitória* [*Victory Carnival*] and *O ritmo do N'Gola Ritmos* [*The Rhythm of N'Gola Ritmos*], both released in 1978, in addition to Ruy Duarte de Carvalho's ethnographically inspired documentary series and fiction film, *Presente angolano, tempo mumuíla* [*Angola Present, Mumuíla Time*] and *Nelisita,* released in 1979/81 and 1982, respectively.

[7] Among the three Angolan titles released in 2004, Orlando Fortunato's *O comboio da Canhoca* has not circulated as widely as the films by Zezé Gamboa and Maria João Ganga nor has it received much critical attention. *O comboio da Canhoca* is a historical film based on a real-life atrocity committed by Portuguese colonial forces in the 1950s involving a mysterious case of asphyxiation experienced by dozens of political prisoners arrested under suspicious circumstances, who are transported on a train from Malanje to Luanda. In 2006 it was released in DVD form in Angola.

[8] See Gamboa's documentaries: *Mopiopio de Angola* (1991), *Dissidência* (1998), *Burned by Blue* (1999), and *O desassossego de Pessoa* [*Pessoa's Disquiet*] (1999).

[9] See the films *A árvore dos antepassados* [*The Tree of Our Forefathers*] (1995), *A guerra da água* [*The Water War*] (1995), and *O acampamento da desminagem* [*The De-mining Camp*] (2004).

[10] See Tony Hodges's *Angola: Anatomy of an Oil State* for one of the most incisive analyses of contemporary Angolan society.

[11] In 2006, the Angolan government released statistics pointing to a total of 62% of the population living in poverty and, of those, 27% living in absolute poverty (as broadcasted by Radio France International's Portuguese Language Service to Africa and Europe).

[12] In 2006, one of the worst cholera epidemics to hit Africa in a decade broke out in Angola, with Luanda's infamous shantytowns as the epicenter. The massive health crisis has been widely reported in the Angolan and world media, but what has greatly astounded observers is the fact that an entirely preventable disease could spread so rapidly in a country awash in oil and diamond wealth. Even though government corruption—where high-ranking officials are believed to hold multimillion dollar Swiss bank accounts—is largely to blame for such a crisis, the civil war destroyed key infrastructure throughout the country and "eviscerated the government's corps of competent managers, leaving disarray," according to Dauda Wurie, project officer for the UN Children's Fund (qtd. in LaFranière's *New York Times* article, "In Oil-Rich Angola Cholera Preys Upon Poorest").

[13] The 1988 tripartite peace treaty signed between Angola, Cuba, and apartheid-era South Africa led to the complete withdrawal of Cuban and South African military forces from Angolan territory, opening the path towards a first ceasefire and peace agreement between UNITA and MPLA in 1991.

[14] Hodges points to statistical estimates provided by the Angolan INE (*Instituto Nacional de Estatística*) that calculate the total population of Luanda (and environs) at more than 3 million (about a quarter of the nation's population) during the late 1990s (22). INE data for 2001 cited by Hodges (35) estimate that 60% of the Angolan population is now concentrated in urban areas.

[15] The first stanza of the Angolan national anthem, written by Manuel Rui Monteiro, reads thus: "Ó Pátria, nunca mais esqueceremos / Os heróis do 4 de Fevereiro / Ó Pátria, nós saudamos os teus filhos / Tombados pela nossa independência. / Honramos o passado e a nossa História, / Construindo no Trabalho o Homem Novo" [Oh Fatherland, we shall never forget / The heroes of February Fourth / Oh Fatherland, we salute your children / Who fell for our independence. / We honor our past and our History, / Through Work in the pursuit of the New Man].

[16] Based on conversations with him in Luanda in May of 2006.

Works Cited

Abrantes, José Mena. *Cinema angolano: um passado a merecer melhor presente.* Luanda: Cinemateca Nacional, 1986.

Andrade-Watkins, Claire. "Portuguese African Cinema: Historical and Contemporary Perspectives—1969 to 1993." *Research in African Literatures* 26 (1995): 134-50.

Azevedo, Licínio. *A árvore dos antepassados.* Mozambique; UK: Ébano Multimedia, BBC/TVE/One World Group, 1995.

———. *O campo de desminagem.* Mozambique: Ébano Multimedia, 2004.

———. *A guerra da água.* Mozambique: Ébano Multimedia, 1995.

Brandão, Rodrigo. "Bringing It All Home." *Reverse Shot* 17 Oct. 2006. <http://www.reverse-shot.com/legacy/summer05/hero_palindromes.html>.

Cruz, José Matos da, and José Mena Abrantes. *Cinema em Angola.* Luanda: Chá de Caxinde, 2002.

Dembrow, Michael. "Sambizanga and Sarah Maldoror." <http://spot.pcc.edu/~mdembrow/sambizanga.htm>. 7 June 2006.

Diawara, Manthia. *African Cinema.* Bloomington & Indianapolis: Indiana UP, 1992.

Duarte de Carvalho, Ruy. *Nelisita.* Angola: Laboratório Nacional de Cinema; TPA, 1982.

———. *Presente angolano, Tempo Mumuíla.* Angola: TPA, 1979-81.

"Entretien avec Rui Duarte de Carvalho." *Cahiers du Cinéma* 274 (1977): 59-60.

Fortunato, Orlando. *O comboio da Canhoca.* Angola; France: Unifrance, 2004.

Gamboa, Zezé. *O heroi.* Portugal; Angola; France: David e Golias; Gamboa & Gamboa; Les Films de l'Après-Midi, 2004.

Ganga, Maria João. *Na cidade vazia.* Angola; Portugal: Animatógrafo II, 2004.

Gugler, Josef. *African Film: Re-Imagining a Continent.* Bloomington & Indianapolis: Indiana UP, 2003.

Hodges, Tony. *Angola: Anatomy of an Oil State.* Oslo: Fridtjof Nansen Institute; Oxford: James Currey; Bloomington & Indianapolis: Indiana UP, 2001 and 2004.

LaFranière, Sharon. "In Oil-Rich Angola, Cholera Preys Upon Poorest." *The New York Times* 15 June 2006: 1, 14.

Maldoror, Sarah. *Sambizanga.* Angola; Congo; France: n.p., 1972.

Moorman, Marissa. "Of Westerns, Women, and War: Re-Situating Angolan Cinema and the Nation." *Research in African Literatures* 32 (2001): 103-122.

Ole, António. *Carnaval da Vitória.* Angola: TPA, 1978.

———. *O ritmo do N'Gola Ritmos.* Angola: TPA, 1978.

Pepetela. *As aventuras de Ngunga.* [1977]. Luanda: Nzila, 2000.

Ukadike, Nwachukwu Frank. *Black African Cinema.* Berkeley: U of California P, 1994.

Vieira, José Luandino. *The Real Life of Domingos Xavier.* London: Heinemann, 1978.

———. *A vida verdadeira de Domingos Xavier.* [1974]. 4th ed. Lisbon: Edições 70, 1988.

Fernando Arenas is Professor of Lusophone African, Portuguese, and Brazilian Studies in the Department of Spanish and Portuguese Studies at the University of Minnesota. He is the author of *Utopias of Otherness: Nationhood and Subjectivity in Portugal and Brazil* (U of Minnesota P, 2003) and co-editor together with Susan C. Quinlan of *Lusosex: Gender and Sexuality in the Portuguese-Speaking World* (U of Minnesota P, 2002). He was awarded a Guggenheim Fellowship in 2005-06 in order to finish his new book, *After Independence: Globalization, Postcolonialism and the Cultures of Lusophone Africa.* Email: arena002@umn.edu

From *Peixefritismo* to Yellow-bean Stew: Angolan National Cuisine in the Pot and in the Novel

Igor Cusack

Abstract: As part of the ideology of nationalism, every nation is supposed to have a national cuisine. During recent decades, African national cuisines have emerged in a number of states, in particular in Lusophone Africa. Cookbooks on African cuisines have been published in Europe and parts of Africa and the national cuisine proclaimed on official websites. This article reviews the appearance of these cuisines and then focuses on the development of the "national cuisine" of Angola and on national dishes such as *muamba de galinha*. Finally, how food is portrayed in a number of Angolan novels is discussed, and the question raised: why should cuisine appear in some works and not in others?

Cozinha Tradicional de Angola (Cabral) assembles a collection of recipes from Angola, a geographical space only finally established in 1891 following the scramble for Africa. In the introduction we are told that "Angola é uma terra de fascínio, cor, alegria; uma natureza vibrante, um povo afável, paisagens lindas. Mas entre as suas muitas riquezas, encontramos verdadeiras pérolas para o paladar. A gastronomia angolana é deliciosa e variada" (11). How then has this "delicious and varied" cuisine emerged?

Catherine Palmer has pointed out that food, landscape, and the body have been aspects of the modern material world that have been important to both individual and collective identities: she calls these the "three flags of

Portuguese Literary & Cultural Studies 15/16 (2010): 215-30.

identity" (183). In the developed world today it is taken for granted that every nation has its own cuisine: an Angolan nation must have its own cuisine. As Ohnuki-Tierney has stressed, it is the sharing of food together that is important: "Commensality is an important cultural institution everywhere, whether at a family table or at a college in Oxford or Cambridge and it is a crucial cultural institution whereby people who eat together become 'we' as opposed to 'they,' and the food shared becomes a metaphor for a social group" (9). As a nation is a group of people so numerous that it can only be imagined (Anderson), for the group to share the same meal the nation's food must be defined as belonging to it and to it alone.

The word "cuisine" itself comes with some baggage and carries with it a hint of elitism and perhaps an association with restaurants, cookery books, and male chefs. In Africa, this "cuisine" is far from the "eating of anything for survival" that many Africans are facing today. Indeed, perhaps discussing a national cuisine at a time of famine would seem to be grossly inappropriate. We are, however, addressing cuisine in the context of the modern state and where the construction of a sense of national identity may be crucial to that state's long-term survival. The building of a notion of a national cuisine is just one, though important, contributor to this project, and even if in some African countries only a small elite actually consume the national dishes, many other people will be aware of their national symbolism.

This article, after a brief review of the emergence of African national cuisines, concentrates on the development of Angolan cuisine and its links to Portugal and Portuguese cuisine. This cuisine makes some erratic appearances in a number of Angolan novels and the article asks why should food and cuisine infiltrate the pages of certain novels and be absent from others.

African national cuisines

When examining African cuisines we are also exploring the relationship of "everyday life" to the social, cultural, and political history of particular parts of Africa. These cuisines are firmly linked to the colonial past as well as to the postcolonial history, globalized food markets, to emergency food aid, to patriarchal, traditional, and religious ideologies, and to many centres of power and their associated or constitutive discourses. However, when examining African cuisine it is inevitably the colonial "inheritance" that comes into focus. For example, the colonial encounter has been crucial to modern Senegalese cuisine. The French began to grow ground nuts about 1870, so that by the 1930s over half of the agricultural land in Senegal was taken up by this crop. Meanwhile, in Indochina, the French were producing rice, so that importing the poor quality broken-rice to Senegal from there made sense, while the premium product, carried in the same ships, was sent on to France. Senegal is now a major importer of broken rice from the Far East. As a result, the government of independent Senegal is burdened with an enormous rice import bill and wants to boost the consumption of local grains such as millet and sorghum (Barrot 93-94).

As I have discussed elsewhere, national cuisines are currently being claimed by a number of African states and official national websites show such cuisines as part of the national cultural heritage ("Recipes" 207-25). Cookery books play an important part in the assembling of national cuisines, as can be seen from the examples of India or Mexico. In recent decades, in the West, there has been a considerable interest in African cuisine and a great number of cookery books has been published—in the US, Britain, France, Germany, Spain, and Portugal. These African cuisines often include African-American, Caribbean, or Brazilian dishes and, indeed, for African Americans, "African" and "African-American" dishes are often conflated. Again in the West, a few country-specific cookery books can also be found. For example, a Tanzanian cookery book has been published in the United States and books on Ghanaian and Nigerian cookery can be found in the UK and US ("Recipes" 223-25). Books on the cuisines of specific North African countries and on Madagascar, Cameroon, Congo, and Mauritius have also appeared in France and at least one on Senegalese cooking in Spain ("Pots, pens" 294-96).

In Anglophone Africa, a considerable number of cookery books has now been published: in Malawi, Zimbabwe, Liberia, Gambia, Nigeria, and especially in South Africa, Ghana, and Kenya ("Pots, pens" 223-225). Fewer cookery books have been traced from Francophone Africa although national dishes appear to be well recognised, perhaps as an overseas extension of French esteem for obscure regional delicacies. Senegal has a number of national dishes including *le thiéboudiene* (rice and fish) and *Poulet Yassa*, from the Casamance region. The very dominance of French culture in its former colonies, and the importance of French cuisine as a component of that culture, may have suppressed the more widespread proclaiming of national cuisines in Francophone Africa.

It must however be remembered that cuisine in Africa is usually handed down orally, mainly from mother to daughter. Radio and television cookery programmes are also common in many African countries, while newspapers and magazines, which have generally flourished in much of Africa in recent years, have also included columns giving recipes.

The cuisines of Portugal and Lusophone Africa

What about the five Lusophone African countries? Here a more developed sense of a national cuisine seems to have emerged. The key is perhaps to be found in the importance placed by Portugal on maintaining cultural links to the Lusophone world. The promotion of a worldwide Lusophone cuisine by the Portuguese might be seen as an echo of the *lusotropicalista* doctrine, and, indeed, the postcolonial Lusophone state's willing compliance with this Portuguese culinary interpenetration might suggest that some remnants of this lusotropicalism still have some purchase in Portugal's former African colonies. However, just as lusotropicalism in Africa was mainly a myth concocted by the ideologues of the *Estado Novo*, the whole history of Portugal's encounter with colonial cuisines was one of separation of the cuisines and, according to Alfredo Margarido, this remained so for the whole period of Portuguese colonialism (42-45). For example, in Angola, if you wanted to become an *assimilado* you had to show you had abandoned native food (42). Notwithstanding this, present-day Portugal remains happy to promote Lusophone cuisines, believing—rightly—that Portugal has been crucial in their construction both through bringing many foodstuffs from the Americas and by directly influencing many recipes.

So what makes Portuguese cuisine different from, say, Spanish cuisine? Is it just a collection of regional recipes, like many other cuisines, drawn together to form what is typically Portuguese? Certainly one of the more widely used cookery books, Maria de Lourdes Modesto's *Cozinha Tradicional Portuguesa* is made up of the "representative," "authentic," and "most characteristic" dishes taken from each region. Great numbers of cookery books on the regional cuisines of Portugal have been published—from Estremadura, Minho, Alentejo, Madeira, etc. Alternatively, perhaps Portuguese cuisine is different because of the influence of the Moors and the Sephardic Jews on some of these regional dishes?

More pertinently for our discussion, has the food of the former empire influenced Portuguese cuisine? Cherie Y. Hamilton points out in her book of Lusophone cuisines that many recipes in the present-day former colonies are based on Portuguese regional dishes. Thus, for instance, *pastelão de atum,* tuna frittata, from São Tomé and Príncipe is an adaptation of a Portuguese *pastelão* but using tuna, palm oil, and a hot sauce (Hamilton 83).[1] However, there seems very little influence the other way around and those other Africans, the Moors, probably have had more impact on Portuguese cuisine. Alfredo Margarido (43) has argued that returning African colonial settlers sneered at dishes such as *muamba* from Angola or *catchupa* from Cape Verde and this may more accurately reflect Portuguese attitudes to "a cozinha dos outros."

Nevertheless, today Portugal seems to be fascinated by the cuisine of its former colonies—and it is the Portuguese input that fascinates—and maintains a number of websites on Lusophone gastronomy. For instance *Portugal em linha—Os Sabores Lusófonos* asserts that it is not just the Portuguese language but other cultural traits, including cuisine, that "characterise the Lusophone peoples." Another active website is the *Roteiro Gastrónomico de Portugal*, which is sponsored by wine-makers, restaurants, food producers and many other groups. Here the choice of web pages offered to the reader is shown on a task bar across the top of the page—"Home // Recipes // Sweets // Regional Recipes // International // *Lusofonia* [my italics] // Restaurants." A click on *Lusofonia* leads you to "*Sabores da Lusofonia*," where a picture of and a quotation from Camões is displayed alongside the flags of the Lusophone world. Clicking on these flags leads in turn to a list of recipes from each country displayed alongside a picture (and biography) of Infante D. Henrique. Thus, for the Portuguese, the cuisines of the Lusophone world are closely linked to the Portuguese age of the discoveries. Marques da Cruz's book, entitled *À mesa com Luís Vaz de Camões ou o romance da cozinha no Portugal das descobertas*, confirms the strong Portuguese association between the "great discoverers" and gastronomy. All this suggests that it is this focus on the former empire, and the importance of that component of Portuguese national identity, that has driven Portugal to nurture the growth of interest in cuisines in its former colonies.

There are a number of cookery books published in Portugal focused on Africa, as well as on other parts of the Lusophone world. Maria Odette Cortes Valente claims that all Lusophone cooking in Africa, Brazil, Goa, Macao and East Timor was the discovery of the Portuguese—as if it would not have existed at all without the Portuguese. Maria de Lourdes Chantre has also written *111 Receitas de Cozinha Africana* and a book on the cuisine of Cape Verde. The most comprehensive book on Lusophone cuisines is probably, however, one published in English, Cherie Y. Hamilton's *Cuisines of Portuguese Encounters*. Here the emphasis is placed on the interrelationship of all the Lusophone cuisines with related dishes from different countries following each other in the text.

Before examining Angolan cuisine in a little more detail, it is useful to briefly recall the role played by the Portuguese in introducing so many foodstuffs, and cuisine, to Africa. Many of the staple foods of Africa came originally from the Americas—peanuts, manioc, corn, and tomatoes for example. Three items were brought by the Portuguese to all the areas they controlled: olive oil, wine, and cheese (da Cruz 154). Hamilton gives an excellent example of Portuguese agency in spreading food culture. She follows the progress of dishes based on okra, a vegetable native to West Africa. The Portuguese first carried okra to Brazil, where it resembled a local plant that was called *caruru* by the local Tupi-Guarani Indians. An Afro-Brazilian shrimp and okra dish was then "concocted" and named *caruru*, only then to be brought back to Angola to become part of Angolan cuisine—the *calulu* of the official Angolan national webpage on the cuisine of Angola under the heading "Art and Culture." The dish then moved on to São Tomé and Príncipe, brought there by contract workers in the cocoa plantations, so that now a chicken and okra dish called *kalulu de galinha* is a typical national dish (Hamilton 10, 119). Thanks to the Portuguese, the okra has moved in a full circle.

Culinária angolana

The anthropologist Mesquitela Lima, writing the introduction to *111 Receitas de Cozinha Africana* in 1981, acknowledges an already existing Angolan cuisine. She writes "[a]ssim se pode falar de cozinha chinesa, africana, hindu, índia das pradarias, russa, portuguesa, cabo-verdiana, guineense, angolana ou de outras que não são mais do que fixações, 'cristalizações' produtos de articulações constantes de procura de misturas de alimentos com o único objectivo de agradar ao paladar, ao gosto dos homens dessas culturas" (Lima 12). Here Angolan cuisine seems to have firmly crystallized alongside Russian and Chinese cuisine.

Angola, which has only just achieved peace after some forty years of liberation and then civil war, might not be seen as a successful attempt at nation-building. Those thousands of Angolans suffering from the recent famine will have had little concern for any notion of an Angolan cuisine. However, the parties that fought the Angolan civil war all fought for control of an Angola set within the fixed boundaries inherited from the colonial power, not just for part of it. The ruling elite's project of nation-building, which has deep roots in the centralised and authoritarian colonial state, will include the assemblage of a national cuisine. We should note that the Angolan novelist and ethnographer, Óscar Ribas, wrote the first short book on Angolan "alimentaçao" in 1965—some ten years prior to independence. Interestingly this was first published as a book by the *Centro de Informação e Turismo de Angola*, showing an early link between tourism promotion and the definition of a national cuisine.

The recently published *Cozinha Tradicional de Angola* (Cabral) was one of a series of cookery books on *Cozinha Internacional*, which also includes Paola Rolletta's *Cozinha Tradicional de Moçambique*. Cabral's recipes are divided into four sections: *Peixe e Marisco*, *Carne*, *Acompanhamentos*, and *Doces*. The recipes include ingredients that would be found in Angola, such as *dinhungo* (*abóbora carneira*) but with suggestions as to substitutes that might be used in Portugal—a large courgette in this instance (8). This is a book aimed at both an Angolan and Portuguese reader—and cook. Cabral writes "[q]ue este livro ofereça a todos os angolanas e portugueses que viveram em Angola pratos com sabor a este belo país, e a todos aqueles que nunca proveram a gastronomia angolana uma oportunidade para o fazerem, é aquilo que desejo" (12). These recipes, like the fifteen Angolan dishes set out in Chantre's 1981 book, have an authentic ring, using palm oil for example, and they appear less adapted to the European—or American kitchen—than many Anglo-Saxon books on African cooking seem to be. To the non-Lusophone reader some of the recipes listed on the website of the *Roteiro Gastronómico de Portugal* might seem more authentically Angolan. For example, in the recipe for an Angolan version of *Galinha de Cabidela* we are told to "[m]ate a galinha e aproveite o sangue, ao qual se deve misturar vinagre para não coagular" <http://www.gastronomias.com/lusfonia/ang013.html>. However, this dish is typically Portuguese, so that this apparent Angolan authenticity is actually that of the Portuguese peasant.[2]

It is not surprising that "Angolan cuisine" is proclaimed, in English, on the official website as an important part of Angolan culture. A list of dishes is provided under the heading "Cuisine of Angola," including Palm Oil Beans, Fish Calulu, Corn Funge, and Chicken Muamba. *Funge* is a type of porridge made of corn or manioc and is eaten with meat and vegetable stews, while *muamba de galinha*, variants of which are common to much of South West Africa, consists of chicken cooked in palm oil, onion, garlic, and okra. This might be claimed as the national dish of Angola and will certainly be found in Angolan restaurants in Lisbon and elsewhere. Another typical dish is the Angolan version of *feijoada* cooked with palm oil (*demdem*), which produces the yellow colour of the yellow bean stew. However, Afonso Praça suggests that there are two essential dishes of Angolan cuisine, the *muamba* and the *mufete*, a dish of grilled small fish and manioc meal. On another website (terravista 1) an anonymous author declares: "Frescura e simplicidade são as caraterísticas chaves da cozinha Angolana. Não há molhos complicados nem decorações sofisticados. É o honesto sabor dos produtos da terra Mãe, subtilmente acentuado com as especiarias apropriadas, que confere aos produtos mais comuns a nota de originalidade própria da Cozinha Angolana." Such claims of simplicity are a common feature of much gastro-nationalism.

Compared with many other African nations, Angola does have a number of widely accepted national dishes: *muamba de galinha*, *feijão com oleo de palma*, *calulu*, and *mufete*—served with toasted manioc meal and palm oil (Hamilton 181). For most of the recipes in the recently published cookery books no specific regional origins are attributed, although many appear to come from the Luanda area. For example, Hamilton often mentions eating a particular dish on the island in Luanda or, for example, that *Doce de Amendoim* "is very popular in Muxiluanda, a suburb of Luanda" (296), or that the *Couves Cozidos com Oleo-de Palma e Amendoim* is a "traditional dish of the Kimbundu people around (…) Luanda" (124). Occasionally she ventures away from the capital. Thus she recalls how, in 1979, she first ate *Muamba de Peixe* (172) with the governor of the district of Moçâmedes. Neither Cabral nor Chantre (*111 Receitas*) gives any comment at all on the regional origins of the dishes. Perhaps this is not surprising for books written in Portugal.

However, in Ribas's *Alimentação Regional Angolana*, as might be expected, some sense of regional origins is given. This is not a cookery book with detailed food recipes but consists of a short introduction, some photographs of Angolan food, along with an alphabetical list headed *Culinária e bebidas*. Here, the male author pays particular attention to the drinks, with descriptions of many Angolan regional spirits and beers along with some details of their preparation: these include the *aguardentes*, *capitica* made from bananas (Cuanza Norte), *caporroto* or *catombe* from maize (Malanje), and *Caxipembe* from sweet-potato (planalto central) and a type of beer made from sorghum called *macau* (Huíla) (23-4, 36). The food includes *Muamba*, *mufete*, *funge* (here *fúnji*), and *feijão de azeite de palma*.

One distinction between recipes is made by Lima when she points out that some of the 111 recipes are "produtos de contactos" while others are "criações no interior das próprias culturas" (16). When it comes to food it would seem however that there are very few dishes that are not products of contact and Hamilton (4) perhaps reflects the position better when she writes that "[what] fascinated me were the prevailing commonalities among so many dishes found in seven Portuguese-speaking countries on three continents."

Many Angolans living in Luanda and other cities will be aware of the many restaurants from different countries that line some streets in Luanda. Italian, Portuguese, Chinese, Indian, Korean, Brazilian, Spanish, Cuban, Vietnamese, as well as Angolan cuisines are on offer. Angolan cuisine can be found, for example, at the takeaway called Pimentinha near the Kinaxixe circle. If local Angolans do venture inside, say to the SoTam 8 Vietnamese restaurant, they will be offered an eclectic menu including Saigon spring rolls, Swedish meat balls, and *Pizza Vesuvio* (see the SoTam8 website and then "click on the dragon to see our menu"). Both the diner and the passer-by in Luanda, as in most African cities, are being reminded that all nations have cuisines.

Apart from the Portuguese effort, no cookery books have been published in Angola. Cuisine was clearly not a priority of the Union of Angolan Writers (*União dos Escritores Angolanos*). However, in 1996, the Portuguese embassy in Luanda published *A Alimentação do Muxiluanda* (Santos), which includes recipes for many local dishes—from those based around the island of Luanda—where many of Luanda's restaurants mentioned above are located. No doubt, as the present oil boom stimulates economic activity, some local publisher will soon produce a more home-grown cookery book and the notion of an Angolan national cuisine will be further solidified.

Cuisine in Angolan Literature

Many novels make no mention at all of any of the daily bodily functions of the hero. Just as visits to the toilet are seldom chronicled (or the absence of such visits noted by the reader) so these same characters can appear to pass through life without any need to eat or drink. It is possible that in African literature, often written in a continent of food shortages and famine, food might play a more central role than elsewhere, although other factors might be more indicative of the appearance or not of food.

How food is treated will vary greatly, starting from just a passing reference, to a brief description of the food, taken to a full recipe with details of the process of cooking and preparation. The narrator may be one of the characters and share activities such as the partaking of food, while with other narrators, such as the *Deus ex machina*, this possibility is excluded. Whom the author is addressing, the narratee, might also be important, and feminist criticism has pointed out, for example, how European and American narratives "posit a male reader" (Culler 87). Sometimes the plot of a novel will depend on food as in Dickens's *Oliver Twist*. In exotic colonial literature, food may appear in abundance where the ethnographic detail sets the colonial subject in an exotic land. In general, food and cooking does not appear in the romantic novel—the romantic hero has other matters in mind—opium not soup is more likely to make an appearance.[3] Perhaps it is to the realist writers that one has to look for cuisine—and here it is the realist writers of Northeast Brazil that are important because of the model set by this large Portuguese-speaking nation for the new Lusophone states of Africa. The aim of nationalist literary entrepreneurs was the same on both continents, which was to fashion a literature specific to the local peoples, built on an experience they could recognise based in their local culture. Here, cuisine has had a part to play.

Great banquets and eating to excess come with carnival, when the populace is given some licence to mock authority. The carnival in Luanda has been established since the early days of the Portuguese presence and has shown remarkable continuity. In Manuel Rui's comic novel about life in "Marxist" Angola, *Quem me dera ser onda*, the authorities are certainly mercilessly mocked. The story is focused on a pig named *Carnaval da Vitória* that is raised illegally by Diogo in a flat where his two children, Zeca and Ruca, do everything they can to protect their new friend, the pig. Indeed, food and drink play a very important role throughout Rui's novel. For instance, we are told details such as the fried fish sandwiches that the children take to school (18). We should note that fried fish has a particular connotation in the novel, that is, of the mundane; furthermore, the consumption of meat, as opposed to fish, connotes wealth, power and perhaps "counter-revolution." Diogo exclaims to his wife "[d]eixa lá os ismos, mulher, que isso não enche barriga. Ismo é peixefritismo, fungismo e outros ismos da barriga da gente" (9). Indeed, Niyi Afolabi has suggested that "peixefritismo is a metaphor of survival" (107).

The children also make attempts to dissuade their father from eating the pig—by obtaining, for example, meat from a smart hotel, which they acquire by claiming it is destined for the "state" police dogs (50). This meat is served by their mother, Liloca along with manioc, all to their father's great delight.

The food preparation is not generally described in any detail though poor *Carnaval da vitória* is finally "well peppered" and grilled on four braziers built on the seventh-floor balcony where he was raised (65).

Manuel Rui's *Crónica de um Mujimbo* is another book where food and drink play a role at the core of the novel. The story revolves around the life of the bourgeois elite of Luanda and of a ministerial department where there is growing concern about an unspecified rumor, or *mujimbo*. Henrique Feijó, a high-level civil servant bemoans the disorder of the neocolonial state while his wife is mainly concerned with losing weight and finding the special fruits she needs to diet (see also Peres 101). A typical passage, as the family picnic on the beach, runs:

> "Que pão é este, mãe?"
>
> "Pão integral, o melhor pão."
>
> "A mãe não trouxe peixe frito?"
>
> "Vê só Rico. Em casa torce o nariz ao peixe frito e aqui apetece-lhe. Deixa prà proxima." (48-49)

Manuel Rui, in depicting and satirizing life in petit bourgeois postcolonial Luanda, focuses on the travails of everyday life, a life where food and drink play a central role. There is no promotion of any romantic utopian view of the future, only a gentle mocking of those who might think they are involved in such a project.

José Luandino Vieira, who was born in Portugal and who was brought up in a *musseque* in Luanda, was an Angolan nationalist. It was in the Tarrafal prison in Cape Verde that he wrote his best known works. Angolan cuisine often appears in his stories in perhaps a little more detail than in Manuel Rui's novels. For example, in *The Loves of João Vêncio*, the hero is in jail in Angola for attempted murder, where he tells of the loves of his life. He is awaiting a visit from his Bailundu girlfriend—the woman he tried to strangle—who is bringing a "muamba supimpa" (35). At the end of the novel he is still waiting and tells us that "minha bailunda vai chegar com suas cúrias da famorosa [sic] muambá do molho d'oiro, moda desses benguelenses-catumbelas, sulanos" (117).

In Luandino Vieira's short stories, *Luuanda*, food again makes its appearance with, for instance, the hungry Zeca watching his friend eating "um guisado de feijão, um cheiroso quitande amarelo" (31).[4] Later, in "estória do ladrão e do papagaio," Kam'tuta, a starving boy with a crippled leg, joins his friends who are going to eat as they "começaram desamarrar o embrulho das coisas: panela de feijão d'azeite-palma, farinha, peixe frito, banana, pão. Comida de gente de musseque" (120). At first he is reluctant to join, but he shivers and "[O] cuspo nasceu na boca, pensou o feijão amarelo a brilhar na panela, a farinha a misturar" (120). Vieira, perhaps looking back on his adopted land from distant Tarrafal prison in Cape Verde, is thinking of yellow bean stew and *muamba*, perhaps today, two essentials of Angolan national cuisine.

Reviewing the great range of work of different genres written by Pepetela, it is difficult, if not futile, to try and categorize him as a romantic, modernist, realist, or even postmodern writer. However, if the focus is purely on his treatment of food, perhaps it is possible to trace a move from romantic utopianism to postmodern pastiche. He does not present food in his early works in the same way as Luandino Vieira as there is no sense of something delicious to be eaten, no saliva. Food is mentioned *en passant.* Perhaps in *Mayombe,* a story of MPLA (Popular Movement for the Liberation of Angola) guerrillas fighting the Portuguese in the jungles of Cabinda you would expect little detail of cuisine, although a central theme is the failure of supplies from the fighters' headquarters across the border in Congo-Brazzaville. Thus, the exhausted guerrillas "[s]ó beberam leite. A comida estava molhada, a xikuonga desfizera-se com a água. Restava-lhes o arroz e as latarias, aliás raras" (54). A typical Pepetela reference to food might also be when the guerrilla leader Sem Medo has a rather sparse dinner with Ondina where they "[c]omiam o pão com chá, em silêncio" (219). And then, in *Yaka,* a family saga of Portuguese settlers covering a period from the late nineteenth century to independence, you might perhaps have expected a little more culinary detail. This is not the case: "[l]eva um prato de comida aí para o cipaio. Mas bem cheio, que ele come muito. Comeram em silêncio" (285). In *O Desejo de Kianda,* Carmina, who has flourished as a party member both in socialist and capitalist Luanda, comes home for lunch "trazendo um termo dum restaurante com comida" (105). Thus here we have a bleak picture of the process of eating, as if eating, especially with women, is to be endured in silence. Now and then, in Pepetela's works, perhaps because of the very extent of his *oeuvre,* just a little more detail is given. For example, in *A Geração da Utopia,* when Sara, a white Angolan doctor, is visiting Aníbal, a disillusioned former guerrilla leader, who now dives in the sea for his food, she regrets the lack of lemon for a grilled fish, a *pargo.*

When we come to the *Jaime Bunda* books, a different world of food seems to emerge. Pepetela has now finally abandoned "romanticism," the struggle for a utopian socialist future for Angola, and veered into writing a postmodern Angolan parody of the mid-twentieth-century American detective novel, which, incidentally, allows him to picture women as available but unreliable sexual objects in an era when such treatment is frowned upon. When Jaime Bunda visits Kiko's bar, a famous restaurant and has "funje de carne seca de pacaça," the reader for the first time feels that the author is imagining an enjoyable meal (32). The secret agent, in a restaurant on the island of Luanda, also greatly savours succulent *muamba de galinha*, accompanied by *funje* (175). In *Jaime Bunda e a morte do Americano*, food and drink are never far away. As soon as Jaime Bunda arrives in Benguela to investigate the death of the American, he is told that the meals in the hotel are splendid. He takes to the terrace where "com o mar lá bem à frente, duas cervejas já derrotadas e muitos pastéis, pica-paus e quitabas ingeridos, Jaime se sentiu melhor" (27). Quitaba is an Angolan snack, a mixture of ground-up roasted peanuts, piri-piri, and salt. Later, "Bunda iniciou as hostilidades gastronómicas com uma entrada de gamas (...) deviam passar imediatamente (...) a anunciada caldeirada de cabrito." The goat-meat stew, greatly appreciated by Jaime Bunda, is a dish often cooked to celebrate the anniversary of Angolan independence, on the 11th of November (Hamilton 117). Perhaps, because of this more "realist" genre of the *Jaime Bunda* novels, Angolan food—with copious whiskey—is allowed to move to the centre. Whiskey, wine, and beer do make frequent appearances in Pepetela's other novels, but for food we need to look at *Jaime Bunda.*

Of the Angolan writers discussed here, we certainly have to turn to José Luandino Vieira to get any sustained notion of Angolan cuisine: maybe it is the realist influence here that is crucial, as Vieira wants to describe the real life of the dwellers in the Luandan *musseques* and uses the street language, a mixture of Kimbundu and Portuguese, as well as the food, to tell the tales.

Conclusions

It is clear that in a number of Lusophone African states, including Angola, a national cuisine is in the process of emerging, encouraged by the former colonial power whose own identity is still firmly linked to the age of the great discoverers. Food was an important part of those "discoveries" and the Portuguese played a crucial role in the globalisation of food some five hundred years ago.

The national cuisine is proclaimed on the official Angolan website and national dishes like *muamba de galinha* are recognised by many Angolans.

In Angolan literature, Luandino Vieira and Manuel Rui, who want to capture an *Angolanidade* in their prose, focus on the everyday life of the ordinary peoples and these writers savour the characteristics of the dishes of their country. Pepetela, while focusing on building a "romantic" utopian socialist future, tends to ignore food, or have his male characters eat in silence with their women. However, in the Jaime Bunda novels, Angolan cuisine emerges to induce the reader's saliva. A nationalism pointing to a glorious socialist utopia for the Angolan people has been replaced by a more mundane gastro-nationalism.[6]

Notes

[1] Margarido would not agree and argues that Portuguese influence is being lost in Brazil (44).

[2] The Brazilian *galinha ao molho pardo* is a variant of the original Portuguese dish.

[3] I would like to thank David Brookshaw for this thought.

[4] *Quintande*, a bean and palm oil stew (Cabral 83).

[5] It was also included in the second of three volumes or pamphlets entitled *Misoso* in 1964 (Ribas 3).

[6] Since the completion of this essay Pepetela's new novel, *Predadores*, has been published. Here food appears a little less frequently than in the Jaime Bunda novels. However, when the main protagonist, Vladimiro Caposso, is taking his new girlfriend Danúzia to a swanky restaurant in Luanda, Pepetela makes the following aside: "Curiosos, os leitores estão ansiosos por uma descrição da ementa e do que comeu o nosso parzinho. Desiludam-se, aqui não entra publicidada de borla. Foi um jantar ligeiro (...) com base em mariscos (...). Mais acrescento, foi jantar internacional, recusados os funjes, cabidelas ou kisakas da tradição" (63).

Works Cited

Afolabi, Niyi. *Golden Cage: Regeneration in Lusophone African Literature and Culture.* Trenton, NJ: Africa World Press, 2001.

Amado, Jorge. *Dona Flor and Her Two Husbands.* London: Serpent's Tail, 1999. [First published in Brazil in 1966 as *Dona Flor e seus Dois Maridos.*]

Anderson, Benedict. *Imagined Communities.* 2nd ed. London: Verso, 1991.

Barrot, Pierre, ed. *L'Afrique Côté Cuisines.* Paris: Syros, 1994.

Cabral, Ana da Costa. *Cozinha Tradicional de Angola.* Mem Martins: Europa-América, 2004.

Chantre, Maria de Lourdes. *Cozinha de Cabo Verde.* Lisbon: Presença, 1989.

———. *111 Receitas de Cozinha Africana.* Mem Martins: Europa-América, 1981.

Cruz, Marques da. *À mesa com Luís Vaz de Camões ou o romance da cozinha no Portugal das Descobertas.* Sintra: Colares, 1998.

Culler, Jonathan. *Literary Theory: A Very Short Introduction.* Oxford: Oxford UP, 1997.

Cusack, Igor. "African cuisines: recipes for nation-building?" *Journal of African Cultural Studies* 13.2 (2000): 207-225.

———. "Pots, Pens and 'Eating out the body': Cuisine and the Gendering of African nations." *Nations and Nationalism* 9.2 (2003): 277-296.

Hamilton, Cherie Y. *Cuisines of Portuguese Encounters.* New York: Hippocrene, 2001.

Lima, Mesquitela. "Prefácio." Chantre 11-17.

Margarido, Alfredo. *A Lusofonia e os Lusófonos: Novos Mitos Portugueses.* Luanda and Lisbon: Edições Universitárias Lusófonas, 2000.

Modesto, Maria de Lourdes. *Cozinha Tradicional Portuguesa.* Lisbon: Verbo, 1994.

Ohnuki-Tierney, Emiko. *Rice as Self: Japanese Identities through Time.* Princeton: Princeton UP, 1993.

Palmer, Catherine. "From Theory to Practice: Experiencing the Nation in Everyday Life." *Journal of Material Culture* 3.2 (1998): 175-99.

Pepetela. *O Desejo de Kianda.* [2000]. 3rd ed. Lisbon: Dom Quixote, 1995.

———. *A Geração da Utopia.* [2000]. 5th ed. Lisbon: Dom Quixote, 1992.

———. *Jaime Bunda, Agente Secreto.* [2001]. 2nd ed. Lisbon: Dom Quixote, 2001.

———. *Jaime Bunda e a Morte do Americano.* Lisbon: Dom Quixote, 2003.

———. *Mayombe.* [1999]. 7th ed. Lisbon: Dom Quixote, 1980.

———. *Predadores.* Lisbon: Dom Quixote, 2005.

———. *Yaka.* [1998]. 4th ed. Lisbon: Dom Quixote, 1985.

Peres, Phyllis. *Transculturation and Resistance in Lusophone African Narrative.* Gainesville: UP of Florida, 1997.

Praça, Afonso. "Saudades da Ilha de Luanda e alguns petiscos angolanas." *Revista de Letras e Culturas Lusófonos* [Instituto Camões] 6 (July-Sept. 1999).

<www.instituto-camoes.pt/revista/saudadilha.htm. Accessed 5/1/2005>.

Ribas, Óscar. *Alimentação Regional Angolana.* 6th ed. Lisbon: Ramos, Afonso & Moita, 1989. [Originally published in Luanda by the *Centro de Informaçao e Turismo de Angola* in 1965].

Rolletta, Paola. *Cozinha Tradicional de Moçambique.* Mem Martins: Europa-América, 2004.

Rui, Manuel. *Crónica de um Mujimbo.* [1999]. 2nd ed. Lisbon: Cotovia, 1991.

———. *Quem me dera ser onda.* [2001]. 6th ed. Lisbon: Cotovia, 1982.

Santos, Ana de Sousa. *A Alimentação do Muxiluanda.* Luanda: Cooperaçao Portuguesa, Embaixada de Portugal, 1996.

Valente, Maria Odette Cortes. *A Cozinha Descoberta pelos Portugueses.* Portugal: Gradiva, 1989.

Vieira, José Luandino. *João Vêncio e os Seus Amores.* Lisbon: Edições 70, 1979.

———. *Luuanda.* [1997]. 10th ed. Lisbon: Edições 70, 1980.

Websites

Angola: official website, cuisine: www.angola.org/culture/foodind.html. Accessed 9/12/2004.

Os Sabores Lusófonos: www.portugal-linha.pt/sabores/. Accessed 5/1/2005.

Roteiro Gastrónomico de Portugal: www.gastronomias.com/index.htm. Accessed 9/12/2004.

SoTam8: SoTam 8 Vietnamese restaurant, Luanda: www.sotam8.com/page2.html. Accessed 20/07/2002. The web page is being revised as at 5/01/2005.

Terravista: www.terravista.pt/guincho/4047/Angola/culinaria.htm. Accessed 20/07/2002. This is longer available (5/02/2005).

US embassy in Angola: "Welcome Packet for U.S. Citizens in Angola. Restaurants, Jazz Clubs and Nightclubs": http://usembassy.state.gov./angola/wwwhrestaurants.html 1-4. Accessed 09/12/2004

Igor Cusack teaches the history and literature of Lusophone Africa at the University of Birmingham. He also teaches the politics of sub-Saharan Africa, the history, politics, and literature of Equatorial Guinea and a course on cuisine, culture, and identity in the Hispanic World at the University of Bristol. After a career in the oil and coal industries working as a geologist, he began research in cultural studies and his recent publications include articles and chapters on African national cuisines, African national anthems, the ideologies associated with the postage stamps of Portugal and its empire, and representations of hegemonic masculinities in Equatoguinean and Angolan literature. Email: Igor.Cusack@bris.ac.uk

Pepetela: Entre a Carnavalização e a Denúncia de um Tempo sem Heróis

Robson Dutra

Resumo: Este texto pretende mostrar que, pelo jogo entre enunciado e enunciação, os romances de Pepetela reescrevem criticamente a História de Angola, denunciando que, embora tenha havido, durante a luta pela independência, um projeto de construção de heróis nacionais, estes nunca conseguiram se erigir totalmente e foram perdendo o contorno épico até se diluírem no clima distópico pós-colonial de uma Angola sem heróis. Para tanto, centramos nossa análise nos romances *Jaime Bunda, agente secreto* e *Jaime Bunda e a morte do americano*, publicados em 2001 e 2003, respectivamente, demonstrado que os heróis dos romances de Pepetela acompanham o movimento da história de Angola, indo de uma atmosfera de contornos épicos subjacentes aos ideais revolucionários do MPLA a traços trágicos que alegorizam o esfacelamento das utopias no presente que os romances que selecionamos como *corpus* literário enuncia.

Pepetela opta, nesses romances, pelo gênero policial, ainda que o faça pela paródia, visto que Jaime Bunda se revela uma imitação jocosa de James Bond, personagem que representa a excelência na investigação secreta e na sedução. Pela paródia, ironia e riso, Pepetela denuncia a corrupção existente em Angola e a dessacralização dos projetos de construção nacional dos tempos revolucionários. Ao publicar *Jaime Bunda, agente secreto* em 2001, Pepetela

Portuguese Literary & Cultural Studies 15/16 (2010): 231-49.

inaugurou o gênero "policial" na literatura angolana, ainda que o tenha feito pela paródia ao gênero literário em questão.

Nesse romance, a trama ficcional se constrói em torno do detetive Jaime Bunda, um negro lerdo e pesado por conta de suas abundantes carnes, que lhe valeram, somadas a seu desempenho medíocre em jogos de voleibol praticados na infância, o singular apelido. A personagem, no entanto, leitora ávida de novelas policiais, incorpora-o pacificamente como sobrenome por acreditar-se, assim, mais próxima de James Bond, o agente secreto do governo britânico, paradigma, assim, de excelência, quer na arte da espionagem, no uso de inventos que lhe permitem escapadas mirabolantes ou na sedução das muitas mulheres que o circundam, características que, por sua vez, personificam os desejos mais íntimos e secretos do detetive angolano.

A necessidade de aproximação a esse ícone da literatura e da cinematografia policialesca faz com que essa personagem da ficção de Pepetela não hesite, tampouco—evocando o conceito de paródia-travestizante de Bakhtin (*Questões* 373)—em imitar as palavras do herói britânico. Se este se apresenta com a expressão *Bond, James Bond*, Bunda o faz com *Bunda, Jaime Bunda.*

A paródia presentifica-se, desse modo, no romance e, seguindo os pressupostos evocados pela pesquisadora canadense Linda Hutcheon (46), cria novos níveis de sentido e de ilusão que retratam uma "realidade modelada" que aponta criticamente para a sociedade angolana contemporânea. Deste modo, a contraposição entre o James Bond original e sua caricatura angolana resulta no riso irônico, *tropo* fundamental para o funcionamento da paródia e da sátira de que Pepetela lança mão e que assinalam o compromisso crítico e agudo de sua literatura com os rumos tomados por seu país nos últimos quarenta anos.

No que se refere à ironia, esta se configura como uma voz que expressa um ponto de vista insustentável que difere do emitido pelo enunciador por subverter o que é e o que não é assumido por este. Como afirma Dominique Maingueneau (77), a enunciação assume palavras, mas não o ponto de vista do que elas representam no contexto, o que a faz, desse modo, tornar-se portadora de novos sentidos. Por reconhecer a ambigüidade basilar da ironia, que pode produzir significados em diferentes planos, Pepetela a utiliza com freqüência para, simultaneamente, veicular seu ponto de vista.

Uma outra característica relevante da ironia que se presentifica nos romances em que Jaime Bunda é protagonista é sua sutileza, que demanda a existência de um destinatário hábil em desvendá-la e de uma enunciação que permite escapar às normas de coerência impostas pela argumentação. Podemos, dessa maneira, afirmar que a ironia demanda tanto do produtor do texto, quanto de seu destinatário uma competência discursiva para compreendê-la ou resgatá-la e, assim, captar os sentidos subjacentes da narrativa. Este pressuposto é também assumido por Sigmund Freud ao definir a ironia como uma "representação pelo contrário":

> a ironia só pode ser empregada quando a outra pessoa está preparada para escutar o oposto, de modo que não pode deixar de sentir uma inclinação a contradizer. Em conseqüência dessa condição, a ironia se expõe facilmente ao risco de ser mal-entendida. Proporciona à pessoa que a utiliza a vantagem de capacitar-se prontamente a evitar dificuldades de expressão direta, por exemplo, no caso das invectivas. Isso produz prazer cômico no ouvinte, provavelmente porque excita nele uma contraditória despesa de energia, reconhecida como desnecessária. (99)

Sendo assim, para que o fenômeno irônico se concretize, torna-se necessário a decodificação dupla: uma de ordem lingüística e outra de natureza discursiva que fazem, por sua vez, com que o leitor atue como co-produtor de significação do texto, instaurando-se como interlocutor e projetando-se, desse modo, para dentro da obra. Semelhante concepção é partilhada por Elisabeth Brait ao postular que

> o percurso em direção à verdade é feito pela contramão, mas que o locutor conta com a sintonia do seu interlocutor. Ou seja: é de fato, no espírito do destinatário que a verdade irônica faz eclodir seu efeito, mas de maneira a estabelecer uma seqüência de três elementos: o eu consciente, o outro e o eu inconsciente. (165)

A ironia assume, dessa maneira, uma dimensão ideológica, social, cultural e histórica, tanto quanto pode ser considerada pelo prisma da subjetividade autoral. O texto irônico serve, ainda, a uma maior conscientização política e social, ao esclarecimento e ao desmonte de discursos tidos como sérios e absolutos, do mesmo modo que pode ratificar ou instaurar conceitos, descrevendo em termos valorizantes uma realidade que ele desvaloriza. Mueck destaca, ainda, uma outra perspectiva, apresentando a ironia do ponto de vista social. Ouçamo-lo:

> A ironia tem basicamente uma função corretiva. É como um giroscópio que mantém a vida num curso equilibrado ou reto, restaurando o equilíbrio quando a vida está sendo levada muito a sério ou, como mostram algumas tragédias, não está sendo levada a sério o bastante, estabilizando o instável, mas também desestabilizando o excessivamente estável. (19)

Podemos perceber que, em última instância, ironizar é dizer algo de forma que ative não uma, mas uma série infindável de interpretações de ordem subversiva que criam, por sua vez, um contraste entre o real e o aparente que pode ser encontrado na mentira, na hipocrisia, nos sofismas, nos equívocos. O que irá diferenciá-los da ironia é o fato de que o "ironista" não quer ser acreditado, mas, sim, entendido como tal. O que não está explícito pretende-se, portanto, entendido e jamais sonegado.

Essas são algumas das premissas de que Pepetela lança mão em sua incursão pelo gênero "policial" e que voltaremos a considerar oportunamente. No que tange ao romance especificamente, o sucesso obtido pelo primeiro livro de aventuras de *Jaime Bunda, agente secreto* e a revelação de muitos outros dilemas dignos de investigação minuciosa na sociedade angolana, levaram Pepetela a, em 2003, lançar outro romance protagonizado pela mesma personagem: *Jaime Bunda e a morte do americano.* A trama narrativa desta obra faz com que o agente secreto dos SIG—Serviços de Investigação Geral, a polícia das polícia—se desloque de Luanda, a capital do país, uma "*Manhattan* hiperbolizada," segunda a voz narrativa (25), para a provinciana cidade de Benguela, também conhecida como "cidade das acácias rubras," a fim de solucionar o possível assassinato de um cidadão norte-americano.

Homicídios são, aliás, os elementos desencadeadores das duas narrativas, visto que em *Jaime Bunda, agente secreto,* a morte de uma adolescente de catorze anos de idade constitui-se o ponto inicial de uma investigação que assume contornos insondáveis, que revelam crimes de maior gravidade, e por isso, acobertados, em Angola. Em *Jaime Bunda e a morte do americano,* Pepetela retoma um tema conhecido no país: o assassinato, na década de cinqüenta, de um engenheiro português em circunstâncias idênticas àquelas enunciadas no romance em questão. A estratégia ficcional em resgatar um evento ocorrido meio século atrás faz valer a epígrafe usada por este autor no romance *A Geração da utopia* de que "só os ciclos são eternos" (9) e, por isso, fatos de outrora são recorrentes e podem servir de reflexão, questionamento e crítica do presente.

Ademais, tendo em vista que a hegemonia lusitana na África até 1975, ano de sua derrocada, pode equivaler à supremacia que os Estados Unidos da América tentam ardorosamente manter na contemporaneidade, a trama romanesca de Pepetela lida, de igual modo, com relações de poder e de dominação. Nossa reflexão parte do pensamento crítico de Edward Said que, ao discorrer sobre a identidade norte-americana nos dias atuais, afirma ser ela "variada demais para constituir algo homogêneo; na verdade, a luta que se trava em seu interior envolve defensores de uma identidade unitária e os que vêem o conjunto como uma totalidade complexa, mas não redutoramente unificada" (27).

O traço comum que une as duas narrativas é a tentativa ávida e obtusa de Jaime Bunda usar o conhecimento oriundo da ficção policialesca no cotidiano de seu trabalho em uma das inúmeras repartições da complexa máquina estatal angolana. A personagem pensa, ainda, poder empregar em seu trabalho como detetive a mesma lógica que crê existir nas novelas de sua predileção, o que constitui-se motivo de riso e de escárnio de seus companheiros de equipe e, em segunda instância, do narrador e do próprio leitor.

Em considerações sobre o riso, Verena Alberti afirma ser ele "o carro-chefe de um movimento de redenção do pensamento," como se a filosofia não mais pudesse se estabelecer fora dele (11), ou seja, o riso reabilita um "nada," uma metade excluída do universo das chamadas "coisas sérias" que só é considerado visível e audível através do riso. A autora afirma ainda que a esperança inicial de apreender a essência do riso e do risível revela-se um lugar melancólico, como aquele que despontara em romances do pós-guerra como *A Geração da utopia*, *O Desejo de Kianda* e *A Montanha da água lilás*, por exemplo, em que o riso distópico se une à constatação da falência dos movimentos de libertação e de sua total exigüidade na contemporaneidade.

Esta é a razão por que o riso não-normativo, o desvio e o indizível fazem parte da existência e estabelecem uma relação entre ordem e desordem que implica pôr em xeque a própria razão humana e o "nada" a que nos referimos anteriormente. Desse modo, o riso e a ironia tornam-se a alternativa escolhida por Pepetela para, mais uma vez, tentar compreender seu país e aclarar os ocultos e densos caminhos históricos traçados por instâncias do poder em Angola.

Mesclando, pois, o riso ao grotesco que envolve personagens antes comprometidos com os ideais revolucionários, a morte da anônima adolescente—ou seja, um crime de importância reduzida—torna-se, em *Jaime Bunda, agente secreto*, a via de acesso ao mundo da corrupção angolana, que oscila dos muitos e pesados cordões de ouro usados, por exemplo, pelo detetive Isidro, um dos colegas de trabalho de Bunda, através de ações ilícitas que lhe assegurarão a aquisição de mais dessas jóias, ao envolvimento de personagens ilustres da sociedade e do universo político angolano em crimes perpetrados contra a nação, que passam, contudo, pela figura risível de Jaime Bunda, que desfila jocosamente entre esses diversos espaços narrativos carnavalizantes e alegóricos.

A carnavalização operada por Pepetela nesses romances retoma as premissas de Mikhail Bakhtin ao considerar a obra de François Rabelais e perceber nela laços densos com a cultura popular medieval, levando em consideração, para tanto, os gêneros literários a ela associados, como a paródia, a sátira e o realismo grotesco. Bakhtin argumenta que, no final da Idade Média e durante o Renascimento, o carnaval desempenhou um papel simbólico fundamental na vida das pessoas visto que, durante estas festividades, elas penetravam brevemente na esfera da liberdade utópica.

Naquela época, a relevância do carnaval representava muito mais do que a interrupção do trabalho produtivo, mas assinalava uma cosmovisão alternativa que se caracterizava pelo questionamento lúdico de todas as formas, por abolir as hierarquias e restrições cotidianas. Por esta razão, durante o carnaval, tudo o que é marginalizado e excluído, como o insano, o não normativo, o indizível e o aleatório se aproximam do centro, numa explosão libertadora. Para o pensador russo, o riso que permeia as manifestações carnavalescas pertence a um tipo especial de riso festivo que vai além da manifestação individual a um evento cômico isolado. Caracteriza-se, também, por uma espécie de alegria cósmica universal que se dirige a tudo e a todos, inclusive aos que tomam parte do carnaval. Dotado de um profundo significado filosófico, esse riso assinala um ponto de vista particular sobre a experiência, não menos profundo que a seriedade e acaba por se constituir uma vitória sobre o medo que torna risível e grotesco tudo que aterroriza, seja o pânico natural sobre o sagrado ou a morte que reduzem simbolicamente a realeza e a nobreza opressoras.

Se pensarmos o herói romanesco na obra de Pepetela, perceberemos que ele oscila do protagonista de traços épicos que caracteriza as narrativas datadas dos anos setenta, como *As Aventuras de Ngunga* e *Mayombe*, como bem assinala Lourenço do Rosário, àquele que se reveste de traços trágicos por perceber a fratura que caracteriza o espaço em que se insere. Nestas narrativas, Pepetela descreve o herói romanesco que habita um mundo degradado, como afirma Lukács, que tenta, em vão, recuperar a unidade de um universo fechado que não mais existe. Pepetela assume o pressuposto luckasiano que atribui às sociedades modernas burguesas o estilhaçamento entre sujeito e objeto, fragmentação e angústia. A utopia ingênua e a falta de mediação entre tomada de posição deste sujeito e a realidade concreta que se presentificam nas obras relativas à gênese da revolução contra o colonialismo cedem lugar à constatação de que é impossível ao herói romanesco alcançar seus objetivos, o que faz com que ele assuma contornos trágicos como os percebidos, por exemplo, no romance *A Geração da utopia*. De acordo com o próprio Pepetela, este romance "não é uma resposta a nada. É apenas uma estória sobre uma geração que fez a independência de Angola e não soube fazer mais" (Chaves e Macedo 35). Por esta razão, a personagem Aníbal, o sábio, cede lugar a Vitor Ramos, o Mundial, ou seja, o local e restrito se fragmentam ante à sedução exercida pelo poder em um universo globalizado que não prestigia mais o particular, mas sim a massificação que se presencia em Angola, a partir do pós-guerra.

A ficção pepeteliana e seu compromisso implícito de analisar criticamente a história de seu país não deixam de assinalar a curva descendente que estes "heróis" empreendem ao longo de seu percurso. Por esta razão, os ideais utópicos que embalaram a revolução deterioraram-se à beira do mar de Benguela, sem que a vitória contra o colonialismo pudesse ser amplamente compreendida e instaurada. Ainda que opte por residir no alto de uma falésia e dela contemplar o mar, como o já aludido Aníbal, de *A Geração da utopia*, ou ainda como o lupi-poeta e o lupi-pensador que passam a habitar o cimo das árvores, em *A Montanha da água lilás*, sem jamais tocar o solo, a trajetória político-literária empreendida por Angola e captada por Pepetela com acuidade, assinala que, em tempos neoliberais, a figuração do herói, neste país, encontra-se desgastada e comprometida.

De acordo, ainda, com a concepção de Lukács sobre o romance, este seria uma das formas de percepção da modernidade. Se para Walter Benjamin, por exemplo, a modernidade é um colapso das experiências de espaço e tempo anteriores, provocado pela revolução industrial e tecnológica, Lukács a problematiza como o último estágio de um processo de decadência e desintegração em que se esvai o sentido de vida e de ruptura entre a verdade e a existência, que lança o indivíduo em uma espécie de desamparo transcendental. Desse modo, o romance também passa a representar uma forma romanesca de desilusão, em uma perspectiva dialética, que deverá encontrar seu momento sintético através de novas experiências e concepções da realidade em que o mundo homogêneo encontra-se desarticulado.

Esta é a razão por que, como protagonista de uma modernidade comprometida e corroída, Jaime Bunda renuncia ao real e não se mostra capaz de compreender as verdades que o circundam, nem mesmo algumas das características que, outrora, eram inerentes ao herói. Em *Jaime Bunda, agente secreto*, por exemplo, Dona Filó, uma anciã, adivinha e representante do saber tradicional angolano, declara explicitamente a Bunda que ele não será capaz de elucidar a morte da catorzinha, tampouco reconhecer seu autor: "Tu não vais descobrir. O medo cobre o rosto do assassino, tu vais olhar no lado, vai lhe ver (...). Quando tiveres medo de te mijar pelas pernas, lembra-te de mim" (61). Ao término da narrativa e após ser reconhecido oficialmente como "herói," Bunda confronta-se com o assim enunciado tenebroso personagem Senhor "T," instante em que, pelo temor sentido, recorda-se da profecia da velha feiticeira. Tomado de pânico, o detetive fraqueja e reconhece sua incapacidade em entender e esclarecer essa intrincada "verdade," um novo enigma que se presentifica.

De modo a exacerbar a crítica social e política através do riso, as múltiplas vozes enunciadoras ressaltam a forma equivocada com que Bunda age, se confrontada com o padrão detetivesco clássico. A personagem tem seu discurso freqüentemente permeado por referências cultas citadas, no entanto, erroneamente, como, por exemplo, ao referir-se a Calígula como um "filósofo lá dos orientes" (29). Bunda subverte, ainda, ditos populares e cria outros como: "nunca ouviu dizer que *dura lex sed lex*, quer dizer a lei dura muito e tem sede de lei? Frase do Aristóteles" (24-25); "como diria Camus, um decadente francês, não há peste sem pústulas" (114) ou, ainda, dentre inúmeras outras exemplificações possíveis, "como diria S. Sebastião, há de sentir o peso de cada flecha que agora disparam" (113). Esta característica ressalta o traço risível da personagem e da ambigüidade do texto que enuncia, visto que seu saber denota a falta de reflexão crítica e criteriosa que resulta no *nonsense* com que conduz suas investigações.

Contudo, apesar de ridicularizado pela narrativa, o estagiário e, posteriormente, denominado pejorativamente como detetive "cototó," causa espanto em seus colegas de repartição ao deslindar uma rede internacional de falsificação de *kwanzas*, a unidade monetária angolana, vindo a receber, por seus feitos e astúcia, o epíteto de "herói nacional." Na estupefação enunciada despontam a representação pelo contrário e a duplicidade de sentido e de significado que a ironia apresenta: o crime inicial não é desvendado, do mesmo modo que todos os demais delitos investigados não serão satisfatoriamente concluídos. A promoção de Bunda, os elogios ao Diretor de Operações, o brinde com o champanhe oferecido pelo senhor "T" e toda comemoração feita resultam apenas numa noção irrisória de satisfação e completude que Pepetela denuncia em sua trama e que alegoriza crimes que nem a mais detalhada e pormenorizada investigação policial aclara.

Ao discorrer sobre o romance policial, Vera Follain de Figueiredo (qtd. in Secco 124) afirma que este subgênero literário é um contraponto aos romances de resistência que caracterizaram o período de distopias, ou seja, de um tempo posterior às utopias dos anos sessenta no Brasil e na América Latina. Se naquele momento era premente subverter a ótica oficial da história fazendo-se ouvir voz dos excluídos e apontar novas "verdades," em seu sentido benjaminiano, a fim de se acentuar o ideal de nação recém-liberta, o esgarçamento e o esfacelamento das utopias no pós-guerra de Angola resultaram em um humor cínico e mordaz que se presentifica na contemporaneidade, assinalando "a dispersão e a banalização de crimes e detetives em tempos neoliberais, onde, em muitos países, a corrupção é generalizada e instituída por poderes paralelos e, até mesmo, centrais" (125).

Pepetela parodia a estética policial para, a partir da morte da adolescente e do norte-americano, iniciar uma investigação que revela não necessariamente seus assassinos, mas uma rede complexa de crimes de maior gravidade e relevância, cometidos, mormente, por personagens antes comprometidas com os ideais utópicos de libertação e de reconstrução de Angola. Por isso, é inevitável a comparação entre personagens de *Jaime Bunda, agente secreto* e *Jaime Bunda e a morte do americano* com Aquiles e Orestes, de *Yaka*; Carmina Cara de Cu, de *O Desejo de Kianda* e seu marido João Evangelista; Malongo e Vitor Ramos, de *A Geração da utopia*, por exemplo, "jacalupis" de uma Angola contemporânea descrente com o fato de ser objetivamente impossível recuperar o passado, visto que a aura de "heroicidade" que as envolvia, quer pela semântica de seus nomes ou pelo papel que desempenharam nos anos anteriores à guerra, não perdurou no período subseqüente à independência.

Dada a tênue linha que separa o *facto* do *ficto*, Pepetela utiliza procedimentos metaficcionais para construir uma ilusão romanesca que será, em seguida, desconstruída, revelando ao leitor como a tecedura ficcional é engendrada. A utilização de fatos e personagens da história, ainda que camuflados pela enunciação feita por múltiplas vozes narrativas, assume um outro sentindo no universo ficcional, já que instaura o contexto histórico para, posteriormente, subvertê-lo ao conferir-lhe um tratamento que se concretiza no desencanto e na reflexão que a literatura faz de si mesma. Tanto em *Jaime Bunda, agente secreto* quanto em *Jaime Bunda e a morte do ame-*

ricano percebem-se claramente fatos do cotidiano angolano, ainda que o "poder" ao qual Jaime Bunda se associa e procura defender seja integrado por personagens anônimas. Suas identidades são, contudo, apontadas sutilmente pela descrição de fatos políticos e sociais de que participam. Desse modo, abundam referências, ao Diretor de Operações (D.O.), ao misterioso comandante do Bunker que, "com seus olhos enormes e redondos como os das osgas, tudo vê e tudo sabe" (*Agente Secreto* 95), e ao tenebroso senhor "T," personagens que, por sua vez, se ligam aos vários departamentos e segmentos da burocracia angolana, conhecidos por siglas como SIG, SRD, SPU, PQP.

Algumas dessas personagens são retomadas, em *Jaime Bunda e a morte do americano* e unidas ficcionalmente a outras como o embaixador americano, o ministro e o governador de Benguela, que, de modo semelhante, não recebem nome. Curiosamente, apenas a "governadora," Dona Nzuzi dos Santos (*A Morte* 91), é nominada dentre aqueles ligados ao poder, talvez porque suas funções oficiais limitem-na a se ocupar dos muitos panos coloridos com que se enfeita e do preparo de pratos típicos da culinária angolana que serve aos convidados do governo, o que, de certo modo, corrobora uma representação exótica de Angola.

A crítica de Pepetela ao sistema governamental angolano também é feita de forma mordaz em duas passagens de *Jaime Bunda e a morte do americano*: a primeira delas se presentifica quando a narrativa se refere à gordura do poder, ou seja, ao excesso de peso dos governantes angolanos, metonimizados no representante máximo de Benguela. Este excesso de calorias é adquirido através de imagens *rabelaisianas* de lautos banquetes custeados pelo Estado e que têm a função simbólica de transferência temporária para um mundo utópico de prazer, abundância e excessos perpetrados por esse mesmo Estado que, entretanto, relega ao povo a fome e a magreza que, na visão irônica do narrador, será por isso "mais saudável e longevo que seus líderes" (55). A segunda crítica também é feita a partir do governador da cidade das acácias rubras e aos gases não nobres por ele expelidos durante as reuniões da cúpula governamental angolana. A curiosidade em conhecer o autor da atrocidade olfativa, associada à improbidade no uso da verba pública, tornou-se, segundo a voz enunciadora, prioridade nos altos escalões do governo que, de posse de sensibilíssimos sensores importados exclusivamente dos EUA para este fim, conseguiram desvendar este "mistério" e manter, conseqüentemente, o governador de Benguela distante do nariz da figura máxima da nação, cujo flato é, irônica e absolutamente, inodoro (86).

Mais uma vez, Pepetela retoma pressupostos bakhtinianos de carnavalização, visto que, durante esta festividade, o princípio corpóreo material como a fome, a sede, a copulação, a defecação e a flatulência, por exemplo, torna-se uma força positivamente corrosiva que, acompanhada do riso festivo e corrosivo, celebra uma vitória simbólica sobre a morte e resulta na dessacralização de dogmas sociais, religiosos e culturais e, em última instância, das várias formas de opressão.

O corpo humano assume, na carnavalização, o que Bakhtin denomina "corpo grotesco" e o "local de vir-a-ser" (*Cultura* 23). Seja na urina vertida por Bunda ao deparar-se com o terrível senhor "T," como o excesso de peso do detetive e do governador de Benguela, os elementos-chave do corpo são os pontos que ele possui e que transgridem seus próprios limites: os intestinos, o falo, as convexidades e os orifícios que ressaltam para o mundo ou que absorvem o mundo. Ao focalizar a vida corpórea, o carnaval oferece uma suspensão temporária da proibição e do tabu, transferindo o que é abstrato para o nível material, neste caso, para a esfera do corpo.

No que se refere, contudo, ao tom "policialesco" da obra, este é alcançado pela utilização de uma outra técnica narrativa que reforça o ar de investigação policial, como a de começar novos capítulos com frases e idéias literalmente descritas no anterior. Como exemplo podemos citar o capítulo quatro de *Jaime Bunda, agente secreto*, que termina com a frase "esse derrame de informações podia chegar a maus ouvidos, por exemplo, de uma certa imprensa pretensamente controlada pelo Honório, que disseminaria os indícios por tudo quanto é canto, perigando o já de si difícil *inquérito*" (40) e o capítulo cinco que é iniciado com "*Inquérito* que estava completamente emperrado" (41). Este mesmo procedimento é retomado entre os capítulos cinco: "Amanhã só vai *entrar por essa porta* o Bunda com aquele sorriso gelado..." (48), e seis: "Não *entrou pela porta.* Telefonou" (49), e ainda, entre os capítulos seis e sete: "Laurinha é só dois anos mais velha que a *menina assassinada*" (54); "(...) *A qual menina* está completamente esquecida" (55). Essa repetição intencional de palavras simula as diversas pistas que detetives, tanto da realidade quanto da ficção, têm de seguir cautelosamente a fim de desvendarem os mistérios que lhes apresentam, criando um jogo de esconde-esconde em que o grande trunfo consiste em decifrar a autoria do crime.

No que se refere ao nível diegético em *Jaime Bunda, agente secreto*, são convocados quatro narradores que dão seus "depoimentos," muitas vezes falseadores, ao leitor que vai, aos poucos, montando o intrincado quebra-cabeça que ronda a morte da menina de catorze anos, por isso conhecida como "catorzinha." Seria a idade da vítima uma alusão à prostituição infantil que cresce alarmantemente em Angola ou uma referência sutil aos catorze anos de revolução que resultaram em violação, degradação e morte metafórica da sociedade angolana? A crítica que Pepetela pode fazer através da idade da menina dialoga com outra, feita à impunidade reinante no país, já que seu assassinato se deu nos confortáveis bancos do imponente automóvel da elite luandense, sem que nada ou ninguém revelasse a identidade de seu autor. Outra interpretação que acreditamos ser pertinente é a de que o estupro da menina se associa à ruptura da lei e dos costumes, hábito que se tem tornado por demais aviltante em Angola. Esta violação afeta, ironicamente, até mesmo o poderoso Senhor "T," que, para ser protegido de seus crimes, é possuído sexualmente pelo *kimbanda* a quem encomendara proteção e que em seu português arrevesado ordena: "baixa as calças e as cueca, põe a mão no braço da cadeira e afasta as perna e fica quieto"... "Eu é que sei. Tratamento para fechar teus caminhos todos. Ninguém depois vai descobrir as asneira que você tem feito" (*Agente Secreto* 69).

É interessante observar que, tal como a estátua *jaga* testemunhara com seus olhos de vidro e silêncio o percurso dos protagonistas de *Yaka*, a gênese e os desdobramentos da guerra contra o colonialismo, o "tratamento" banto ora descrito é acompanhado, na contemporaneidade, por outra estátua: um *nkisi* do Congo, crivado de pregos enferrujados, que, de cima da secretária, contempla, com seus olhos de espelho, mais esta violação (70).

Quaisquer que sejam, no entanto, as respostas para os muitos questionamentos que a leitura do texto pepeteliano suscita, estas parecem ser conhecidas apenas pelo "mega-narrador" que rege a enunciação de *Jaime Bunda, agente secreto*, cujo discurso onisciente, impresso em itálico e entre colchetes, convoca outros narradores a relatar o que sabem, ao mesmo tempo em que este opina, traduz, corrige, suprime vozes e relatos, sem que, contudo, os enigmas propostos sejam devidamente aclarados. Ao contrário, os diversos capítulos, intitulados "livros dos narradores," criam e ampliam teias intrincadas que frustram as muitas tentativas de deslindamento da trama romanesca e apontam para a recorrência de muitas "verdades" que, mais uma vez em acepção benjaminiana, a narrativa desvela. Por esta razão, o leitor é incitado a participar da "perseguição" aos possíveis criminosos, cujas pistas são deixadas por toda Luanda, do sofisticado bairro do Alvalade, onde reside o Senhor "T," ao popular mercado Roque Santeiro, às margens da baía de Luanda, onde desembarcam mercadorias contrabandeadas.

Este mesmo recurso, diga-se de passagem, já fora empregado anteriormente pelo autor como, por exemplo, em *O cão e os caluandas*, em 1985, em que Pepetela no capítulo "aviso ao leitor," com que inicia a obra, informa que "os que conheceram o cão pastor-alemão deixaram os documentos escritos ou gravados" que este resumira e publicara (9). Estes relatos, guardados por anos em uma gaveta—o que faz com que muitos de seus autores não possam mais ser localizados, fato que, ironicamente, dificulta qualquer reclamação de seus possíveis herdeiros—são constituídos por anúncios de jornal, cartas, depoimentos, etc, que, reunidos pelo narrador, compõem a obra.

O poder auferido ao "mega-narrador" não se restringe apenas às quatro vozes enunciadoras por ele comandadas: por vezes, este se dirige ao leitor com o intuito de repreendê-lo por fazer interpretações diferentes das suas, coibindo, inclusive, aqueles que, porventura, saltaram páginas do romance, a fim de, como é comum em novelas policiais, "descobrir viciosamente como acaba a história" (*Agente Secreto* 274).

Suas restrições e interrupções ao primeiro narrador fazem com que este seja "demitido" de suas funções, visto que seu depoimento revela mais do que recomenda a prudência das testemunhas dos relatos (pseudo)-históricos. A segunda voz narrativa apresenta um enredo já descrito pelo primeiro narrador, mas que é apresentado sob nova perspectiva que revela a multiplicidade de interpretações possíveis de uma mesma história. Os fatos ali evidenciados não se referem, especificamente, ao assassinato da jovem Catarina Kiela, mas descrevem o contrabando, a falsificação de dinheiro e o envolvimento de figurões da elite angolana em atividades comprometedoras. Com os desdobramentos da narrativa, percebemos que quem escreve é Malika, personagem de uma trama a princípio secundária à do romance, mas que se avulta consideravelmente ao longo do texto, revelando que enredos menores também interferem na história principal. Ao utilizar o depoimento oficial da personagem, detida pelos SIG para investigação dos crimes de corrupção, Pepetela fragmenta ainda mais a narrativa, visto que aufere dupla função a esta personagem-narradora e à significância dos fatos que relata.

A terceira enunciação é retomada pelo primeiro narrador que retorna à diegese após ser repreendido pelo "mega-narrador" que lhe faz "necessários acertos e infindáveis recomendações" que resultam em um texto cético e mordaz. A autoconsciência narrativa faz com que este enunciador reconheça o depoimento da segunda narradora e una o relato de Malika aos fatos que, por sua vez, evidenciará. Por fim, cabe ao quarto narrador concluir a história, tentando encadear os fatos já enunciados. Sua tentativa, no entanto, se mostrará frustrada, visto que a verdadeira conclusão a que se chega é o "desvendamento pelo leitor da enunciação polifônica do romance que, operando com o fingimento escritural, sinaliza para o cinismo social e a descrença no poder instituído de Angola" (Secco 129).

No epílogo de *Jaime Bunda, agente secreto*, o discurso é retomado por um falso autor que aparecera explicitamente no prólogo do romance para contar o trágico fim da catorzinha e que, ao longo da narrativa, teve sua presença marcada por uma série de interrupções e observações que evidenciaram que os esforços de Jaime Bunda em desvendar o assassinato o afastavam cada vez mais deste crime para aproximá-lo da potente rede de corrupção em Angola.

De forma semelhante, em *Jaime Bunda e a morte do americano*, as investigações do detetive protagonista o conduzem à solução da morte do americano, assassinado, por razões pessoais, por um compatriota e não por motivação política, como quisera crer o governo norte-americano. No entanto, a obra apresenta dois epílogos e o primeiro deles dá conta de que um culpado, Júlio Fininho, fora encontrado a fim de satisfazer o desejo do governo estadunidense, temeroso, tanto na ficção quanto na realidade, de ataques inimigos. A revelação do nome do assassino, coagido, contudo, a confessar o crime após intermináveis sessões de tortura, acaba por preservar o bom relacionamento de Angola com o governo norte-americano, fazendo, segundo palavras do D. O. a Bunda, "pouco importar se o criminoso é inocente ou culpado" (219).

Apenas o segundo epílogo possível aponta para o verdadeiro assassino do engenheiro, evidenciando, mais uma vez, a existência de uma pluralidade de "verdades" que nem sempre podem ser vislumbradas, conforme afirma o pseudo-autor no fim do romance, posto que "nosso mundo é regido por forças que sempre nos escaparam" (261). Mais uma vez, Pepetela retoma a estratégia ficcional empregada em *O cão e os caluandas*, de apresentar dois finais possíveis: "Pus as duas versões. O júri são vocês, leitores" (179). Através dela, a enunciação, que, a princípio dirige-se a um público angolano, é ampliada, passando a envolver outra categoria de leitores, que passa a auferir valor às possíveis interpretações que as diversas narrativas que compõem a obra suscitam.

Tanto *Jaime Bunda, agente secreto* quanto em *Jaime Bunda e a morte do americano* apresentam uma trama principal e outras secundárias que lhe servem de contraponto. No primeiro romance, a morte da adolescente é secundada pela corrupção em Angola, pelo relacionamento entre Malika e o jovem Tozé, protegido do Senhor "T" e também pela ligação pseudo-amorosa entre Jaime Bunda e Florinda. Ironicamente, ao contrário de sua "matriz" britânica, o detetive da polícia das polícias demonstra ser incapaz de seduzi-la e, por isso, contrata um marginal para surrar e quebrar a perna do marido de sua pretensa amante, sofrendo, contudo, ele mesmo o mal que encomendara ao rival. Em *Jaime Bunda e a morte do americano*, o protagonista tenta arduamente incorporar os encantos sedutores de Bond, envidando os mais árduos—e risíveis—esforços na conquista de Shirley, a detetive do FBI enviada para Angola a fim de supervisionar as atividades da polícia local. Esta, no entanto, opta pelos encantos da *Miss* Benguela, rechaçando por completo as diversas investidas amorosas do detetive. O êxito, portanto, em descobrir as falcatruas de "T" e o assassino do americano não se repete nas artes amorosas em nenhuma das duas narrativas, fazendo com que Bunda se contraponha a James Bond em mais este quesito e não alcance a plenitude de vitórias inerentes aos protagonistas da ficção policial.

Uma outra narrativa que se associa a esta e à da personagem Robin dos comboios—alusão a outra personagem da ficção, no caso, Robin Hood—e que se refere ao contrabando de crianças angolanas para o exterior, com vistas ao abastecimento do tráfico internacional de órgãos humanos. A ironia da enunciação une Arsênio do Carmo, aliciador dos menores e sobrinho da empregada do engenheiro americano assassinado, a um membro da tradicional e secular família Bragança, herdeiro, portanto, da elite lusitana que, no entanto, segundo a enunciação, gerou "reis e príncipes incapazes de governar por deficiências genéticas" (*A Morte* 260).

A trama narrativa de *Jaime Bunda e a morte do americano* é engendrada por narradores de *Jaime Bunda, agente secreto*. A primeira e a terceira vozes enunciadoras do primeiro romance são outra vez ouvidas neste segundo. Tomamos conhecimento de sua existência pela afirmação feita, que relata ao leitor que este narrador fora demitido anteriormente pelo autor por descrever fatos que este não apreciou. Por isso, e a fim de se redimir, o narrador em questão, outra vez contratado, procura agradar ao pseudo-autor que, tal como Pepetela, é nascido na cidade de Benguela. Desse modo, a enunciação tece loas a esta cidade, à culinária local, além de optar por variantes lingüísticas do português benguelense que resulta no uso, por exemplo, do vocábulo "mataco" em vez de "bunda" para se referir às grandes dimensões glúteas de

Jaime. No entanto, os esforços dessa voz narrativa parecem ter sido em vão, visto que, no segundo epílogo, o pseudo-autor dá-se conta do estilo exacerbadamente superficial deste narrador que teve o azar de apresentar aos leitores. Por esta razão, é ele mesmo, o pseudo-autor, quem conclui a narrativa, evidenciando, com isso, a parcialidade dos depoimentos e a multiplicidade de olhares e "verdades" dos fatos enunciados.

Essa premissa, cremos, vai ao encontro dos postulados de Theodor Adorno ao afirmar que o narrador no romance contemporâneo representa a "resposta antecipada a uma constituição do mundo em que a atitude contemplativa tornou-se um sarcasmo sangrento," posto que "a permanente ameaça da catástrofe não permite a observação imparcial" (61), característica, portanto, das obras de que nos ocupamos. O filósofo alemão ainda levanta outra questão que se presentifica nas obras em questão ao comentar que, no romance contemporâneo, a subjetividade liberada é levada por sua própria força gravitacional a converter-se em seu contrário, assemelhando-se, dessa maneira, àquilo que ele denomina epopéias negativas uma outra característica da ficção pepeteliana.

No que diz respeito ao tempo cronológico, lemos tanto em *Jaime Bunda, agente secreto* quanto em *Jaime Bunda e a morte do americano*, o relato de fatos ocorridos no momento da enunciação. As vozes narrativas informam, ironicamente, ao leitor, por exemplo, que o assassinato da adolescente ocorreu no feriado do dia 11 de novembro (*Agente Secreto* 307), data em que é celebrada a Independência de Angola. As demais referências relativas ao pretérito tempo das utopias restringem-se à menção de "Esperteza do Povo" e ao socialismo esquemático dos anos de guerra. "Esperteza do Povo" é-nos apresentado como um ex-guerrilheiro, tio de Bunda, que, deslocado no pós-guerra, foi convidado a trabalhar nas fileiras policiais em que, por acaso, começou a cultivar a leitura dos romances detetivescos que o sobrinho herdaria posteriormente. Parte da derrocada do projeto utópico é assinalada ao longo do primeiro romance protagonizado por Bunda, através de uma série de referências a pequenos delitos cometidos pela população, ainda sob efeito da guerra colonial e da revolução civil que a sucedeu, que fez uso de "pistolões" para a compra de residências abandonadas pelos antigos colonos, para a obtenção de empregos e até mesmo para a venda de armas de guerra.

Em *Jaime Bunda e a morte do americano* surge outra referência aos tempos do socialismo e das utopias pretéritas. Julio Fininho, o Robin dos comboios a que nos referimos, assume-se "homem de princípios, formado nos tempos do socialismo esquemático, esperança de Homem Novo que nele desabrochava" (39), mas que, contudo, não encontrou meios de subsistência após ser desmobilizado do exército angolano, exceto viver dos pequenos furtos cometidos ao longo dos caminhos de ferro angolanos e, posteriormente, maximizados pelo jornalismo obtuso e pretensioso de Charlô Qualquer Coisa.

Estas referências ao passado dialogam com uma outra superposição temporal que se dá entre contemporaneidade e ancestralidade. Em *Jaime Bunda, agente secreto,* conforme nos referimos no início do texto, Jaime Bunda não compreende o vaticínio de Dona Filó, a adivinha da Ilha de Luanda, de que ele tremeria quando estivesse diante do culpado pela morte de Catarina Kiela. Bunda dá-se conta da importância dessas palavras apenas ao deparar-se com "T" e quase, ironicamente, desmaiar, no momento em que se celebrou o "êxito" das diligências policiais no desmantelamento da rede internacional de contrabandistas que o próprio Senhor "T" capitaneava. O medo sentido pelo detetive nesta ocasião é idêntico ao pânico que o havia feito urinar-se calças abaixo quando o armazem com o dinheiro clandestino trazido a Angola fora invadido pela polícia.

A palavra profética da anciã foi o motivo da busca da proteção do soturno Sr. "T," que ouviu da boca do *kimbanda* a quem recorrera, haver na Ilha de Luanda uma velha cujo poder lhe poderia lhe ocasionar problemas. O livro do quarto narrador, contudo, afirma que o assassino confesso da catorzinha, o filho de um político do partido majoritário angolano, havia sido preso com a ajuda da mesma D. Filó, que, ao passar as mãos pelo banco do carona do carro do rapaz, sentira as vibrações do corpo da menina. A trama policialesca se faceta ainda mais nesse momento, ressaltando, outra vez, a existência de crimes de maior gravidade que o assassinato da adolescente, cometidos pela classe hegemônica angolana que, através de saberes ancestrais, tentara encobrir as falhas do presente.

Em *Jaime Bunda e a morte do americano,* a anciã da Catumbela, responsável pelo feitiço engendrado por Josefina para prender Julio Fininho junto a si, não escuta a personagem requerer o amante preso para sempre "junto a si" porque no momento em que o final da frase é proferido, um avião passa sobre a casa e encobre, ironicamente, a voz da pedinte. Este detalhe irrelevante torna-se, no entanto, o motivo da prisão perpétua de Fininho e razão por que um evento ocorrido cinqüenta anos atrás tornara a se repetir, fazendo com que, mais uma vez, "os ciclos se eternizassem" em uma sociedade regida por forças que nos escapam e que, por vezes, encobrem a própria ancestralidade.

Por fim, cabe-nos ressaltar a permanência das utopias ainda que difusas nessa Angola violada e que são alimentadas por personagens marcadas pela poeticidade e pela crença em um porvir que resgate sonhos idênticos aos do passado. Em *Jaime Bunda e a morte do americano*, a primeira voz a se pronunciar sobre ao assassinato do americano e as demais questões por ele suscitadas é a de Julião Domingos de Souza, o poeta da Massagalala, que ao afirmar que "um gringo a menos sempre melhora a qualidade do ar" (10), exterioriza mais uma crítica ao imperialismo americano que subjuga os países considerados denominados periféricos. Julião, Mané do Corinje—personagem que rechaça veementemente a comida consumida em restaurantes—e o "mais velho" Raul Dândi são vozes de resistência que integram o grupo dos "Línguas de Fogo" e rejeitam categoricamente a dominação e a aculturação que vêem, no presente que a enunciação traduz, se agigantar em Angola.

Em *Jaime Bunda, agente secreto* essa incumbência é delegada por Pepetela a Gégé—o irmão mais novo, irreverente e "subversivo" de Bunda—que, tal qual este, é igualmente herdeiro do tio "Esperteza do Povo." Como redator de um jornal popular de esquerda, caberá à personagem cuidar do registro de mais fatos ignorados pela história oficial, nessa saga africana que revela "verdades que incomodam e que devem ficar pudicamente sobre sete véus" (312). Como é freqüente no gênero policial, Pepetela termina sua narrativa com mais um enigma, embora este fuja ao gênero referido: será Gégé um mero repetidor das idéias ligadas ao saber folhetinesco dos romances herdados por Bunda ou atualizará ele no presente angolano as mesmas utopias vividas pelo tio e evocadas pelos poetas de Benguela, as quais se revelarão a verdadeira e suprema "sabedoria do povo"?

Obras Citadas

Adorno, Theodor. "Posição do narrador no romance contemporâneo." *Notas de literatura*. São Paulo: Editora 34/Duas Cidades, 2002.

Alberti, Verena. *O Riso e o risível na história do pensamento*. Rio de Janeiro: Jorge Zahar, 2002.

Bakhtin, Mikhail. *A Cultura popular na Idade Média e no Renascimento*. São Paulo: Hucitec, 2002.

———. *Questões de literatura e de estética—a teoria do romance*. São Paulo: Hucitec, 1993.

Benjamin, Walter. *Obras escolhidas*. 3 vols. São Paulo: Brasiliense, 1997.

Brait, Beth. *A Ironia em perspectiva polifônica*. Campinas: Unicamp, 1996.

Chaves, Rita e Tânia Macedo org. *Portanto... Pepetela*. Luanda: Chá de Caxinde, 2002.

Freud, Sigmund. "Os chistes e sua relação com o inconsciente." *Obras completas de Sigmund Freud.* Vol. 3. Rio de Janeiro: Imago, 1969.

Hutcheon, Linda. *Uma teoria da paródia* [1985]. Lisboa: Edições 70, 1999.

Luckács, Georg. *Teoria do romance.* São Paulo: Editora 34, 2002.

Mangueneau, Dominique. *Novas tendências em análise do discurso.* São Paulo: Pontes, 1997.

Pepetela. *A montanha da água lilás.* Lisboa: Dom Quixote, 2000.

———. *As aventuras de Ngunga.* Lisboa: Edições 70, [s.d.].

———. *Jaime Bunda e a morte do americano.* Lisboa: Dom Quixote, 2003.

———. *Jaime Bunda, o agente secreto.* Lisboa: Dom Quixote, 2001.

———. *Mayombe.* Lisboa: Dom Quixote, 1997.

———. *O desejo de Kianda.* Lisboa: Dom Quixote, 1995.

———. *O cão e os caluandas.* Lisboa: Dom Quixote, 1995.

———. *Yaka.* Rio de Janeiro: Ática, 1984.

Rosário, Lourenço do. "Pepetela: o homero angolano." *Portanto, Pepetela.* Ed. Rita Chaves e Tânia Macedo. Luanda: Chá de Caxinde, 2001. 255-58.

Said, Edward. *Cultura e Imperialismo.* São Paulo: Companhia das Letras, 1995.

Secco, Carmen Lucia Tindó Ribeiro. "Entre crimes, detetives e mistérios..." *A Magia das letras africanas—ensaios escolhidos sobre as literaturas de Angola, Moçambique e alguns outros diálogos.* Rio de Janeiro: ABE Graph Editora, 2003.

Robson Dutra é Doutor em Letras Vernáculas pela UFRJ, com ênfase em Literaturas Africanas. Professor do Mestrado em Letras e Ciências Humanas da Unigranrio, tem participado ativamente de eventos nessa área no Brasil e no exterior. É autor de diversos artigos sobre Portugal e África, bem como do livro *Pepetela e a elipse do heroi*, publicado pela União dos Escritores Angolanos, em 2009. Email: robson.dutra@oi.com.br

Colonial Representation and Conquest in Pepetela's "As Cinco Vidas da Teresa"

Phyllis Peres

Abstract: This article offers a reading of one of Pepetela's first literary publications, the short story "As cinco vidas da Teresa," originally published under Pepetela's legal name, Artur Carlos Pestana, in 1962.

In a column published on the occasion of Luandino Vieira's long-awaited novel, *Nosso Musseque* (2003), Leonel Cosme criticizes the writer for a narrative *regresso* instead of a promised *ruptura.* After more than two decades following the publication of *Lourenthinho, Dona Antónia de Sousa Neto e Eu,* Cosme argues that Luandino's return to the colonial past represents a double regression, not only to the narration of a creolized *musseque* space but also to the threads of a previously published text. The critic, moreover, knows of what he speaks since the text to which he refers, "Os miúdos do Capitão Bento Abano," appeared in *Novos contos d'África* (1962), an anthology of short stories edited by Cosme and Garibaldino de Andrade.[1] Luandino's prolonged silence is compounded, according to Cosme, by his dislocation from Luanda to Alto Minho, and led to the expectation of a "explosive text," particularly since "outros camaradas seus, da literatura e da acção política, já tinham 'actualizado' as fontes de inspiração e a profissão de fé com o desejado sucesso" (44).

If Luandino's *Nosso Musseque* marks a regression to the roots of the hybrid and ambivalent *angolanidade* of texts such as *Luuanda, Nós os do Makulusu,*

Portuguese Literary & Cultural Studies 15/16 (2010): 251-57.

and *Macandumba*, which ruptured the conceptual binary oppositions of Portuguese colonial discourse, it is a return that is at once both nostalgic and essentializing. The *musseque* of Luandino's earlier works, primarily written in the prisons of Luanda and Tarrafal, was an interstitial space, the narrative site of the cultural and linguistic processes of an imagined *angolanidade* and a textual reclaiming of both geographical and cultural location. That reclaiming, however, was always ambiguous and self-questioning at every narrative turn. Forty years after the rupture of *Luuanda*'s *estórias* and the inevitable breakdown of the collective subject in *Nós os do Makulusu,* the regression to *Nosso Musseque*, originally written while Luandino was imprisoned in Luanda, but rewritten in Alto Minho, essentializes the very *nós* of Angolan collective identity.

Without entering further into the "regresso" versus "ruptura" debate posed by Leonel Cosme, my intent here is another return, in this instance to an early text published by Pepetela, one of Luandino's literary and political contemporaries whose works of fiction are foundational narrations of Angolan nation-ness. The text, "As cinco vidas da Teresa," appeared in the same aforementioned 1962 anthology along with short stories by a pantheon of then emergent Angolan writers including Mário Antônio, Arnaldo Santos, Henrique Guerra, Henrique Abranches, Ernesto Cochat Osório, Fernando da Costa Andrade, and Antônio Jacinto. Pepetela's narrative pre-dates the adoption of the *nome de guerra* that would also become his literary pseudonym and is published under his birth name, Arturo Carlos Pestana. In the accompanying bio note, the author's birthplace and date are listed—"Benguela a 29 de Outubro de 1941"—along with summary literary credentials: "É estudante da Faculdade de Letras de Lisboa. Tem colaboração em *Mensagem*, boletim da Casa dos Estudantes do Império" (44).

The focus of this present work on "As cinco vidas da Teresa," represents, in fact, more of a turn than a return. The short story has not received critical attention nor is it acknowledged formally as part of Pepetela's literary production. My intent here in the first instance, therefore, centers both on recuperating an early text by a writer whose narrative fiction is intricately linked to emergent national literature and to offer a preliminary reading that draws upon the critical paradigms of postcolonial theory to engage the text with questions of representation both from a colonial and nascent Angolan perspective. Of particular interest will be the ambivalent representations of the feminine, geographical location, and the masculine colonial conquest.

The narrative line is relatively familiar in the context of contemporary Angolan texts; Teresa, a young woman, has relocated to Benguela from then Nova Lisboa. On her daily route to work, Teresa meets Manuel, a young Portuguese office-worker and recent settler in Angola, who pursues and seduces her. The set of mutually exclusive expectations notwithstanding—Teresa believes herself to be in love and that the sexual encounter would result in marriage, whereas Manuel, who is portrayed with more ambiguity and depth, acts out his colonial role in terms of exploitation and power—the narrative plays repeatedly with intertwined notions of sexual and colonial conquest as part of a larger discourse of masculine imperial *aventura* again, both in terms of Teresa's body and the geographical space of Benguela.

This discourse of colonial conquest is evident from the beginning of "As cinco vidas da Teresa," which opens with the perspective of the masculine gaze: "Viu-a à saída do emprego. Seu corpo jovem, alegre, era um mundo de quentes promessas mal disfarçadas pelo vestido de chita" (45). In the gaze of the Portuguese settler, Teresa's body is part of the colonial landscape and that which may be conquered and colonized. In this opening passage, Manuel follows Teresa through the streets of Benguela until she reaches the "extremo da cidade branca" and watches her "tomar o caminho para a sanzala da Cambanda" (45). Benguela, itself, emerges in these beginning lines as a major character in the text, and supports a reading of geographical conquest and colonization.

As Alfred Crosby and others have iterated, the enterprise of colonization centers as much on the natural environment as it does on the "native peoples" and results in what he terms "ecological imperialism." Crosby, of course, builds on the work of the pioneering theorist of colonization, revolution, and decolonization—Frantz Fanon. Fanon, in particular, wrote extensively about the colonial conquest of the natural environment as linked to economic exploitation and argued that "hostile nature, obstinate and fundamentally rebellious, is in fact represented in the colonies by the bush, by mosquitoes, natives and fever, and colonization is a success when all this indocile nature has finally been tamed (*Wretched* 201).

In Angola, the conquest of nature and natives was always intrinsically fundamental to Portugal's participation in the Atlantic slave trade and, in the latter stages of colonialism, to the exploitation of African labor. Benguela, the setting for "As cinco vidas da Teresa," was one of the major slave ports of Angola; in the narrative, this history haunts Teresa at every corner in the "white city": "Benguela, o Mercado de triste memória, amedrontou-a com seus fantasmas do passado, saídos dos soturnos quintalões, tilintando com fúria as grilhetas que os manietaram" (46). The history of enslavement is hidden in the "civilized city," but is transmitted, as the elders tell Teresa, through memory and blood from generation to generation of Angolans (46).

Teresa's movement twice daily from the "sanzala" to the white city further situates the narrative in the context of environmental conquest and the establishment of colonial settlements. For Fanon, colonial cities were always paradigmatic of relationships of conquest and power as they were divided between two towns, those of the settlers and those of the natives (*Wretched* 30). The "Settlers' Town" encompasses privileged zones that are built and maintained by "natives" but from which they are excluded. Teresa may work as a domestic laborer in the urbanized section of Benguela, but in the evening she returns to the "sanzala," never seen in the text but understood by even its designation to be "native" and "untamed." Interestingly enough, in relation to Pepetela's later works, the "untamed" and "uncivilized" space is always depicted as such in colonial terms; in the recuperation of African space, those territories become revolutionary space, whether it be the forest of Mayombe in the text of the same name or the *chana* where Mundial, one of the guerrillas of *A geração da utopia*, recoups and regains his revolutionary vision.

That "As cinco vidas da Teresa" takes place almost entirely in the colonial "cidade branca" reinforces the space of sexual conquest and exploitation as the site of an inherent practice of colonization in all of its stages. Manuel follows and accompanies Teresa through the paved streets as she walks in the evenings towards the *sanzala*, but always stops at the border. Teresa, for her part, continues on the unpaved path—"lingua de terra batida entre o capinzal doirado"—imagining a possible life with Manuel and the world that he describes to her. As the narrative line ensues, the more that Manuel desires Teresa's body, the more she imagines her life with Manuel, "igual à de seus pais que desceram juntos para a cova" (49). For Teresa, whose parents died—"libertados pela febre"—when she was a child, the prospect of true love with Manuel is fraught with ambiguities. Is she betraying her community and "os sentimentos da raça" as she longs for a world to which she does not belong (48)? This incipient sense of betrayal is mitigated by her conclusion—"Mas ela ama Manuel" (48).

Manuel's motive is more explicitly played out as conquest in his thoughts as he sits at a café in "esplanada barulhenta" of the colonized city: "Deseja-a. Adivinhou nela uma virgem y saboreia antecipadamente a violência da posse" (49). From the very opening of the text when Manuel places Teresa's body in his sight, the pursuit toward conquest is heightened by the fact that her body is "untouched" and "unconquered." In Pepetela's narrative, however, Teresa's questioning of her feelings for Manuel as an abandonment of the *sanzala* community and all that this would entail finds its ambivalent counterpart in Manuel's self-questioning: "Ter-se-á também apaixonado?" (49). Ultimately, however, he rejects this notion "com repugnância" and resolves to "possess" Teresa the following day.

Their sexual encounter, which should be read as part of the colonial pattern of violent conquest, takes place in that border zone between the white city and the *sanzala*—"quando ultrapassaram a última fila de casas e a sua frente apenas a estrada vermelha se avista" (50). Manuel's exploitative purpose is revealed to Teresa when she attempts to kiss him and sees "a reacção dele, o ríctus de nojo que a Lua iluminou" (51). His explanation—"Mas eu prometi a mim mesmo só beijar aquela com que casasse" (51)—ruptures the landscape of Teresa's imagined entry in the colonial city and world. As she flees into the *sanzala*, Manuel first questions whether he has abused her, but then relegates Teresa to the world of his "passatempos," not to the colonial world in which marrying an African woman would have cost him his privileged life as a Portuguese settler in Benguela. To complete his colonization of Teresa, Manuel brags to his Portuguese buddies of his conquest and tells that she would accept the first one of them who went after her. Manuel acts with complete awareness that he is sacrificing her future for his own colonial privilege, since as Pepetela describes, he must mitigate his remorse by passing Teresa on to the next Portuguese man. The closing paragraph of the story mirrors the opening; as he watches Teresa re-merging into the *sanzala* landscape, Manuel's gaze turns to a vision of an imagined world of the "grilhetas dos escravos, os lamentos e gritos dos torturados" (54). For Manuel, however, "em breve essa visão fugidia desaparece" and his desire for Teresa would no longer threaten his privilege.

The title of Pepetela's story refers to the various overlapping colonial spaces that Teresa crosses in the space of the narrative text. The first is the world of a domestic female laborer in the white city in which she is exploited by her boss. The second, "o seu Mundo" is that of the "sanzala miserável" and what she sees as her narrow family life with her brother and sister-in-law. Teresa's third life takes form through Manuel's discourse of the expansive colonial world, while the fourth is the imagined future marriage and life with Manuel. Her fifth life is the one of sexual exploitation and conquest that she could not imagine, the one to which Manuel condemns her in order to extricate himself from the contradictions of his own guilty conscience. In the space of ten pages, as Teresa traverses the divided colonial city of Benguela, but not the colonial divide, she negotiates five lives and an affirmation of her own blood line of exploitation and possession.

Published in 1962, "As cinco vidas da Teresa" predates Pepetela's revolutionary narratives that violently negate colonial identities as they express revolutionary *angolanidade* with equal violence. A reading of the short story, however, might posit that the early text is essential to an understanding of Pepetela's narrative progression. Undoubtedly influenced by Franz Fanon's writings during his revolutionary training and study in Algeria in the late 1960s just prior to his return to Angola, "As cinco vidas da Teresa" points to the questions of identity that mark his later works and could well draw upon Fanon's treatise on colonial Manichean representations and the construction of self-identity in *Black Skin, White Masks.* Trapped within the colonial gaze, Teresa questions her own African identity and world as miserable and small, and envisions her release from the *sanzala* via the imagined life of privilege as the wife of a Portuguese settler. That this imagined life is a betrayal to her own selfhood, her community, and the generations of exploited and enslaved Angolans who have come before her also represents the bridge to the beginning of her fifth life of sexual exploitation and, perhaps, self-hatred. The narration also enters with more detail into Manuel's thoughts as he moves from the desire of possession to its violent enactment. If Manuel is to truly assume the role of colonizer, he must forgo any sense of Teresa as an individual with her own self-identity. Rather, the Teresa that Manuel captures in his gaze is primitivized, de-civilized and, ultimately, essentialized as an Angolan woman whose representation must always be both submissive and promiscuous if his own position of privilege, however ambivalent, is to be secured.

In this early text by the writer who would become Pepetela, the colonial representations of women, history, and urban space form an essential and essentializing part of the discourse of violence, conquest, and power. The Angolan contestations, articulated through political theory, violence, and discourses of utopia in Pepetela's later questioning narratives, are only hinted at in "As cinco vidas da Teresa." That the unseen *sanzala* is the hidden site of resistance to the locus of power in the *cidade branca* revitalizes the potential of Angolan self-identity and that Teresa, perhaps, in the future revolutionary location of Pepetela's narrative discourse, might have a possible sixth life.

Note

[1] The short story to which Cosme refers was published in 1962, but was not the first appearance of the narratives that were to become part of *Nosso Musseque.* In 1961-1962, Luandino published a series of *contos* in the *Jornal de Angola* with interrelated characters and geographical locations. One of the stories, for instance, "Os amores de Silva Chalado," refers to characters in "Os miúdos do Capitão Bento Abano," as is the case with, "Meninos de muceque," also cited as excerpted from the "romance inédito de Luandino Vieira."

Works Cited

Andrade, Garibaldino de, and Leonel Cosme, eds. *Novos Contos d'África.* Sá de Bandeira: Imbondeiro, 1962.

Cosme, Leonel. "O regresso de Luandino." *A Página* 125 (Aug.-Sept. 2003): 44.

Crosby, Alfred. *Ecological Imperialism: The Biological Expansion of Europe 900-1900.* Cambridge: Cambridge UP, 1986.

Fanon, Frantz. *Black Skin, White Masks.* New York: Grove, 1991.

———. *The Wretched of the Earth.* Hammondsworth: Penguin, 1967.

Pepetela. "As cinco vidas da Teresa." Andrade and Cosme 44-54.

———. *A Geração da Utopia.* Lisbon: Dom Quixote, 1992.

———. *Mayombe.* Lisbon: Edições 70, 1982.

Vieira, José Luandino. "Os amores de Silva Chalado." *Jornal de Angola* 30 Sept. 1961: 3.

———. "Meninos de muceque." *Jornal de Angola* 30 June 1962: 6.

———. "Os miúdos do Capitão Bento Abano." Andrade and Cosme 162-178.

———. *Nosso Musseque.* Lisbon: Camhinho, 2003.

Phyllis Peres is Vice Provost for Undergraduate Studies at American University. She is the author of *Transculturation and Resistance in Lusophone African Literatures.* Email: pperes@american.edu

Book Reviews

Pedro Meira Monteiro. *Um moralista nos trópicos: o visconde de Cairu e o duque de La Rochefoucauld.* São Paulo: Boitempo and Fapesp, 2004.

André Botelho

In his latest book, Pedro Meira Monteiro offers a solid and stimulating analysis of the intersections between literature, morals, and society. He discusses the semantic artifacts that create moral norms in the construction of meaning through the intersubjective experience of social agents. He also discusses how morals operate in the structuring of their reflexive ability and how they are rendered manifest in the successful communication between literature and society. These relationships are the basis for understanding the "moral catechism" compiled by José da Silva Lisboa, which is based on Roman Catholic doctrines. Lisboa was a Viscount of the Brazilian Empire, and his prose symbolically deals with morals intertextually, as an orientation of conduct and social organization, as shown in Monteiro's book.

In this study, the writings of the Viscount of Cairu cast a new historical and discursive light on Brazil's transition from colonial society to independent state. Monteiro emphasizes the search, implicit in this state-in-the-making, for a moral basis that could contribute to the containment of the "collective fabric" in the blossoming national political community. *Constituição Moral, e deveres do cidadão* [*Moral constitution and obligations of the citizen*] was first published in 1824, when, two years after Brazil declared its independence from Portugal, the country "was granted" its first constitution. Cairu's writings, then, arise in the context of the institutional and political architecture of that new state, or perhaps even in opposition to it, if we consider that, in appealing to Catholic morals, Cairu's work questioned the liberal principles according to which good institutions are enough to generate virtuous societies and citizens. Taking morals not only as the theme but, specifically, as the motivation that led Cairu to take up his quill, Monteiro correctly refers to a "moralistic campaign" whose main objective was to allow young "Brazilians" to conceive of themselves as members of a collectivity.

Portuguese Literary & Cultural Studies 15/16 (2010): 261-63.

The mediations that confer intelligibility to Cairu's moral prose and make possible a communication between literatures and societies are explored from an intertextual perspective that Monteiro calls "crossed readings." These serve as one of the book's original contributions on the methodological level. This does not mean that Lisboa's prose (and literature in general) are taken simply as "independent" of society. But from Monteiro's perspective, it means that literary analysis has obligations of its own that cannot be escaped. This explains his option to leave to historians the task of retracing the connections between text and context. The Maxims of La Rochefoucauld are not the only crossing of readings, as can be seen in Cairu's (chapter 1) use of the collection entitled *Júbilos da América* [*Jubilations of America*], published in Brazil in the mid-eighteenth century, and the meaning of its use. In fact, the Maxims are the main references for understanding Cairu's publication. The comparative intertextual perspective employed does not fit easily into the conventional mold of studies on literary "diffusion," or "reception," although Monteiro's approach does use some of their analytic resources. This is not only because he goes into detail (in chapter 2) about the complexity of the Maxims in the Duc's universe, but also because, by tracing their evolution over time and in space, he renews the reader's understanding of French classicism itself. In particular, at no moment does he ignore the characteristics that may particularize the Maxims as a literary genre in the midst of the diversity of their configurations and intellectual references in Western history.

More than in the sociological mechanisms of transmission, then, the notion of "crossed readings" deals with the "selectivity" proper to this literary genre. Maxims function as an analytic angle to capture experiences, nuances, distinctions, and even new perspectives of composition that symbolically encode dynamic behaviors in time and space. They do so even at the cost of changing their meanings in the final analysis of what was retained of the "original" and what was changed. This holds true for the "shifts" from the "pessimism" associated with the feeling of the eclipse of a civilization (La Rochefoucauld) to the "optimism" stirred up in creating a new one (Cairu), which wishes to be "something else" even if it is built on the ruins of the former (chapter 3). This is also true for shifts from the "individual" as the target of the discourse (La Rochefoucauld) to the "political community" as its unity (Cairu), as well as for the "critical effort" of the Maxims in revealing the falseness of human virtues and the "edifying warning" in the Brazilian catechism.

It is not a question of literary form and its cultural variants, in a structural, functional, or historicist sense. The attempt is to show in these intertextually mediated "shifts" that morals allow/demand the experience of *difference* in the same way that the selectivity of the Maxims allow/demand the *contingency* of the all-too-human. *Crossed readings*: the prose of Cairu, the sonnets of the Academy of the Select, La Rochefoucauld's Maxims, and the Brazilian Empire, then, all allow for multiple, but not infinite, discursive relationships of meaning. Monteiro's book is marked by its ability to identify in the text the finest threads of the warping of meanings among literature, morals and society, rather than the abrupt contrasts that are common in analyses of genres such as moralizing literature. With grace and precision he shows that—paraphrasing Simmel—the finest threads of historical semantics are indeed the strongest.

André Botelho teaches for the Programa de Pós-Graduação em Sociologia e Antropologia at the Universidade Federal do Rio de Janeiro. He is author of *O Brasil e os Dias: Estado-nação, Modernismo e Rotina Intelectual* (2005). Email: andrebotelho@digirotas.com.br

Maria Helena Mateus and Ernesto d'Andrade. *The Phonology of Portuguese*. Oxford: Oxford UP, 2002.

José A. Elías-Ulloa

The Phonology of Portuguese is intended for students of phonology, for researchers in Romance languages, and for the linguistic community in general. It presents the main aspects of Portuguese phonology, including those processes that affect segments, syllables, and stress, as well as morphophonological aspects, discussing their implications in phonological theories. Although the book is mainly about European Portuguese (as spoken in the Lisbon area), comparisons are made with Brazilian Portuguese so that the reader obtains an idea of what is similar and what is not between these varieties.

The book presents Portuguese phonology from the point of view of non-linear phonology and within a computational framework that resorts to the ordering of rules. The authors make use of the following theories: Constriction- -Based Model of Feature Geometry (Clements and Hume) joined with Radical Underspecification (Archangeli); X-Skeleton Syllable Theory (Levin); "Grid-Only" Metrical Theory (Prince; Selkirk); and Lexical Phonology (Kiparsky; Mohanan).

Chapter 1 explains the aim of the book as well as provides a brief overview of previous studies of Portuguese phonology. Chapter 2 describes the segmental inventory, the main phonotactic patterns and phonological phenomena, previewing how they can be analyzed in the light of Feature Geometry and Radical Underspecification.

Chapter 3 accounts for syllable structure and discusses phonological aspects within this domain (for example: glide insertion; diphthongization; diphthongs with different weights and their relation with stress). Chapters 4 and 5 provide information about the intricacies of Portuguese morphology and discuss its interaction with phonology. The former chapter addresses inflectional morphology whereas the latter, derivational morphology.

Portuguese Literary & Cultural Studies 15/16 (2010): 265-67.

In Chapter 6, the authors present the word stress of Portuguese as being actually two stress systems, one for nouns and adjectives and the other for verbs, a situation also found in other Romance languages such as Spanish (Hualde). One of the most interesting points made in this chapter is the discussion of why Portuguese is not a quantity-sensitive language. The authors argue, instead, for a morphology-oriented account of Portuguese stress.

Chapter 7 accounts for the main phonological processes of Portuguese. In contrast to the previous chapters, which address phenomena that are morphologically-conditioned or conditioned by the interplay of morphology, lexical marks, and prosody, this chapter presents phenomena that are only conditioned by prosodic factors. Nasalization, vowel reduction in unstressed syllables, processes sensitive to syllable structure (point of articulation and voicing of codas, palatalization of coronal onsets) and connected speech (coalescence, haplology, etc.) are all investigated.

Although one of the authors' stated aims is to discuss Portuguese phonology in the context of evaluating modern phonological theory, they do not explain their neglect of Optimality Theory (Prince and Smolensky) nor do they establish a dialogue with its proponents. Thus, the reader is unable to benefit from evaluating the pros and cons of differing approaches. Even within the representational theories they use, no explanation is provided as to why they reject other more widely accepted alternatives (for example, the use of the Skeleton-Syllable Theory for syllable structure and syllable weight instead of Moraic Theory [Hayes]).

Having said that, this book provides a wealth of empirical data, enlightening descriptive generalizations, and clever analytical insights. In particular, the discussion of stress is revealing and it will serve as an obligatory point of reference for any linguist interested in metrical phonology. Overall, the book is a success and definitely a must-have for those linguists interested in Romance phonology in general and especially for those who study the phonology of Portuguese. The authors do an excellent job in presenting the main aspects of Portuguese phonology. They emphasize characteristics particular to Portuguese. Undoubtedly, the authors make a significant and up-to-date contribution to the understanding of Portuguese phonology.

Works Cited

Archangeli, D. "Aspects of Underspecification Theory." *Phonology* 5 (1988): 183-208.

Clements, G. N., and E. Hume. "The internal organization of speech sounds." *The Handbook of Phonological Theory.* Ed. J. A. Goldsmith. Cambridge, MA and Oxford, UK: Blackwell, 1995. 245-306.

Hayes, B. "Compensatory Lengthening in Moraic Phonology." *Linguistic Inquiry* 20 (1989): 253-306.

———. *Metrical Stress Theory: Principles and Case Studies.* Chicago: U of Chicago P, 1995.

Hualde, J. I. *The Sounds of Spanish.* Cambridge: Cambridge UP, 2005.

Kiparsky, P. (1982a). "From Cyclic Phonology to Lexical Phonology." *The Structure of Phonological Representations.* Eds. H. van der Hulst and N. Smith. Dordrecht: Foris, 1982. 1:131-175.

———. "Lexical Phonology and Morphology." *Linguistics in the Morning Calm.* Ed. I. S. Yang. Seoul: Hanshin, 1982. 2:3-91.

Levin, J. B. *A Metrical Theory of Syllabicity.* Cambridge, MA: MIT, 1985.

———. *Reduplication and Prosodic Structure.* Cambridge, MA: MIT, 1983.

Mohanan, K. P. *The Theory of Lexical Phonology.* Dordrecht: Reidel, 1986.

Prince, A. "Relating to the Grid." *Linguistic Inquiry* 14.1 (1983): 19-100.

Prince, A., and P. Smolensky. *Optimality Theory: Constraint Interaction in Generative Grammar.* Oxford: Blackwell, 2004.

Selkirk, E. *Phonology and Syntax: The Relation between Sound and Structure:* Cambridge, MA: MIT, 1984.

José A. Elías-Ulloa is Assistant Professor in the Department of Hispanic Languages and Literature at SUNY–Stony Brook. He is a formal linguist, whose specialization is metrical phonology. His main interests are the study of prosody (syllable weight, metrical stress, intonation) and the interaction with segmental phenomena. Email: Jose.Elias-Ulloa@sunysb.edu

Rui Zink, ed. *Até ao Oriente & outros contos para Wenceslau de Moraes*. Lisbon: Dom Quixote, 2004.

Daniela Kato

This anthology of short stories by eight contemporary lusophone writers was commissioned in the context of Wenceslau de Moraes's 150th anniversary (1854-2004) celebrations, an initiative that took place in Portugal and Japan throughout 2004 and included a number of exhibitions, concerts, conferences, and publications under the auspices of Instituto Camões. The reader might thus be led to expect the habitual panoply of encomia that we find in most works on Moraes. The commissioner of the celebrations, Pedro Barreiros, however, seems to disclaim such intent in his brief introduction to the anthology when he suggests that the commemoration aims to inaugurate a new cycle in the study of Moraes's life and works. And, indeed, when we look at the IC's official website (http://www.instituto-camoes.pt/iniciativas/wenceslau.htm), the emphasis is not so much on Moraes the chronicler of Japanese folk traditions as on Moraes the connoisseur of the "real" Japan—the great visionary whose thinking allegedly foresaw the huge changes that would take place throughout the twentieth century. Yet, despite its innovative ambitions, the ideological agenda falls back on the stuffy old narrative of Portuguese "universal humanism" when it consistently claims for Moraes the single role of promoter of mutual understanding between the two civilisational poles, East and West. As usual, little or no attention is paid to the thematic and political contradictions and rifts in the writings of Moraes, in favour of a sanitized image fit for all times and political regimes.

The reader may nevertheless find in *Até ao Oriente* a brief respite from such worn-out clichés. In fact, most of the short stories that comprise the collection—apart perhaps from Mário Cláudio's more conventional approach in "Os Leques"—have little to do with the Moraes of literary critics and their accolades or with Moraes *tout court*, for that matter. As Rui Zink points out in his introductory note, the only thread or *leitmotif* linking the eight stories together is the free exploration of "the spirit of Moraes" [o espírito de

Portuguese Literary & Cultural Studies 15/16 (2010): 269-70.

Moraes], a concept that the editor very conveniently (for him)—and provocatively—leaves undefined. Hence, each story gives a different fictional shape to the various themes, obsessions, and contradictions of Orientalist discourse: exile and home, fact and fantasy, center and margin, identity and alienation, orientation and disorientation. Paraphrasing Zink's account, we might say that Luís Cardoso asks the question: "what does somebody do when away from home?"; Inês Pedrosa reformulates: "what does a woman do when away from home?"; Richard Zenith adds a different nuance: "what makes somebody leave home?"; Eduardo Brum focuses instead on the question: "what makes somebody become afraid of leaving home?"; and Marilene Felinto wonders: "how long do you have to endure till you find yourself at home?" Based on a Japanese experience of his own, Jacinto Lucas Pires gives us an intriguing film noir and detective story. Possidónio Cachapa picks up a "translation" of a Bashô *haiku* by Moraes and writes on two lovers transfixed in a moment of time. Mário Cláudio, in turn, interrogates himself: "what is it like to live and write in Japanese *ink*?"

The reader will most probably finish the book without an answer to any of the above questions. Yet, it is well worth following the editor's advice: take each story as a small fragment of that huge "Map of the Orient" called fiction and (dis)orientate yourself in the best possible way.

Daniela Kato has degrees in Law (Catholic University of Portugal) and Modern Languages and Literatures—Portuguese and English Studies (University of Oporto). She is currently a doctoral candidate in English Literature at the University of Oporto. Her research interests include Anglo-American modernism and the twentieth-century epic; contemporary poetry and poetics; nationalisms and linguistic and cultural minorities in Britain. She has published articles on modern poetry and literary theory. Email: ytd.kato@mail.telepac.pt

Rosa Maria Martelo. *Em Parte Incerta—Estudos de Poesia Portuguesa Moderna e Contemporânea*. Porto: Campo das Letras, 2004.

Helena Lopes

Moving along a wide time frame that comprises Pessoa as well as Herberto Helder, this collection of essays on major voices of contemporary Portuguese poetry is also an insightful reflection on the questions of reference, authorship, and modernity in literature.

In the several essays concerning Carlos de Oliveira's work, Rosa Maria Martelo focuses on the poet's realism as an estrangement from a traditional poetics of representation. The progressive loss of circumstantiality in the course of the poet's work is read as a swerving from orthodox neorealism through a denial of an ontologically strong Marxist version of the world and a search for a broader and more complex referentiality that implies envisaging poetical form as an Adornian space of resistance. This is a reading that can contribute to a new appraisal of neorealist literature insofar as it draws attention to the underlying consciousness that the strengthening of bonds between poetry and the extra-literary world can only be carried out through a discoursive practice.

Martelo also explores Carlos de Oliveira's rewriting of his own work as the reconstruction of his implied author. The same metonymical sliding of the empirical to the textual author that Martelo recognizes in José Gomes Ferreira's self-portrait, here read as the creation of a verbal image designed to efface its real-life model, could be discerned in her interpretation of Carlos de Oliveira's work as the emergence of an author-in-the-text in the manner of a Demanian "figure of reading." In fact, it is as if the researcher's experience of the poets abridged in this collection of studies shapes an approach to the text where the unraveling of meaning echoes a textual becoming subsumable in difference and deferral, since, to displace Martelo's remark to António Franco Alexandre's poetry:

Portuguese Literary & Cultural Studies 15/16 (2010): 271-73.

> A distância e o diferimento estão tão presentes entre os interlocutores do poema como entre o discurso e os seus referentes, discursivos ou não. Como entre o leitor e o texto. (233)

In "Corpo, velocidade e dissolução," Al Berto's poetics of discursive deceleration is read as a search for the possibility of a signature in the context of an urban experience textually reconstructed as velocity at odds with the integrality of its subject. Al Berto's movement towards identity is compared with Herberto Helder's intensification of discursive speed, approached as the embracing of a subjectivity fearless of disintegration. A similar value is ascribed to Luiza Neto Jorge's fractured syntax, whose impending disruption is analyzed as the weaving of a discursive excess capable of engendering a textual otherness that claims corporeal sexuality as a means of recapturing the power of insurgency. The body is also under consideration in the comparative study of Eugénio de Andrade and Fernando Pessoa, where Martelo argues that in Pessoa's work the body accompanies the disruption of subjectivity like a specter. Rather than an effacement of the body, she acknowledges in Pessoa's work "a ambiguidade de uma presença da ausência do corpo" (135), which, after all, is a crucial element in sensationism. The poetry of Luís Miguel Nava entices further attention to the complex role of the body in the construction of subjectivity, since Nava's work is regarded as approaching the sublime by weaving a network of significants of excess where the spiritual and the material are no longer separable, thus challenging the Kantian notion of sublimity as an immensity that cannot be comprehended by the senses.

The last and, to my mind, most pathbreaking section of this volume concentrates on the idea of literary modernity in its broadest sense and attempts to map out routes in recent poetry. Martelo remarks how the poetics of Romanticism already presupposes a stranded subjectivity to be acted on by the reader by expecting the "I" in the text to be subsumed in the addressee. She proceeds to interpret the turn to "figurative poetry" set off in the 1970s and characterized by an effort of concretion and a foregrounding of the "I" (often managed through a recourse to autobiographical materials) as a strategy to enhance communicativeness in poetry that can be subsumed in the Demanian notion of "de-facement." Bearing in mind that the circumstantiality in the poem remains but a textual fiction, the reader is then allowed to reconstruct it upon his or her own experience, thus creating an effect of realism that no longer relies on an ontologically strong model of the world and of the self but rather builds on the modernist shifting of subjectivities.

Though most of the essays develop a thesis, the text breeds a profound openness to dialogue by welcoming voices from varied critical schools. On the whole, this work stands out in the landscape of Portuguese criticism as it puts into practice conceptual tools forged by great contemporary thinkers such as Deleuze and José Gil and suggests a thorough assimilation of landmarks in modern literary theory, namely Derrida and Paul de Man.

I would say this is an essential work for the study of the poets under discussion and also a very inspiring and juicy read for those interested in literary criticism in general.

Helena Lopes is currently preparing a PhD dissertation on Literature and Film under the title *Há um filme neste texto? Aspectos cinematográficos na obra de Paul Auster e de Rubem Fonseca* at the Universidade do Porto, Portugal. She is also part of the national research project *Utopias literárias e pensamento utópico: a cultura portuguesa e a tradição intelectual do Ocidente*. Email: cityofglass@clix.pt

Pedro Eiras. *Esquecer Fausto—a fragmentação do sujeito em Raul Brandão, Fernando Pessoa, Herberto Helder e Maria Gabriela Llansol.* Porto: Campo das Letras, 2005.

Luis Maffei

Li, inteiro, *Esquecer Fausto.* Notícia óbvia, pelo suposto que é um recenseador ter lido a obra sobre que/a partir da qual escreve. Mas notícia que possibilita um viés, ou ponto de vista, que a mim interessa deveras; leio na introdução: "(...) se não há fragmento nem totalidade *por si próprios,* se ambos dependem de uma *diferança* que os desconstrói, o objecto de estudo é menos a totalidade ou os fragmentos do que o modo pelo qual a escrita/leitura os inventa" (32). Repito, com Pedro Eiras: "modo pelo qual a escrita/leitura os [fragmentos e ou vs. totalidade] inventa." Este será, a meu ver, um modo privilegiado de abordar o livro: a invenção, pela escrita, duma tensão nunca excludente mas sempre problemática entre "fragmentos" e "totalidade" na própria constituição de *Esquecer Fausto.*

A propósito, o livro origina-se duma Tese de Doutoramento, o que poderia pressupor a existência nele de alguns vícios acadêmicos. Rechaço tal hipótese por duas razões: 1) não acredito tanto assim em "vícios acadêmicos," pois a Academia é menos afeita a (escrevi *menos afeita* pois não quero grafar, já que não a considero, *desafeita* ao que digo na seqüência) vícios do que supõe uma sub-reptícia, a ela e a instâncias a ela exterioras, voz; 2) havendo tais vícios, isso pouco diz a Pedro Eiras, ensaísta dos mais criativos e corajosos.

Volto à constituição de *Esquecer Fausto* como organismo em estado de *opera,* portanto como *obra,* não como Tese, pois ali não há exatamente defesas, mas leituras: por um lado os fragmentos, por outro a totalidade. Linhas acima, pus *versus* entre uma possibilidade e a outra, mas devo repensá-lo imediatamente, pois "o modo pelo qual a escrita" deste livro se coloca não os opõe, mesmo que os difira. O fato é que existe, na própria escolha temática, uma espécie de fragmentação, pois toda escolha acaba por ser, com efeito, ato fragmentário, ao menos no nível do recorte. Fragmenta-se, portanto, a literatura portuguesa do século XX para que se ponham a ler Raul

Portuguese Literary & Cultural Studies 15/16 (2010): 275-78.

Brandão, Fernando Pessoa/Bernardo Soares, Herberto Helder e Maria Gabriela Llansol. Fragmenta-se ainda mais, pois cada um dos autores comparece com uma obra, ou "Texto" (536), se eu quiser falar mais uma vez com Eiras, que fala aqui, por sua vez, com Roland Barthes: em ordem cronológica são lidos *Húmus*, *Livro do desassossego*, *Photomaton & Vox* e *Lisboaleipzig*—não obstante as iluminadoras leituras que Eiras realiza do demais das obras de cada um de seus contemplados autores, acabando por lê-las, em certa medida, como *todos*: de novo em relação os fragmentos e a totalidade.

Sublinho que *Esquecer Fausto* é um livro de 757 páginas, da quais 691 de texto e as restantes de generosíssimas bibliografias. Falo de generosidade, falo mais: antes da abordagem do primeiro autor estudado, Raul Brandão—e também no correr dos capítulos—Eiras realiza um notável passeio pela história do pensamento que se terá debruçado especialmente sobre os temas do fragmento, da totalidade, da subjetividade e da linguagem. Ponto nodal da *opera*: o autor, mesmo quando discorda, mesmo quando afasta sua leitura de outras, fala *com*, não apenas *com* os autores a que se dedica com sensível paixão e nenhuma ingenuidade, mas também com os que pensaram antes certos temas urgentes para o livro. Exatamente por isso, a adoção do plural majestático (por alguém, faço questão de assinalar, useiro e vezeiro, em diversos outros trabalhos, no uso da primeira do singular) é às vezes redundante, às vezes modalizadora demais das novidades que o ensaio apresenta: único vicio acadêmico daquilo que foi uma Tese?

Mas isto não importa, é uma tola filigrana. O que importa é o quanto de informação Eiras recolhe para falar *com*, e falar desde um tempo que é o seu, num entendimento notável da "catastrófica descrição de Gilles Lipovetsky" (687) do homem pós-moderno como já não analogizável a Fausto, mas sim a Narciso. Entendimento, claro, pelo ensaísta re-entendido e deslocado, pois o "mito de Narciso enfatiza a distância infinita entre o sujeito e ele mesmo (...), não um mito de unidade egótica. Ler o texto é compreender de que modo essa ficção se faz nele" (691).

Tal compreensão permite ao autor, por exemplo, perceber a questão da necessidade de uma operação moderna de luto, presente em Brandão (que "não explora uma verdade certa da crise de valores, mas uma incerta crise da verdade dos valores" (72) e Pessoa/Soares "não admira que (...) o semi-heterônimo concilie o entusiasmo modernista que o faz sonhar projectos de Livro total e o cansaço decadentista de quem se sabe nascido tarde demais para qualquer revolução estética ou política" (344), *desde* a pós-modernidade.

Aproveito para ressaltar: a Pedro Eiras não assusta pensar em pós-modernidade, e ele o faz de modo raramente lúcido.

Desde específicos *lugar* e *tempo* de escrita, o ensaísta pode localizar, já que o "luto do sujeito forte não é um projecto, mas um facto, e por isso *já não há luto*" (684), um sujeito forte em Herberto Helder, radicalmente criado pelo texto (que é criador também dum mundo, pois, no caso herbertiano, "o mundo como 'movimento e transmutação' não existe *per si*, mas é criação da escrita" (432), e a assunção de figuras na obra de Llansol, em quem é afirmada a "polissemia" e a "relativização" de uma "leitura logocêntrica: se há negatividade, ela subordina-se a uma educação da (des)leitura. *Lisboaleipzig* invalida assim a angústia da perda e do luto que gera textos como *Húmus* ou *Livro do desassossego*" (552).

Agora é já tempo de afirmar o que comecei a sugerir com a referência ao tamanho do livro e à gênese abrangente que o constitui, mesmo bibliograficamente: ao estudar o fim da ambição fáustica de totalidade, e também ao fragmentar a história de uma literatura, Pedro Eiras acaba por criar uma espécie de totalidade em problema, pois seu livro acusa a impossibilidade do total sendo, ele mesmo, um "Texto" em certa medida totalizante daquilo que estuda. E talvez seja esse o dado mais espantosamente *novo* do ensaio: sem já acreditar naquilo que a própria modernidade acabou por entender como falácia, e sem, tampouco, extremar a crença arriscada de que o fim das metanarrativas seja por si só uma redenção, *Esquecer Fausto* não deixa de possuir, de algum modo, a pretensão de dar conta a fundo, ou, se eu quiser brincar com a idéia fáustica por excelência, *totalmente* de seus objetos de estudo.

Portanto, não é casual que dois dos autores ali comparecentes, Pessoa/Soares e Herberto Helder, pensem no livro total. Tampouco é casual que o ensaísta detecte a impossibilidade do projeto do primeiro, e, na abordagem do segundo, recolha um livro que não é o *Livro* herbertiano (Eiras discordaria desta minha grafia com maiúscula, suponho...), a *Poesia toda*, mas *Photomaton & Vox*, lugar notável da ironia de Herberto Helder. Do mesmo modo, é o livro constantemente mudado de Raul Brandão que se privilegia no longo ensaio, e a autora que o encerra, Maria Gabriela Llansol, é aquela que, dada a "unidade de todos os livros desde *O Livro das Comunidades*," investe na "dissolução das formas" (538). Não faz sentido, evidentemente, falar do projeto da enciclopédia renascentista, escrita universalizante capaz mesmo de aspirar a certa metafísica. Mas, caso houvesse uma atualização de tal projeto, e se essa atualização fosse capaz de reconhecer a maravilha que é um sujeito como função e, por vezes, ficção, isto estaria, certamente, muito próximo do magnífico trabalho de Pedro Eiras.

Luis Maffei é doutor em Literatura Portuguesa pela Universidade Federal do Rio de Janeiro, com tese sobre Herberto Helder. É também poeta, tendo estreado com *A* (Oficina Raquel, 2006). Tem artigos publicados em diversos periódicos especializados.
Email: luis.maffei@terra.com.br

De São Paulo: cinco crônicas de Mário de Andrade, 1920-1921. Organização, introdução e notas de Telê Ancona Lopez. São Paulo: Editora Senac São Paulo, 2004.

Pedro Meira Monteiro

"Sugestões tão inéditas como os versos de Mallarmé." Esta a cifra com que Mário de Andrade, em verdadeira contemplação amorosa, evoca a cidade de São Paulo, anunciando, numa crônica de novembro de 1920, a "Paulicéia" desvairada dos poemas que comporiam, dois anos depois, um dos livros mais notáveis do modernismo brasileiro. Ler estas cinco crônicas do jovem poeta, que a Editora do Senac e o Sesc de São Paulo trazem em preciosa edição anotada por Telê Ancona Lopez, pode ser uma aventura parecida às entradas com que os bandeirantes, partindo do planalto paulista, rasgaram o continente americano, no século XVII. Há mesmo uma espécie de bandeirismo sublimado nisto que é o relato, ora sôfrego ora plenamente lírico, do burburinho fecudante dos modernos paulistas, didaticamente apresentados por Mário de Andrade aos leitores da *Ilustração Brasileira*, importante revista do Rio de Janeiro em que foram publicadas aquelas crônicas, entre 1920 e 1921.

De fato, um gesto heróico parece esconder-se, como um acorde desmaiado, atrás de cada linha. A Terra inculta que os paulistas arrostam, numa curiosa figuração da cena cultural brasileira, configura a Esfinge com que os poetas modernos se regozijam, herdeiros, muitas vezes confessos, do simbolismo finissecular que, como a água insalubre das barrocas dos sertões, guarda e sacraliza o Mistério e, com ele, o enigma das forças superiores ao indivíduo. Jogo quase indecifrável, a um só tempo verbal, arquitetural, musical ou pictórico: é a cidade a desdobrar seus tentáculos, oferecendo em seus antros e reentrâncias os recantos uterinos em que o indivíduo vislumbra a imagem da Beleza perdida. O cronista Mário de Andrade não esconde, antes revela com volúpia, a sensualidade das linhas com que a cidade se expressa, em silhueta plural e misteriosa, guardando em si tempos passados e futuros. É a cidade no instante, no tempo: a *crônica* em sua perfeição.

Portuguese Literary & Cultural Studies 15/16 (2010): 279-82.

Não apenas os versos "arlequinais" da *Paulicéia desvairada* (*Hallucinated City*, na tradução de Jack Tomlins) se anunciam, quase inteiros, nestas crônicas, como também o olhar do contista-cronista Mário de Andrade, jogado entre belas e más artes, se deixa flagrar na mirada desejante que recai sobre a jovem paulistaninha, imigrantezinha cuja dissimulação nem uma cascata de diminutivos lograria esconder: "Paulicéia é como brasileirinha nascida nessa idade-média em que uma parte de Minas adormeceu: alonga os babados da saia escura para fechar no segredo a volta sensual do tornozelo, mas traz nos lábios a rosa provocante das espanholas."

Fechando-se a cidade, sisuda e cinza, abre-se de repente a rosa misteriosa, no movimento espasmódico de um amor pulsante, à cata do momento de gozo, que é a epifania que busca o poeta: "dizem-na fria...Dizem-na tristonha, escura...Mas no momento em que escrevo, novembro anda lá fora, desvairado de odores e colorações. Eu sei de parques esquecidos em que a rabeca dos ventos executa a sarabanda por que pesadamente bailam os rosais...Eu sei de coisas lindas, singulares, que a Paulicéia mostra só a mim, que dela sou o amoroso incorrigível e lhe admiro o temperamento hermafordita...."

O amor é, nestas crônicas, pleno, ambíguo, pansexual. E a cidade é ela mesma personagem, imenso corpo, jardim de signos por que vaga o poeta. Cantar a cidade, narrá-la, é narrar a si mesmo, nela perdido. Supremo paradoxo do amante (aqui, no fim das contas, tão masculino): o gozo vem de si, porque é impossível atingir completamente o outro. Amando o outro, não há entrega completa, porque eu regresso teimosamente a mim: como na crônica sobre a arquitetura, de fevereiro de 1921, em que Mário de Andrade se perde em divagações, para chegar à conclusão de que não fala senão de si. Trata-se então de um impressionante torneio metalingüístico, quando o cronista revela que a cidade amada não pode ser senão a construção de uma crônica, que é, novamente, a construção do instante em toda sua significação, o eu-lírico funcionando como ponto de fuga da composição: "Mas isto é falar de mim...Ia eu dizendo que..."; "...afinal, estou muito longe do meu fim,"; "Apenas: eu me perdi novamente..."

Falando de si, Mário de Andrade fala da construção moderna do texto, expondo a crônica em suas engrenagens. E expõe também a cena literária paulistana em pleno funcionamento, alegorizada na magnífica crônica sobre o Trianon e a festa em torno de Menotti Del Picchia, de março de 1921, ou descrita, belamente mas não sem uma dose de provincianismo, na crônica seguinte, quando São Paulo revela ao mundo que tem também seu salão literário: a vila Kyrial. Mas neste livro há mais. Chama a atenção, e põe a pensar, o tamanho da introdução, a precisão das notas, o aparato crítico enfim que envolve e esclarece o texto. Lendo-o, podemos pensar que não lemos mais apenas Mário de Andrade, mas lemos um autor já numa forma que a crítica ajuda a dar, daí nascendo a pergunta angustiante de todo organizador: até onde aditar comentários, explicar? Por que entregar menos bruta a pedra ao leitor?

A edição de Telê Ancona Lopez, incompreensível fora do esforço crítico que, a partir do Instituto de Estudos Brasileiros (IEB) da Universidade de São Paulo, concorre para a organização do legado de Mário de Andrade, prova que é desejável, assumidos os riscos da empreitada, cercar o texto de um grande autor com um grande aparato. Vale notar, a propósito, a dedicatória do estudo introdutório marcando um bonito momento, nesta espécie de longa passagem imaginária do bastão, que é a preservação crítica dos documentos por toda e qualquer equipe competente, formada por várias gerações de pesquisadores. (O ensaio que serve de introdução ao livro é dedicado a dois pesquisadores mais jovens do IEB.)

O resultado é que se fornece ao leitor um certo Mário de Andrade, atrás do qual ele, leitor, buscará o seu próprio Mário. O desafio de um aparato crítico, aliás, estará porventura expressando o paradoxo da própria crítica, da qual se espera que seja completa e densa, mas não tanto que abafe a obra ou que a faça curvar-se com o peso das opiniões, das adições ou das explicações. Uma edição anotada, como esta, faz pensar na necessária angústia do organizador, que a etimologia ajuda a compreender: o "aparato" é o resultado de uma *preparação*. O crítico prepara, entrega o que preparou, e sai de cena, ruminando dúvidas sobre o que fez.

A introdução ("Mário de Andrade, cronista do modernismo: 1920-1921") busca justamente fixar aquilo que são os primeiros gestos dos modernistas paulistas, especialmente o autor da *Paulicéia desvairada*, e, ao fazê-lo, inscreve-se, a si própria, na historiografia que auxilia a compreensão do movimento. A introdução se cola ao texto de Mário não como aposto desajeitado, ela mesma sendo, *enquanto* (insista-se no aspecto temporal da conjunção conformativa) introdução, uma intervenção crítica, isto é, a um só tempo mapeamento do campo literário e convite à leitura.

A autora do estudo introdutório não pode furtar-se à condição de intérprete mais importante do poeta e cronista, devedora (e recriadora) portanto de certa leitura do movimento, que reforça quase sempre o seu caráter de ruptura e renovação. Mas o que é interessante é que a introdução não se nutre de alguma certeza sobre a vitória do modernismo, o que levaria ao aplastamento crítico pela teleologia (isto é, buscar as sementes do que se sabe de antemão vitorioso), sabendo, antes, respeitar certo ritmo indeciso, tateante mas vigoroso, que é o dos escritores que inauguram a cena moderna e que, para tanto, devem crer na absoluta novidade de seu próprio gesto. O vigor e o ímpeto renovadores, vistos através das lentes que nos fornece esta edição, não escamoteiam contudo o *quantum* de indeterminação que faz, da cena descrita pelas crônicas, algo vivo, tornando São Paulo, entre provinciana e cosmopolita, o campo de ensaio de idéias novas e velhas, palco principal das vanguardas brasileiras.

Conectando as crônicas ao cenário intelectual que as acolhe, mas também aos textos que concomitantemente se gestam no imaginário do poeta, a introdução ao livro revela que a crônica pode ser o instantâneo da criação literária, espécie de laboratório poético em que flagramos o escritor em seus passos iniciais, que depois se configurarão na poesia que hoje conhecemos. Sendo a figuração do instante, as crônicas são espaço privilegiado para que o leitor, valendo-se do aparato que ora as cerca, compreenda a densidade e a complexidade do tempo que este livro evoca e mobiliza, ao apanhar, em toda sua potência, a experiência moderna do gozo com a metrópole.

Pedro Meira Monteiro é professor-associado de Literatura Brasileira no Department of Spanish and Portuguese Languages and Cultures, Princeton University, autor de *A queda do aventureiro* (Editora da Unicamp, 1999) e *Um moralista nos trópicos* (Boitempo Editorial, 2004) e co-editor do volume da Coleção Correspondência de Mário de Andrade (IEB/USP) que conterá as cartas trocadas entre o autor de *Macunaíma* e o historiador e crítico literário Sérgio Buarque de Holanda. Email: pmeira@princeton.edu

Eduardo Pitta. *Fractura: A Condição Homossexual na Literatura Portuguesa Contemporânea*. Coimbra: Angelus Novus, 2003.

Ana Reimão

Curiosamente, *Fractura* inaugura os estudos *gays* na literatura portuguesa alegando que não existe uma literatura portuguesa *gay*. Neste ensaio, Eduardo Pitta começa por tecer algumas considerações sobre os motins de Stonewall, que tiveram lugar em Junho de 1969, na cidade de Nova Iorque, e que contribuíram para a emergência duma cultura assumidamente *gay*. À maturidade que estas circunstâncias provocaram no discurso existente à volta dos estudos *gays*, no contexto anglo-americano, onde as barreiras do indizível foram há muito ultrapassadas—e a prová-lo está a inclusão dos estudos *gays* e lésbicos nos currículos académicos de várias universidades—Pitta contrapõe o silêncio da realidade portuguesa que ele próprio vem quebrar.

Pitta encara o termo "gay" como característico de uma realidade que não se deve aplicar ao padrão português sem mais considerações. Para o autor, a sociedade portuguesa é uma "sociedade tradicionalmente hipócrita e sexualmente repressiva (...), onde o inenarrável *trash* televisivo dos últimos anos tem feito mais pela 'libertação' dos interditos do que a revolução de 1974," o que parece explicar a inexistência até agora de um discurso sobre a homossexualidade na literatura. Com a liberdade que pode ter alguém que inaugura um discurso, Pitta propõe uma distinção entre literatura *gay* e literatura homossexual. Para o autor, literatura *gay* é aquela que reivindica direitos de cidadania, enquanto a literatura dita homossexual apenas "reflecte sensibilidades e experiências isentas de sentido político pré-determinado." E é precisamente de literatura homossexual, ou seja, das representações literárias da homossexualidade, que se pode falar em respeito à especificidade portuguesa.

Assim, após apresentar uma breve genealogia da literatura homossexual portuguesa em que se incluem nomes como o do português António Nobre ou dos brasileiros Gregório de Matos e Adolfo Caminha, Pitta faz uma incursão pelo cânone português contemporâneo, exemplificando através de

Portuguese Literary & Cultural Studies 15/16 (2010): 283-84.

excertos bem comentados a forma como a condição homossexual é retratada. Arrancando com *A Confissão de Lúcio* de Mário de Sá-Carneiro, passando por *Mau Tempo no Canal* de Vitorino Nemésio, *Sinais de Fogo* de Jorge de Sena, pela primeira parte da obra de Al Berto, pela obra de António Franco Alexandre, Eugénio de Andrade, Manuel Magalhães e Luís Miguel Nava, entre outros, o autor vai tecendo as suas considerações ressalvando que não pretende apresentar uma lista exaustiva.

No final do ensaio, volta-se à questão da especificidade do termo "gay" como representante de uma comunidade próspera e bem estabelecida, social e economicamente, que exclui aqueles que não correspondem ao padrão da "normalidade gay": "Não vale a pena dourar a pílula: a cultura gay está associada a um estatuto económico *well-off* que deixa de fora parte não negligenciável da comunidade homossexual." Características que, diz Pitta, estão completamente ausentes da literatura portuguesa. A "fractura" entre classes característica da cultura *gay* anglo-americana é inexistente nos textos portugueses.

Para além do mérito de ter desbravado o terreno numa área, até aqui, por estrear, Eduardo Pitta deixa também a vontade de ouvir mais esclarecimentos em relação a estas questões que vai levantando no seu ensaio, deixando o espaço e as pistas necessárias para que ele próprio, ou outros, continuem a percorrer esse caminho. Faz-se ainda notar que, apesar de o conteúdo do ensaio referir que se vai tratar exclusivamente da homossexualidade masculina na literatura portuguesa, não é isso que se entende pelo seu título, deixando, por isso, algo a desejar relativamente às questões da homossexualidade feminina na literatura, que não são de todo abordadas aqui.

Ana Reimão ensina português na Universidade de Liverpool. Email: anareimao@gmail.com

Sérgio Paulo Guimarães de Sousa. *Literatura & Cinema: Ensaios, Entrevistas, Bibliografia.* Coimbra: Angelus Novus, 2003.

Ângela Sarmento

Beginning with its title, Sérgio Sousa's book is a call for a comparative approach to two autonomous art forms. The author offers his own version of genre intertwining through texts that are hybrid themselves: theory and practice are mixed in the essays, the interviews imply the conjunction of oral and written modes as well as the presence and absence of the speakers, and then there is the bibliography, brief yet enriching.

These diverse registers are articulated by "a kind of parallel editing," and there is no lack of photographic images, as close-ups preceding the interviews. In this way, the writing travels mimetically, as if it were the "stylo-caméra" mentioned in the book, inverting Astruc's original concept of "caméra-stylo." So, the book must be considered within a range of traditions of writing: about directors who are writers; or about writers who are directors; or about literature and cinema in general.

In the first essay, Sérgio Sousa studies the influence the seventh art has exerted on literary composition techniques. He chooses *Azul-Turquesa*, by Jacinto Lucas Pires, as an example of "a book that is almost a film," in the wake of authors like Hemingway or Faulkner or even the Portuguese neo-realistic writers, who make use of "behaviouristic" speech, concentrating on external focalization, on the "a-psychology" of the characters, in short, on the "objective" representation of the real. Literary speech is considered to operate in a "showing" format, marked by the non-existence of the narrator and the consequent lack of "deictics," which contribute to the concreteness of the audio-visual image. The reader of such texts also becomes a spectator, facing the spatialization of time and the temporalization of space, in which the anaphoric and cataphoric circumvolutions and the progression of the plot are indicated by visual icons, within a paratactic discourse of an eternal present, broadly speaking, like an editing technique.

Portuguese Literary & Cultural Studies 15/16 (2010): 285-87.

The author emphasises that this is *one* possible reading/watching of a literary text. He does not ever negate the possibility of other discursive strategies in the text, at the very level of cinematographic code importation, which he mentions further on during his interview with Lucas Pires.

In the second essay, Sousa considers film transpositions from literary texts. He questions the concept of "fidelity," supported by several semiotic theories from both literary and cinematic studies (Bazin, Zumalde, Genette, Greimas), and tries to establish limits between an "adaptation" and an "inspiration," that is to say, he tries to distinguish between heuristic and hermeneutic liberty and libertinism, which the reader/director should be allowed to perform. He reminds us that, in spite of traditional closed theories (tending to open gradually), in practice there have been prolific betrayals and sterile fidelities.

The interviews allow the author to explore these questions in a more direct tone. It is as if a camera shot in a continuum the spontaneous interactions between the two speakers, led by the interviewee. Nevertheless, you immediately realise that the interviewer is subtly commanding the movements and the editing; not much, though just the amount necessary to give coherence to the whole, like bringing verisimilitude to the "spoken world." Over a three-year time span, five people are interviewed, all differently connected with writing and cinema. Jacinto Lucas Pires, the aforementioned author of *Azul-Turqueza* is a protean creator who feels nearer to directors than writers; Artur Ribeiro is a Portuguese director living in New York, who tells the difference between adaptation and inspiration based on his own practice; Adília Lopes is writer of multiple genres, strongly influenced by cinema; Manuel António Pina is a multimode writer as well, who preferred to use e-mail to answer the questions posed; and Anabela Dinis Branco de Oliveira is a specialised reader and commentator, who develops a thesis about the reception of the cinematic technique and language in Portuguese contemporary novels.

The central question of the relationship between literature and cinema is therefore spread in different directions. Starting from the autonomous claim of each of the two art forms, their main difference is considered in terms of "means," as it was for Aristotle in his matrix of all aesthetics. Other themes are connected with this one, such as technological development or communicative ability, either more or less mediated. You are then confronted with the problem of language and writing genres, with the specificities of the cinematic versus the literary codes and with those of other genres as well. Other questions arise, about the themes that motivate each artistic representation, questions of boundaries, of hybrid nationalities, or about the difference (or not) between male and female expressions, or the different worlds and functions of the (two) art forms.

The bibliography presents titles related to these topics. In general, they represent very recent works, or classics, and they point to a variety of methodologies, focusing more on theory *or* on practice, on literature *or* on cinema. Essential references also appear at the end of the two essays as well as scattered throughout the interviews.

Ângela Sarmento is a research assistant at the Institute of Comparative Literature, Oporto University, with an MA in Brazilian poetry. She is currently preparing a doctoral thesis on literature and cinema. Email: asarmento@letras.up.pt

Margarida Calafate Ribeiro and Ana Paula Ferreira, eds. *Fantasmas e Fantasias Imperiais no Imaginário Português Contemporâneo*. Porto: Campo das Letras, 2003.

Claire Williams

This extremely important and varied collection of essays includes papers presented at two interdisciplinary conferences that were held at King's College London in 2000 and 2001 as part of a series on European identities and former empires. Although excluded from Said's canonical texts, like the Spanish empire, the Portuguese empire was one of the most interesting and unusual, not least because the Portuguese penetrated first and furthest into new territories and wrote detailed accounts of their travels and encounters. Due above all to the language barrier, Portuguese colonial and postcolonial experiences and materials have been neglected by international critics and theorists dealing with globalisation and empire, apart, maybe, from in the works of Boaventura de Sousa Santos, Maria Alzira Seixo, and Paulo de Medeiros.

The processes of winning, managing, defending, and finally losing their sovereignty in far-flung territories marked the Portuguese sense of national and personal identity irreparably, as the fifteen essays in this collection show. They (psycho)analyse the relics and ghosts haunting contemporary literature and the visual arts, history and philosophy, historiography and anthropology, memoirs and travel narratives. The strength of the collection is in its variety, its attention to all the corners of the former empire (in Africa, Asia, and South America) and the use of postcolonial theories to reveal and confront the dreams lost and traumas exposed, especially by the colonial wars and the events of the immediate post-Revolutionary period. References in the introduction and the chapters themselves remind the reader how the lost empire constantly resurfaces in public events such as the 1998 Lisbon Expo and the 2000 commemorations of 500 years since the "discovery" of Brazil.

The impressive list of essayists is composed of experts in the area from Europe and the United States, and well-known and highly esteemed members of Portuguese academic circles. Some of the contributors (Lisboa, Sousa

Portuguese Literary & Cultural Studies 15/16 (2010): 289-90.

Rebelo, Medeiros, Brookshaw, Owen, Rothwell, Bastos) draw conclusions from close readings of one text, writer or artist; others use the evidence of several texts to consider a common concept (Ribeiro, Bethencourt, Vecchi, Jackson, Vakil); and others work at a more theoretical level (Lourenço, Labanyi). The excellent introduction, in particular, provides an extremely useful history (and bibliography) of the evolution of postcolonial theory in Portugal, suggesting ways of moving forward rather than dwelling on the past and what has been lost.

One aspect that recurs in several chapters is the misogyny of empire and the strategies used by women writers such as Lídia Jorge (Medeiros), Maria Ondina Braga (Brookshaw), and Teolinda Gersão (Owen), and the painter Paula Rego (Bethencourt, Lisboa) to highlight and criticise it. The focus of such artists on the domestic as a microcosm of the nation, as well as the recourse to nostalgia by means of pseudo-autobiographical narratives/images are further tools by which they comment on the inequalities of the colonial system.

Several of the critics employ psychoanalytic theory in their approaches to the Portuguese experience of the loss of empire and how it surfaces in the contemporary "imaginary" mentioned in the title. Vecchi, for example, believes that there is a need to find symbolic "bodies" in order that mourning, and subsequently closure, can take place. The essays in this volume exemplify the quantity, variety, and complexity of existing material and will surely trigger further research into the area within and outside Portugal and, by discovering and analysing the ghosts and fantasies of empire, help lay them to rest.

Claire Williams is University Lecturer in Brazilian Literature and Culture at Oxford University. A fellow of St Peter's College, she is author of *The Encounter between Opposites in the Works of Clarice Lispector*. Email: claire.williams@mod-langs.ox.ac.uk

Portuguese Literary & Cultural Studies

www.plcs.umassd.edu

Portuguese Literary & Cultural Studies 1
Fronteiras/Borders.

Portuguese Literary & Cultural Studies 2
Lídia Jorge in other words / por outras palavras.
Guest Editor: Cláudia Pazos Alonso, Oxford University

Portuguese Literary & Cultural Studies 3
Pessoa's Alberto Caeiro.

Portuguese Literary & Cultural Studies 4/5
Brazil 2001. A Revisionary History of Brazilian Literature and Culture.
Guest Editor: João Cezar de Castro Rocha, Universidade do Estado do Rio de Janeiro

Portuguese Literary & Cultural Studies 6
On Saramago.
Guest Editor: Anna Klobucka, University of Georgia

Portuguese Literary & Cultural Studies 7
A Repertoire of Contemporary Portuguese Poetry.

Portuguese Literary & Cultural Studies 8
Cape Verde: Language, Literature & Music.
Guest Editor: Ana Mafalda Leite, Universidade de Lisboa

Portuguese Literary & Cultural Studies 9
Post-Imperial Camões.
Guest Editor: João Ricardo Figueiredo, Universidade de Lisboa

Portuguese Literary & Cultural Studies 10
Reevaluating Mozambique.
Guest Editor: Phillip Rothwell, Rutgers University, New Brunswick

Portuguese Literary & Cultural Studies 11
Vitorino Nemésio and the Azores.
Guest Editor: Francisco Cota Fagundes, University of Massachusetts Amherst

Portuguese Literary & Cultural Studies 12
The Other Nineteenth Century.
Guest Editor: Kathryn Bishop-Sanchez, University of Wisconsin, Madison

Portuguese Literary & Cultural Studies 13/14
The Author as Plagiarist—The Case of Machado de Assis.
Guest Editor: João Cezar de Castro Rocha, Universidade do Estado do Rio de Janeiro

Portuguese Literary & Cultural Studies 15/16
Remembering Angola.
Guest Editor: Phillip Rothwell, Rutgers University, New Brunswick

Forthcoming (in alphabetical order)

Controversies in and about Luso-Afro-Brazilian Studies.

Economies of Relation: Money and Personalism in the Lusophone World.
Guest Editor: Roger Sansi-Roca, Goldsmiths, University of London

Facts and Fictions of António Lobo Antunes.

Parts of Asia
Guest Editor: Cristiana Bastos, ICS, University of Lisbon

Transdisciplinary Readings of Garrett's Travels in My Homeland.

Adamastor Book Series

www.plcs.umassd.edu

Eduardo Lourenço. *Chaos and Splendor and Other Essays.*
Edited by Carlos Veloso, New York University
ISBN: 0-9722561-1-3

Producing Presences. Branching out from Gumbrecht's Work.
Edited by Victor K. Mendes and João Cezar de Castro Rocha
Afterword by Hans Ulrich Gumbrecht, Stanford University
ISBN: 1-933227-22-2

Luís de Camões. *Sonnets and Other Poems.*
Translated by Richard Zenith
ISBN: 1-933227-26-5

The Traveling Eye: Retrospection, Vision, and Prophecy in the Portuguese Renaissance.
Fernando Gil, EHESS, Paris and Helder Macedo, King's College, London.
ISBN: 978-1-933227-29-0

António Vieira. *The Sermon of Saint Anthony to the Fish and Other Texts.*
Translated by Gregory Rabassa
ISBN: 978-1-933227-30-6

Forthcoming (in alphabetical order)

A New History of Brazilian Literature
Edited by João Cezar de Castro Rocha, The University of Manchester

Joaquim Nabuco: An Intellectual Between Two Cultures
Edited by João Cezar de Castro Rocha, The University of Manchester

Machado de Assis & Eça de Queirós: The History of a Debate
Edited by Frank F. Sousa, University of Massachusetts Dartmouth, and
João Cezar de Castro Rocha, The University of Manchester

Eça de Queirós. *The Correspondence of Fradique Mendes*
Translated by Gregory Rabassa

Portuguese Language Textbook Series

Francisco Cota Fagundes. *Um Passo Mais no Português Moderno: Gramática Avançada, Leituras, Composição e Conversação.*

Portuguese in the Americas Series

Portuguese-Americans and Contemporary Civic Culture in Massachusetts.
Edited by Clyde Barrow, Center for Policy Analysis,
University of Massachusetts Dartmouth
ISBN: 0-9722561-0-5

Through a Portagee Gate.
Charles Reis Felix
ISBN: 0-9722561-4-8

In Pursuit of Their Dreams: A History of Azorean Immigration to the United States.
Jerry R. Williams
ISBN: 0-9722561-6-4

Sixty Acres and a Barn: A Novel.
Alfred Lewis
ISBN: 0-9722561-5-6

Da Gama, Cary Grant, and the Election of 1934.
Charles Reis Felix
ISBN: 0-9722561-8-0

Distant Music
Julian Silva
ISBN: 0-9722561-9-9

The Representation of the Portuguese in American Literature
Reinaldo Silva
ISBN: 1-933227-18-4

The Holyoke
Frank X. Gaspar
ISBN: 1-933227-20-6

Two Portuguese-American Plays
Paulo Pereira and Patricia A. Thomas
ISBN: 1-933227-21-4

Tony: A New England Boyhood
Charles Reis Felix
ISBN: 1-933227-24-9

Community, Culture and The Makings of Identity: Portuguese-Americans along the Eastern Seaboard
Edited by Kimberly da Costa Holton, Rutgers University, Newark and Andrea Klimt, University of Massachusetts Dartmouth
ISBN: 1-933227-27-3

The Undiscovered Island
Darrell Kastin
ISBN: 1-933227-23-0

Forthcoming

So Ends This Day: The Portuguese in American Whaling 1765-1927
Donald Warrin

Move Over Scopes and Other Short Fiction
Julian Silva

The Marriage of the Portuguese (Extended Edition)
Sam Pereira

Being "Azorean": Identity Politics in the United States and Brazil
João Leal

Home Is an Island, 2nd Edition
Alfred Lewis

The Complete Poetry of Alfred Lewis
Alfred Lewis

The University of Massachusetts Dartmouth

Center for Portuguese Studies and Culture

Founded in 1996, the University of Massachusetts Dartmouth Center for Portuguese Studies and Culture is a multidisciplinary international studies and outreach unit dedicated to the study of the language, literatures and cultures of the Portuguese-speaking world comprised of over 200 million people in eight countries on four continents.

The Center publishes four different collections, to wit: the peer-reviewed journal *Portuguese Literary & Cultural Studies* and the Adamastor Book Series, both edited by Victor K. Mendes, the Portuguese Language Textbook Series, and the Portuguese in the Americas Series. The Center aims to develop pedagogical materials to aid in teaching and learning Portuguese, and supports the development and dissemination of knowledge regarding the Portuguese-speaking communities in the United States.

The Center further sponsors and organizes the Summer Program in Portuguese, colloquia, concerts, art exhibitions, dance performances and theatrical productions, in addition to administering the Hélio and Amélia Pedroso/Luso-American Development Foundation Endowed Chair in Portuguese Studies. Recently the Center proposed and led the effort to create the Ferreira-Mendes Portuguese-American Archives at the Claire T. Carney University Library.

The activities of the Center for Portuguese Studies and Culture are made possible in part by the commitment and generosity of Portuguese-Americans and institutional supporters, including the Luso-American Foundation of Lisbon, the Foreign Ministry of the Government of Portugal, and the Government of the Autonmous Region of the Azores.

For more information, visit www.portstudies.umassd.edu.